Life and Ideas

The Anarchist Writings of Errico Malatesta

Edited by Vernon Richards

Foreword by Carl Levy

Life and Ideas: The Anarchist Writings of Errico Malatesta
Edited and translated by Vernon Richards

ISBN: 978-1-62963-032-8
LCCN: 2014908067

PM Press
PO Box 23912
Oakland, CA 94623
www.pmpress.org

Originally published by
Freedom Press
Angel Alley
84b Whitechapel High Street
London E1 7QX
www. freedompress.org.uk

Cover by John Yates/stealworks.com
Layout by Jonathan Rowland

10 9 8 7 6 5 4 3 2 1

Printed by the Employee Owners of Thomson-Shore in Dexter, Michigan.
www.thomsonshore.com

CONTENTS

of anarchist and syndicalist repertoires of action, thought, and culture in the Global South as well as the tracing of transnational networks of libertarian diasporas in port cities and elsewhere.[3] Malatesta's life is emblematic of this process that allowed anarchists and syndicalist currents to have far greater influence on the global Left than mere numbers would suggest. A sociology of these networks reveals several generations of intellectuals like Carlo Cafiero,[4] Francesco Saverio Merlino,[5] and Luigi Fabbri,[6] who were ideological comrades and sounding boards for his ideas, and several generations of self-taught workers and artisans from the anarchist seedbeds of Liguria, Tuscany, Umbria, the Marches, and Rome who kept his presence alive in Italy even if he rarely set foot in his native land.[7] And one of these self-taught anarchists was Emidio Recchioni, the father of Vernon Richards, the author and editor of this very book.[8] Malatesta never finished his medical degree at the University of Naples and became an artisan: he trained as a gas-fitter and electrician, and between his stints as an organizer and radical newspaper editor he always returned to his trades, even in old age in Rome during the 1920s. Like the Russian populists he sought to declass himself and go to the people, and he feared and detested the development of a class of left-wing professional journalists, orators, and politicians who fed off the social movements and betrayed their principles.

Malatesta lived in a modern, globalized world of the steamship, the railroad, the telegraph, and dynamite.[9] And although he fought a brave battle against the anarchist terrorism and expropriation inspired by Ravachol and Henry in the 1890s or in the new century of Parisian tragic bandits and Latvian revolutionaries turned robbers consumed in the fires of the Siege of Sidney Street, he never endorsed pacifism, wrote long articles against the followers of Tolstoy, and remained a revolutionary inspired by, though critical of, the followers of Mazzini during the Risorgimento. Like many Italian anarchists of his generation, his political apprenticeship was forged in the disappointing aftermath of the Italian struggle for unification and independence.[10] Although he renounced Mazzini and the Republicans when the old nationalist revolutionary disavowed the Paris Commune for its atheism and promotion of class war, Malatesta always retained deep ethical and voluntarist strains in his thought and political action, maintained a fruitful dialogue with the Italian

Republicans, and indeed formed an alliance through a mutual struggle against the Savoy dynasty. Thus in 1914 this alliance of anarchists, anti-militarists, syndicalists, republicans, and maverick socialists nearly brought the regime to a crisis before the First World War rearranged the political field. But even after the war, during the *Biennio Rosso* and the years leading to the creation of Mussolini's dictatorship (1922–26), Malatesta sought alliances with the maverick left and the republicans to prevent or overthrow the growing power of the new Fascist movement and its installation in power with the support of the Savoyard king in Rome.[11]

Malatesta advocated the establishment of a national federation of anarchist groupings—internationalists, anarchist socialists, and then plain anarchists—in Italy from the 1870s to the 1920s, and for this he received strong criticism and indeed abuse from the individualists, Stirnerites, and the affinity group anarcho-communist anarchists associated with his old comrade Luigi Galleani.[12] But he was not an advocate of an anarchist revolution as such. The social revolution would be guided by small-'a' anarchist methods but an anarchist party would not be the invisible pilot behind its success. That is why he later looked back on the quarrels between Marxists and Bakuninists in the First International and felt them both to be in the wrong. He argued with Mahkno and the Platformists in the 1920s because they seemed to be advocating an anarchist form of Leninism. The denouement of the Bolshevik Revolution did not surprise him. Like Bakunin, he predicted that a Marxist revolution would result in a dictatorship of a New Class of ex-workers, intellectuals, and politicos. All social organisations might be prey to an "iron law of oligarchy," as German sociologist Robert Michels termed it. Albeit, Malatesta took exception to the concept of "iron laws" in political and social life; thus he objected to his fellow London exile Kropotkin's marriage of biological concepts of mutual aid with the open-ended business of human politics. He fought all determinisms and indeed foreshadowed the critique of many recent post-anarchists who have lambasted "classical anarchism" for its determinism, essentialism, and Whiggish teleology. Nevertheless, Malatesta argued that anarchist or syndicalist trade unions would be prey to the same maladies as the moderate, socialist, or communist ones. The only remedy was for anarchists to work in "ginger groups" in all trade unions and promote libertarian methods: rank and file control, circulation of leadership, and low salaries for these temporary leaders.[13]

Trade unions were important for Malatesta. Although he never renounced the role of insurrection in making the revolution, by the 1880s and 1890s, with the massive London Dock Strike of 1889 in mind, he advocated a syndicalist strategy to the first generation syndicalist French anarchist exiles in London during the 1890s. When syndicalism grew worldwide in the early twentieth century he pointed out the theoretical and practical weaknesses of its workerism (the revolution was broader than that) and the fact that a peaceful general strike would merely result in the starvation of the urban working classes and the collapse of the strike if it wasn't brought to a quicker termination by the State's armed forces and vigilante groups. When the factories of northern Italy were occupied in September 1920, Malatesta suggested that the workers recommence production and distribution links and not await events or negotiations. The modern city had to be restarted by the revolutionaries on their own initiative if the occupation was not to falter and lead to an inconsequential negotiated settlement.[14]

But Malatesta did not ignore the countryside and, like Bakunin, saw the tremendous revolutionary potential in the peasantry, and some of his most widely read pamphlets were aimed at landless laborers and smallholders. Unlike the Italian Socialists in 1919–20, he warned against the promotion of the rapid socialisation of the land which drove the smallholders into the hands of the Fascists. A class war between the landless laborers and the smallholders was a war between the poor and the poorest and allowed Fascism to sweep away the Red Zones around Bologna and Ferrara in the spring of 1921; starting a rapid process to allow the former and largely discredited radical socialist Benito Mussolini in 1919, ascend to prime minister by the autumn of 1922.[15]

Malatesta also argued that small-'a' anarchism was the only method by which the reformists had won their dubious victories: the expansion of the suffrage to the male British working class or the struggle for female suffrage in early twentieth century Britain, which Malatesta witnessed and had known many of the key personalities in the fight, had been won from the ruling classes through direct action not peaceful petition and rallies, he argued, over and over again. But he was not averse on occasion to forming alliances with moderate socialists, anti-clericals, and even liberals if the State threatened the space of civil society in which the anarchists could organize and make their case. Thus he endorsed such broad alliances in Italy when civil liberties were threatened during the 1890s,[16] during the road to Fascism in the early 1920s, and under the Fascist regime from his condition of near–house arrest in Rome from 1926 to his death in 1932. But Malatesta would under no conditions stand as a protest electoral candidate as suggested by the former anarchist intellectual and activist Saverio Merlino, who by the turn of the century endorsed a maverick form of libertarian social democracy. Of course Malatesta was not naive: he was no admirer of liberal politicians, such as Lloyd George, whom he termed a hypocrite. He understood the realities of the republican United States in the Gilded Age: industrial welfare, lynch law, nativism, and the unbridled racist jingoism of the Spanish- American war were commented on by Malatesta, who had spent 1900–1901 in the Italian anarchist colony of Paterson, New Jersey, and in U.S. occupied Havana. He knew full well that his near-deportation from London in 1912 was prevented by a united front stretching from MPs such as Ramsay MacDonald and Keir Hardie in the British Labour Party, trade unionists both moderate and syndicalist, Radical Liberals and less radical liberals of the broadsheet press, and even his neighbourhood Islington's "free-born Englishman" (*sic*) Fair-Trade Unionist (Tory) newspaper. But a united front which involved a careful calibration of direct action when the British government was threatened by industrial unrest, the troubles in Ireland and the suffragettes as well as the pressure of radical and liberal elite networks (indeed one might add "old boy's networks"), which worked to Malatesta's advantage.[17]

The First World War brought a major split among the most famous personages of international anarchism, especially a fierce debate against Kropotkin, who not only endorsed the Entente and Allies but became a bitter-ender and demanded a continuation of the war in 1916, even when some senior British Tories were demanding a truce and a negotiated settlement. Malatesta remained opposed to the war and witnessed how the war reactivated the industrial radicalism of pre-war syndicalism in the factory council movements and free soviets of Italy and the wider world.[18] He felt in 1917 that the expelled anti-parliamentary socialists and anarchists of the

London congress of the Second International in 1896,[19] in which he fought on the anarchist side, had been vindicated as wartime and (later) post-war socialist and industrial radicalism seemed to be adopting or perhaps adapting pre-war anarchist and syndicalist positions. But by the 1920s and the triumph of Fascism and Bolshevism and the decline of anarchism in many of its former strongholds, Malatesta returned to the basics and engaged in some of his most penetrating journalism on themes of the essence of anarchism, anarchism and violence, and the role of liberalism and spaces for anarchism in civil society. When classical insurrectional anarchism faded after 1945, Malatesta's legacy of an open-ended and non-scientistic anarchism was adapted by "reformist" anarchists such as Colin Ward.[20] One of Ward's closest comrades in the post-1945 British anarchist movement was Vernon Richards.

Vero Benevento Constantino Recchioni was born in London in 1915 and later anglicized his name to Vernon Richards.[21] As previously mentioned, Emidio Recchioni had been an active anarchist mainly in Ancona before his arrival in London in 1899, which had been preceded by his imprisonment on the penal island of Pantelleria where he made the acquaintance of Luigi Galleani, a fellow prisoner. During the 1890s Emidio had been employed with the Italian railroads, and this facilitated easy access to other comrades throughout the anarchist seedbeds of central Italy. During the 1890s he may have been involved in an attempt on the life of the authoritarian prime minister Francesco Crispi. In London he quickly opened a noted Italian delicatessen, King Bomba, which became a meeting place for two generations of anarchists and radicals, including Malatesta's inner circle when they visited London and the local Malatestan anarchists, and later in the 1920s and 1930s Sylvia Pankhurst, whose partner, Silvio Corio, was another Italian anarchist exile in London, and Emma Goldman and George Orwell. The financial success of the shop allowed Recchioni to help finance Malatesta's major newspapers in Italy in 1913–15 (*Volontà*), 1919–22 (*Umanità nova*), 1924–26 (*Pensiero e Volontà*), and later funded several attempts on Mussolini's life.[22] Under the pen-name "Nemo," Recchioni was an avid contributor to the Italian anarchist press and to *Freedom*, the newspaper founded by Kropotkin in London in 1886. His contributions to the newspaper are still of great interest, especially an article in 1915 in which he predicted a new form of radicalism in a post-war Europe, rather close to the council communism and militant factory shop stewards movements of the period 1917–20 before they were undermined by the rise of Leninist communism and suppressed by the restoration of the bourgeois order.[23] He died in 1934, but his son Vero carried on the family politics.

Vernon Richards received his education at Emmanuel school in Wandsworth and then graduated in civil engineering from King's College London in 1939. In his youth he was an accomplished violinist but later let this lapse. In 1934 he became active in the struggle against the Fascist regime of Mussolini and was deported from France where he fell in love with the daughter of the anarchist Camillo Berneri, Marie-Louise. Camillo Berneri was from the next generation of Italian anarchists after Luigi Fabbri and helped modernize its scope with important works on inter-war anti-Semitism, a critique of "worker-worship" and the adaption of the concepts of mass society, psychoanalysis, and totalitarianism for understanding the rise and strength of Fascism and Stalinism in the 1930s. He was murdered in Spain during the May Days of 1937 in Barcelona, most probably by Stalinist agents disguised as Spanish Republican Guards. Berneri had criticised the policies of the CNT-FAI: the joining of the Popular Front government, the lack of a guerrilla war, the sacrifice of the social revolution for a militarised war effort and the lack of a campaign to undermine Morocco, the original base of the Nationalists and the Army of Africa, by engaging in anti-imperialist agitation in the Spanish-controlled portion of that country.[24] These critiques would reappear in one of Vernon Richards's most cited works, *The Lessons of the Spanish Revolution*, first published in 1953.[25] Before his death Emidio had helped Berneri's various plots against Fascist and Royal luminaries. Vero/Vernon was deported from France in 1935 but not before a joint collaboration with Camillo Berneri and Marie-Louise Berneri on the anti-Fascist, newspaper, *Free Italy/Italia Libera*. When the Spanish Civil War began in 1936, he collaborated with veterans of *Freedom*, which had ceased effective publication in 1932, with the new fortnightly, *Spain and the World*, which then became *Revolt!*, before becoming the rather popular *War Commentary* during the Second World War: in 1945 the title reverted to *Freedom*.

In 1945 Vernon, Marie-Louise, Philip Sansom, and John Hewetson were charged with trying to disaffect members of the armed forces and were defended by a campaign which included George Orwell, Michael Tippett, T.S. Eliot, and Benjamin Britten. Vernon, Samson, and Hewetson were convicted and served nine months in jail, whereas Marie was acquitted on a technicality. After serving his sentence, instead of pursuing a career as a civil engineer, he ran the family business, which was sold in the 1950s. He then worked as a freelance photographer, which included a series of famous early photographs of Orwell in his Islington flat.[26] Later he became an organic gardener and a travel courier. For the last thirty years of his life he lived in a smallholding in Suffolk. In the late 1940s the small but dynamic Freedom group included the likes of Colin Ward, George Woodcock, and Alex Comfort. At the height of his fame, one the founders of the Institute of Contemporary Arts and the guide to the great British and American public on Surrealism, Cubism, and all things modern in art, Herbert Read, was a major contributor to Freedom's publication house, which over the decades published a formidable array of books and pamphlets.[27] Marie-Louise died of a viral infection in 1949 shortly after losing a child at birth,[28] but she left behind a literary legacy, most notably a fine study of utopias, which is still a wonderful read.[29]

From 1951 Vernon edited *Freedom* as a weekly but quit as editor in 1964 only to resume the editorship sporadically for many years to come. He stopped writing for the newspaper in the 1990s. He was a difficult person to work with: most of his closest colleagues such as Sansom, Hewetson, and Woodcock were not on speaking terms at their deaths, and his famous longstanding quarrel with the former contributor to *Freedom*, Albert Meltzer, was legendary. Although endorsed by *Freedom*, Colin Ward's 1960s *Anarchy* tried to make anarchism and its method relevant to the newer generation of the welfare/warfare state, engaging with social scientists, architects, and designers and opening up to university students who would be involved in the social and radical currents of 1968's New Left.[30]

Although one might assume that Emidio was the key influence in Vero's politics, it was in fact Malatesta who was the central figure in his political life. Vero knew him personally and told me that as a tiny child he sat on Malatesta's shoulders watching the "zepps" (the German zeppelins) bombing London.[31] Malatesta never wrote a book or memoir. His written work consisted of journalism and important pamphlets. Richards translated several of the pamphlets and most importantly two collections of his newspaper articles.[32] The second collection focussed on his writings from 1924 to 1931.[33] The collection here is compiled not in a chronological sense but under twenty-seven topics derived from translated sections of articles taken from throughout his life such as "Anarchism and Anarchy," "Ends and Means," "The Anarchist Revolution," "Anarchists and the Working Class Movements," "Workers and Intellectuals," "Anarchism and Science," etc. This is followed by notes on a biography and Malatesta's relevance for anarchists today. Now surely much of the introductory and concluding material is rather old hat, with an annoying sectarian point-settling air to proceedings, including a rather uncharitable dig at my teacher James Joll,[34] and a rather curious, dated museum-piece polemic with George Woodcock over whether or not anarchism was dead as he had announced in the first edition of his history of anarchism of 1962. Woodcock's timing was poor: small-'a' anarchism informed much of the early participatory democratic Anglo-American New Left and Civil Rights movements, and nearly destroyed the Gallic Gaullist State in a few heady weeks in May 1968, something Woodcock admitted in later editions of his popular history.[35]

The value of this collection is the pithy overview of Malatesta's thought and also the appendices, which reproduce among other things, Malatesta's longish essay of assessment and memories of Kropotkin written a year just before the death of the Italian anarchist. In this collection, one gets an excellent feel for the non-sectarian, open-ended, and thoughtful consistency of Malatesta's anarchism. But this volume can be supplemented with the volume of Malatesta's writing edited by Davide Turcato, *The Method of Freedom* (2014), which reproduces a selection of articles in a chronological fashion within the various phases of his political militancy. Richards's edition gives the reader a sense of Malatesta's political ideas, whereas Turcato's volume is an English overview of his major project to reproduce all his writing, interviews, and correspondence in ten volumes, of which three have been published in Italian.[36] With Richards's pioneering efforts and with Turcato's overview of his ongoing massive, definitive, scholarly, and historically contextual project, the English reader will now appreciate the Malatestan "method of freedom" in all its clarity and good sense.

Endnotes

1. The most extensive biography of Malatesta is in Italian. See Giampietro Berti, *Errico Malatesta e il movimento anarchico italiano e internazionale 1872–1932* (Milan: FrancoAngeli, 2003). See also Errico Malatesta, *Autobiografia mai scritta. Ricordi (1853–1932)*, Piero Brunello and Pietro Di Paola, eds. (Santa Maria Capua Vetere: Edizioni Spartaco, 2003); and Davide Turcato, *Making Sense of Anarchism: Errico Malatesta's Experiments with Revolution, 1889–1900* (New York: Palgrave Macmillan, 2012).
2. On Malatesta in London, see Carl Levy, "Malatesta in Exile," *Annali della Fondazione Luigi Einaudi* 15 (1981): 245–70; Carl Levy, "Malatesta in London: The Era of Dynamite," in *A Century of Italian Emigration to Britain 1880–1980s*, eds. Lucia Sponza and Arturo Tosi, special supplement of *The Italianist* 13 (1993), 25–42; Carl Levy, "Da Bresci a Wormwood Scrubs: Il 'Capo' dell'anarchismo mondiale a Londra," in *"Lo sciopero generale armato": Il lungo esilio londinese, 1900–1913* (vol. 5 of *Errico Malatesta, Opere complete*), ed. Davide Turcato (Milan: Zero in Condotta, 2014). On Malatesta and the Italian colony of anarchists in London, see Pietro Di Paola, *The Knights Errant of Anarchy: London and the Italian Anarchist Diaspora (1880–1917)* (Liverpool: Liverpool University Press, 2013).
3. Carl Levy, "Anarchism and Cosmopolitanism," *Journal of Political Ideologies* 16, no. 3 (2011): 265–78; David Berry and Constance Bantman, *New Perspectives on Anarchism, Labour and Syndicalism: The Individual, the National and the Transnational* (Newcastle upon Tyne: Cambridge Scholars Publications, 2010); Steven Hirsch and Lucien van der Walt, eds., *Anarchism and Syndicalism in the Colonial and Postcolonial World, 1870–1940: The Praxis of National Liberation, Internationalism, and Social Revolution* (Leiden: Brill, 2010); Constance Bantman and Bert Altena, eds., *Reassessing the Transnational Turn: Scales of Analysis in Anarchist and Syndicalist Studies* (London: Routledge, 2015).
4. Pier Carlo Masini, *Cafiero* (Milan: Rizzoli, 1974).
5. Giampietro Berti, *Francesco Saverio Merlino: dall'anarchismo socialista al socialismo liberale (1856–1930)* (Milano: FrancoAngeli, 1993).
6. Maurizio Antonioli and Roberto Giulianelli, eds., *Da Fabriano a Montevideo. Luigi Fabbri: vita e idee di un intellettuale anarchico e antifascista* (Pisa: BFS, 2006).
7. Levy, *Malatesta in Exile*, 258–59.
8. For accounts of Emidio Recchioni's life, see Pietro Di Paola, "Recchioni, Emidio," in *Dizionario biografico degli anarchici italiani*, eds. Maurizio Antonioli, Giampietro Berti, Santi Fedele, and Pasquale Iuso (Pisa: BFS, 2004), 418–20; Erika Diemoz, *A morte il tiranno. Anarchia e violenza da Crispi a Mussolini* (Turin: Giulio Einaudi, 2011).
9. Richard Bach Jensen, *The Battle against Anarchist Terrorism: An International History, 1878–1934* (Cambridge: Cambridge University Press, 2014).
10. Misato Toda, *Errico Malatesta da Mazzini a Bakunin* (Naples: Guida, 1988).
11. Carl Levy, "Charisma and Social Movements: Errico Malatesta and Italian Anarchism," *Modern Italian* 3, no. 2 (1998): 205–17.
12. Ugo Fedeli, *Luigi Galleani: Quarant'anni di lotte rivoluzionarie 1891–1931* (Cesena: AntiStato, 1956); Paul Avrich, *Sacco and Vanzetti: The Anarchist Background* (Princeton: Princeton University Press, 1991).

13. Carl Levy, "The Rooted Cosmopolitan: Errico Malatesta, Syndicalism, Transnationalism and the International Labour Movement," in *New Perspectives on Anarchism, Labour and Syndicalism*, eds. Berry and Bantman, 61–79.
14. Levy, *Charisma and Social Movements*, 214.
15. Levy, *The Rooted Cosmopolitan*, 69.
16. Levy, "Malatesta in London," 37–39.
17. Levy, *Da Bresci a Wormwood Scrubs*.
18. Carl Levy, "Errico Malatesta and the War Interventionist Debate: 1914–1917," in *Anarchism 1914–1918*, eds. Matthew Adams and Ruth Kinna (Manchester: Manchester University Press, forthcoming).
19. Carl Levy, *Malatesta in London*; Davide Turcato, "European Anarchism in the 1890s: Why Labor Matters in Categorizing Anarchism," *Working USA: The Journal of Labor and Society* 12 (2009): 459–62 ; and "The 1896 London Congress: Epilogue or Prologue?," in *New Perspectives on Anarchism, Labour and Syndicalism*, eds. Berry and Bantman, 110–25.
20. Carl Levy, ed., *Colin Ward. Life, Times and Thought* (London: Lawrence and Wishart, 2013).
21. The details of Vernon Richard's life in the next paragraphs can be found in Colin Ward, "Vernon Richards," *The Guardian*, 4 February 2002.
22. Di Paola, *Recchioni, Emidio*, 419; Diemoz, *A morte il tiranno*, 277–81, 297–332.
23. "Between Ourselves," *Freedom*, September, 1915.
24. Berneri needs an English language biography, but see: Carlo De Maria, *Camillo Berneri: tra anarchism e liberalism* (Milan: FrancoAngeli, 2004); Massimo Granchi, *Camillo Berneri e i totalitarismi* (Reggio Calabria: Cittanova, 2006).
25. *Lessons of the Spanish Revolution* (London: Freedom Press, 1953).
26. Vernon Richards, *George Orwell at Home (and among the Anarchists): Essays and Photographs* (London: Freedom Press, 1998).
27. For the trial in 1945 and the Freedom Group in the 1940s see, Pietro Di Paola, "'The man who knows his village': Colin Ward and Freedom Press," in Levy, *Colin Ward*, 28–52.
28. Pietro Di Paola, "Marie Louise Berneri e il gruppo di Freedom Press,' in Carlo De Maria, *Maria Luisa Berneri e l'anarchismo inglese* (Reggio Emilia: Biblioteca Panizzi/ Archivio famiglia Berneri-Aurelio Chessa, 2013), 133–57.
29. Marie Louise Berneri, *Journey through Utopia* (London: Freedom Press, 1950).
30. David Goodway, "Colin Ward and the New Left," in Levy, *Colin Ward*, 53–71.
31. For a recent account of the "zepps" see Jerry White, *Zeppelin Nights: London in the First World War* (London: The Bodley Head, 2014).
32. For example, *Anarchy* (London: Freedom Press, 1974).
33. *The Anarchist Revolution: Polemical Articles 1924–1931* (London: Freedom Press, 1995).
34. James Joll wrote a letter to Margaret Cole, the wife of historian G.D.H. Cole, who had taught at Nuffield College, Oxford, and was a maverick Fabian and former Guild Socialist, and whose immense multi-volume history of socialism was quite sympathetic

to the anarchists, indeed concluding with a plea for libertarian socialism in an era of nuclear terror. The letter is dated 5 January 1965 from St Anthony's College Oxford, just after the publication of Joll's book *The Anarchists* and, as we will see, just after a damning review in Ward's *Anarchy* by Vernon Richards:

"Your letter came at a most opportune moment, when *Anarchy* had devoted two long articles to demolishing me and the book, so that it was very encouraging to know that a serious historian of the working-class movement had not thought that that I was unsympathetic to the ideas I was describing!" (Papers of Margaret Cole, Archive collections of Nuffield College, Oxford: MIC/E4/3/1).

On Cole's relationship to anarchism, see Leonie Holthaus, "G.D.H. Cole's International Thought: The Dilemmas of Justifying Socialism in the Twentieth Century," *The International History Review* 36, no. 5 (2014): 858–75.

35. George Woodcock, *Anarchism: A History of Libertarian Ideas and Movements* (Harmondsworth: Penguin, 1962).
36. Davide Turcato, ed., *The Method of Freedom: An Errico Malatesta Reader* (Oakland: AK Press, 2014). Besides the fifth volume of Zero in Condotta's complete works of Malatesta mentioned in endnote 2, two other volumes have been published: Vol. 3, "*Un Lavoro Lungo e Paziente*": *Il socialism anarchico dell'Agitazione 1897–1898*, introductory essay by Roberto Giulianelli (2011); and Vol. 4, "*Verso l'Anarchia*": *Malatesta in America 1899–1900*, introductory essay by Nunzio Pernicone (2012).

Editor's Introduction to the First Edition

Since the end of World War II the number of major works on anarchism and anarchists published in English is impressive. I will not attempt to list them all, but we have George Woodcock's biographies of Godwin, Proudhon and Kropotkin and Richard Drinnon's biography of Emma Goldman; then there is Maximoff's huge volume of Bakunin's selected writings, Eltzbacher's *Anarchism*, Stirner's *Ego and His Own* and Kropotkin's *Memoirs of a Revolutionist* (edited), and Irving Horowitz's 600-page anthology on and by *The Anarchists*; and finally there are the histories: G.D.H. Cole's second volume in his "History of Socialist Thought," which deals with *Marxism and Anarchism* (1850–1890), Woodcock's *Anarchism: A History of Libertarian Ideas and Movements*, and James Joll's *The Anarchists*. To this list one must add the literature on the Spanish Civil War, at least that part of it which recognises the anarchist contribution to the struggle, and at the top of this list I would put Burnett Bolloten's *Grand Camouflage*, Orwell's *Homage to Catalonia* and Brenan's *Spanish Labyrinth* (the latter two being post-war reprints). One has only to look up at one's bookshelves to realise that I should have mentioned Herbert Read's *Anarchy and Order*, Marie-Louise Berneri's *Journey through Utopia*, Rudolf Rocker's *London Years*, etc., etc.!

And the longer the list becomes the greater is my surprise that no one should have long ago thought that Errico Malatesta deserved a place in that distinguished company, for he is acclaimed by the historians I have mentioned as one of the "giants" in the giant-studded 19th century revolutionary movement. The fact that he is seen by the historians more as a revolutionary agitator than as a thinker, explains in part their superficial treatment of his role in what they call the "historic anarchist movement." Then there is the question of language. It is noteworthy that English social historians are not linguists, and Italian is not an international language (and neither are Italians good linguists) and so, in spite of the fact that the Italian anarchist movement has produced probably more valuable and thought-provoking writers than any other movement, their names, let alone their ideas, are virtually unknown outside their country (the exception being the Spanish speaking movement).

However, the principal disadvantage with which Malatesta has had to "contend" is that he did not conform to the pattern set by 19th century revolutionary thinkers and revolutionary leaders which would have ensured him his place among the historians' "great men." He was, first of all, too good a revolutionary, to even think of keeping a diary; and he was too active to be allowed to live the kind of settled life that would have allowed him carefully to file away his correspondence for posterity and the convenience of historians. Furthermore, though he was in his 79th year when he died he had never found the time (nor, I suspect, felt the inclination) to write his memoirs, which his closest friends, as well as publishers with an eye on a best seller, had, for their different reasons, been urging him to do for many years. And last, but not least, he earned his living as a skilled worker and not as a writer. If it is thought that I exaggerate the disadvantages, I would refer the reader to Cole's valuable History (Vol. II), to the "Principal Characters" a list of more than 60 names with which he prefaced his text, and invite him to apply the various "tests" I have suggested.

Now let me enumerate some of the reasons why I think it high time not only that historians should accord to Malatesta his proper place in the movement (obviously I cannot oblige them to agree with me, but I hope the publication of this volume of his writings will now make it virtually impossible for them to ignore him as a thinker) but more important, that anarchists in the English speaking world should have something more than a pamphlet by which to study his ideas.

For nearly sixty years Malatesta was active in the anarchist movement as an agitator and as a propagandist. He was, as a glance through the files of the anarchist press will show, one of the movement's most respected members as well as remaining to the end one of its most controversial. He was active in many parts of the world, as well as the editor of a number of Italian anarchist journals including the daily *Umanità Nova* (1920–22). Half his life was spent in exile and the respect he was accorded by governments is surely evidenced by the fact that he spent more than ten years in prison, mainly awaiting trial. Juries, by contrast, showed a different respect, in almost always acquitting him, recognising that the only *galantuomo*, that the only honest man, was the one facing them in the prisoners' cage!

I have, in this volume, purposely soft-pedalled the man in order to emphasise his ideas, because everybody recognises Malatesta as *the man of action* but few realise how valuable, and original, and realistic were his *ideas*. Yet if there is merit in his ideas, the principal source is his experience in the day-to-day struggle and his identification with the working people *as one of them*. In my opinion Bakunin and Kropotkin, in spite of their prison experiences, remained aristocrats to the end. What George Woodcock refers to as Kropotkin's "weakness for oversimplification in almost all the issues he discussed" are the attributes not of the saint but of the aristocrat. And indeed even he suggests that one should not "be content with the impression of Kropotkin as a saint. Obstinacy and intolerance had their place in his character. . . ."

Malatesta had no illusions about the "historic role of the masses" because he shared and understood their lives and reactions. But because he also understood how their oppressors "reasoned," and how the "in-betweeners" preached what they were too privileged, socially and materially, to practice, he expected more from the organised workers, but nevertheless he directed his propaganda to *all* men of good-will.

This volume is divided into three parts. The first consists of selections from his writings, the second, Notes for a Biography of Malatesta, and the third part is an attempt to make an assessment of Malatesta's ideas and tactics in the light of present-day experience.

It is obvious that even the most scrupulous editor cannot avoid reflecting his own preferences in making a selection. But I have done my best to limit this intrusion by attempting to present a "complete" picture of Malatesta's most important ideas and arguments, rather than selecting a limited number of articles from his extensive Writings. And I arrived at the 27 sections in which the ideas have been grouped by the simple process of reading his articles and classifying the subject matter within each article under as many headings as seemed appropriate. The next stage was to condense the material within each classification and then to reduce the number of headings, either by combining some, or by deciding that the material in others was not sufficient or especially interesting to justify inclusion. The picture that emerged was one of Anarchist Ends and Means, and I therefore grouped the sections accordingly, and ending with the complete text of the Anarchist Programme which Malatesta drafted and which was accepted by the Italian anarchist Congress in Bologna in 1920, for it seems to me to synthesise Malatesta's ideas and his commonsense approach to anarchist tactics.

If Malatesta has been badly served by the English speaking movement, quite apart from the historians, the same cannot be said of the Italian movement. After his death all his writings from 1919 to 1932 were collected and published in three volumes (totalling more than 1,000 pages). And after the War two large volumes compiled by the late Cesare Zaccaria and Giovanna Berneri appeared in Naples, containing as well as much of the material that appeared in the first three, many of Malatesta's articles from the *Volontà* (1913–14) period as well as from *l'Agitazione* (1897). I have been able to supplement these with a file of *Volontà*, as well as with odd copies of Bertoni's *Risveglio* (Geneva) and Fabbri's *Studi Sociali* (Montevideo) and the magazine *Volontà* (Naples) in which a number of the earlier articles were reprinted. So though conscious of not having read all Malatesta's writings, I have read enough to feel sure that I have not missed some major aspect of his thought.

Some readers may think that in presenting extracts rather than selections one is presenting Malatesta out of context as well as doing him an injustice as a writer. The latter point seems to me to be a valid one, for in spite of being a reluctant writer, the lucidity of the language and the construction of his articles make them worth reading as literature, and as a propagandist and polemicist he was a master of his craft. Perhaps one of these days it will be possible to make good this "injustice."

As to the extracts being out of their context and needing copious footnotes giving the background in which the articles from which they have been taken, were written, I have resisted doing this partly because this volume would have then appeared to be a work for scholars instead of the undisguised anarchist propaganda it aims at being, but also because it seems to me that the reader himself or herself can easily put these extracts in their context by a quick glance at the foot of the page. For apart from his writings after 1924, one can say that whenever Malatesta took up his pen it was either because the situation was ripe for revolutionary action, or that he saw possibilities, for effective anarchist propaganda. The critics will reply that the fact that Malatesta's writings referred to particular historical situations means the arguments cannot be relevant to, or that they have no bearing on, economic conditions or the political situation today. I take the opposite point of view because I find the ideas of the practical anarchists of the past more stimulating, as well as being able to relate much of what they say to the present, than their starry-eyed contemporaries whose ideal futures had no practical basis even in the present from which they were launched.

Much more than the political background, what should commend Malatesta to our consideration today is his way of thinking. Irving Horowitz in the long Introduction to his above mentioned anthology, seems to have discovered the place Malatesta's ideas should rightly occupy, apparently on the strength of his pamphlet *Anarchy*, when he describes him as "the great Italian anarchist who bridges 19th- and 20th-century European thought as few of his peers did." To determinism Malatesta opposed free will; to "scientism" he opposed the scientific approach. I feel that Malatesta, who when he was over 70 declared that: "to be told that I have a scientific mind does not displease me at all; I would be glad to deserve the term; for the scientific mind is one which seeks the truth by using positive, rational and experimental methods . . ." would have been happy to read the remarks with which Dr. Alex Comfort, in 1948, prefaced a long extract from an article he wrote in 1884 on the subject of "Love": "Malatesta, though not a social psychologist, gives a statement of the anarchist case [on marriage] which is possibly more balanced than any since

Godwin"; or that a political scientist in an article on "Anarchism and Trade Unionism" written in 1957, considers that not only were Malatesta's writings on the subject "a useful starting point" but that he should also conclude that his "main contentions still hold good."

Malatesta was a propagandist not a professional writer. Enzo Santarelli, the Italian Marxist historian contemptuously refers (1959) to the limitations of Malatesta as a thinker and writes him off as a revolutionary agitator, but in the process Malatesta emerges as the central character and thinker in Santarelli's 300-page volume. What a glorious "failure"!

Part Two of this volume: "Notes for a Biography" is even more modest than its title could imply. It reflects in the main the questions I asked myself about Malatesta's life in the course of reading him and the extravaganzas by the historians. Again most of the answers were to be found in the biographies and the articles published by his friends. Acknowledgement is made in the Source Notes, but I would like to mention specially three invaluable biographers and interpreters, Luigi Fabbri, Max Nettlau, and Armando Borghi (the latter still with us, and the octogenarian editor of the Italian anarchist weekly, *Umanità Nova*) who have done all the hard work. I have only selected, and if I have not retailed the human anecdotes and have presented Malatesta's Life in some twenty-odd unconnected bits, it is that while I think Malatesta's life illumines his ideas, the neglect he has suffered as a man of ideas in the English speaking world is, in part, due to the emphasis laid on his political notoriety by the historians and some of the anarchists. It seemed to me that what was required was to seek to debunk the popular "image" of the man and his background, as well as to situate him in the political picture of his time.

The Notes are followed by the Appendices. The first two in reply to Kropotkin's first world war attitude (which were written specially for *Freedom* and are, with the letter to that journal and Malatesta's account of the "Red Week" in Ancona the only texts by Malatesta which have not been translated from the Italian original for this volume) have been included in this part for convenience since they are referred to in the Notes. The article on Kropotkin, as well as being an important document for anarchists also belongs to this part of the book.

Part Three, the last forty pages, is not what I had hoped to write, which was an *Assessment* of Malatesta's ideas in terms of present-day realities. What I have produced is a rambling piece which ideally I would have wished to hold back to expand and clarify. I have not done so for a number of reasons.

Firstly because it does try to relate Malatesta's ideas to the problems of today; secondly because it deals with his ideas on the General Strike as a revolutionary tactic and in the process gives me, thirdly, the opportunity to question the thoroughness with which we anarchists study the efficacy of the tactical weapons we advocate in our propaganda. And lastly, I have included this piece aware as I am of its structural defects, because if this volume meets with the success I want it to have, it will be reflected in growing activity in the groups, a more efficient use of their energies, more coordination between groups nationally (as distinct from the organisational mania). For, even more than in the 19th century (when the anarchist movement was truly Internationalist) to survive and develop we must explore how to coordinate all our activities internationally, not by the show of internationalism—Congresses and telegrams soon evaporate—but by actions which prove our resolve beyond any shadow of doubt. Part Three, then, is not directed to the "outsiders" who may chance on this volume, but to all revolutionists, and in particular to anarchist comrades and friends wherever they may be.

It is not a criticism of the "Idea," about which the historians write their learned tomes, but an attempt to get those of us who think anarchism a wonderful way of life and also want to do something to try and change things, to take stock and seek to make the best use of our resources. The necessary decisions and action must stem from us. And Malatesta, I am convinced, is the most realistic of guides.

London, February 1965
V.R.

Malatesta outside Bow Street Police Court London (1912) where he appeared on a criminal libel charge. He was awarded a three month prison sentence and recommended for deportation. The deportation order was quashed as a result of an energetic campaign in the radical press (notably Lansbury's *Daily Herald* and the *Manchester Guardian*) and by the workers' organisations culminating in mass demonstrations in Trafalgar Square.

Editor's Introduction to the Third Edition (1984)

Nearly twenty years have passed since I wrote the Introduction to the first edition of this book. The May 1968 days have come and gone as have also the Gurus from the other side of the Atlantic such as Reich and Marcuse. Murray Bookchin and Emma Goldman still have their followers while the Germaine Greers are apparently recanting in middle age. Malatesta fortunately has not become a cult figure but his ideas are being slowly recognised by a new generation of anarchists and libertarian socialists in many parts of the world.

This Freedom Press publication has made a modest contribution to a better understanding of Malatesta's ideas in that there have been editions in Italian (Pistoia, 1968 and long out of print), in Dutch (Baarn, 1980—not a success), in Spanish (Barcelona, 1975—more than 6,000 have been sold and it is still in print), in French, as a series of pamphlets (Annecy, 1982).

The most notable effort to make Malatesta's writings available has been made in Italy where the three-volume edition of *Scritti* (first published in 1934–36) was at last reprinted in 1975 by the Movimento Anarchico Italiano, and is an invaluable source work. The late Gino Cerrito contributed a short introduction to this edition while retaining the important original introductions to each of the volumes written by Malatesta's closest friend and biographer Luigi Fabbri. Two volumes of Selections edited by Cerrito have also been published in Italian: *Scritti Scelti* (Rome, 1970) and *Rivoluzione e Lotta Quotidiana* (Revolution and Daily Struggle) (Milan, 1982). And a third volume of anti-militarist writings *Scritti Anti-Militaristi* (Milan, 1982). The *Selected Writings* have also appeared in a German edition (Berlin, 1977 and 1980).

The French group published two other volumes of selections: one of 400 pages with the title *Anarchistes, socialistes et communistes* the other of 128 pages *Pour ou Contre les Elections* (For or against voting). In all 800 pages of Malatesta's writings in French—an achievement without parallel. In addition the French paperback publishers *10/18* issued (in 1979) a 400-page volume *Articles Politiques* selected, translated and introduced by Israel Renof.

In 1982 the fiftieth anniversary of Malatesta's death was commemorated in Italy with special issues of anarchist journals, public meetings in Ancona, and a week-end Seminar organised by the Centro Studi Libertari "G. Pinelli" of Milan.

The growing awareness even among some academics that Malatesta was a considerable exponent of anarchist ideas as well as a man of action can be seen in the inclusion of extracts from his writings in recent anthologies, and such volumes as Professor Woodcock's *Anarchist Reader* (1977). But more importantly Malatesta's analysis of the political situation in the Western world and his realistic approach to the role that anarchists could play in changing that society are as valid today as ever they were.

Colchester February 1984

V.R.

PART ONE

For anarchy to succeed or simply to advance towards its success it must be conceived not only as a lighthouse which illuminates and attracts, but as something possible and attainable, not in centuries to come, but in a relatively short time and without relying on miracles.

Now, we anarchists have much concerned ourselves with the ideal; we have criticised all the moral lies and institutions which corrupt and oppress humanity, and have described, with all the eloquence and poetry each of us possessed, a longed-for harmonious society, based on goodness and on love; but, it must be admitted that we have shown very little concern with the ways and means for the achievement of our ideals.

(*Pensiero e Volontà*, 1924)

Introduction
Anarchy and Anarchism

Anarchism in its origins, its aspirations, and its methods of struggle, is not necessarily linked to any philosophical system. Anarchism was born of a moral revolt against social injustice. When men were to be found who felt as if suffocated by the social climate in which they were obliged to live; who felt the pain of others as if it were their own; who were also convinced that a large part of human suffering is not the inevitable consequence of inexorable natural or supernatural laws, but instead, stems from social realities dependent on human will and can be eliminated through human effort—the way was open that had to lead to anarchism.

The specific causes of social ills and the right means to destroy them had to be found. When some thought that the fundamental cause of the disease was the struggle between men which resulted in domination by the conquerors and the oppression and exploitation of the vanquished, and observed that the domination by the former and this subjection of the latter had given rise to capitalistic property and the State, and when they sought to overthrow both State and property—then it was that anarchism was born.[1]

I prefer to discount uncertain philosophy and stick to the common definitions which tell us that *Anarchy* is a form of social life in which men live as brothers, where nobody is in a position to oppress or exploit anyone else, and in which all the means to achieve maximum moral and material development are available to everyone; and *Anarchism* is the method by which to achieve anarchy through freedom and without government, that is without authoritarian organisms which, by using force, even, possibly for good ends, impose their will on others.[2]

Anarchy is *society organised without authority*, meaning by authority the power to *impose* one's own will and not the inevitable and beneficial fact that he who has greater understanding of, as well as ability to carry out, a task succeeds more easily in having his opinion accepted, and of acting as a guide on the particular question, for those less able than himself.

In our opinion authority not only is not necessary for social organisation but, far from benefitting it, lives on it parasitically, hampers its development, and uses its advantages for the special benefit of a particular class which exploits and oppresses the others. So long as in a community there is harmony of interests, and no one has either the desire or the means to exploit his fellow beings, there is no trace of authority; when, instead, there are internal struggles and the community is divided into conquerors and conquered, then authority appears and is of course used for the advantage of the strongest and serves to confirm, perpetuate and strengthen their victory.

Because we think in this way, we are anarchists; were we to believe that organisation was not possible without authority we would be authoritarians, because we would still prefer authority, which fetters and impoverishes life, to disorganisation which makes life impossible.[3]

How often must we repeat that we do not wish to impose anything on anybody; that we do not believe it either possible or desirable to do good by the people through force, and that all we want is that no one should impose their will on us, that no one should be in a position to impose on others a form of social life which is not freely accepted.[4]

Socialism (and it is even more true of anarchism) cannot be imposed, both on moral grounds in regard to freedom, as well as because it is impossible to apply "willy-nilly" a regime of justice for all. It cannot be imposed on a minority by a majority. Neither can it be imposed by a majority on one or more minorities.

And it is for this reason that we are anarchists, that is we want everybody to possess the "effective" freedom to live as they wish. This is not possible without expropriating the present holders of social wealth and placing the means of production at the disposal of everybody.[5]

The fundamental basis of the anarchist method is freedom, and we therefore combat, and will go on combating, all that which violates freedom (the equal freedom for all) whatever the dominant regime: monarchist, republican, or any other.[6]

We do not boast that we possess absolute truth; on the contrary, we believe that *social truth* is not a fixed quantity, good for all times, universally applicable, or determinable in advance, but that instead, once freedom has been secured, mankind will go forward discovering and acting gradually with the least number of upheavals and with a minimum of friction. Thus our solutions always leave the door open to different and, one hopes, better solutions.[7]

The factors of history are too numerous and too complex and human wills are so uncertain and indeterminable, that no one could seriously undertake to prophesy the future. But we do not want to harden our anarchism into dogma, nor impose it by force; it will be what it can be, and will develop, to the extent that men and institutions will become more favourable to integral freedom and justice. . . .[8]

We aim at the good of all, the elimination of all suffering and the extension of all the joys that can depend on human actions; we aim at the attainment of peace and love among all human beings; we aim at a new and better society, at a worthier and happier mankind. But we believe that the good of all cannot be really attained except by the conscious participation of everybody; we believe there are no magic formulae capable of solving the difficulties; that there are no universal and infallible doctrines applicable to all men and to all situations; that there do not exist providential parties and individuals, who can usefully substitute their will for that of the rest of humanity and do good by force; we believe that social life always assumes forms that result from contrasting the ideal and material interests of those who think and who make demands. And therefore we call on everybody to think and to want.[9]

By definition an anarchist is he who does not wish to be oppressed *nor wishes to be himself an oppressor*; who wants the greatest well-being, freedom and development for *all* human beings. His ideas, his wishes have their origin in a feeling of sympathy, love and respect for humanity: a feeling which must be sufficiently strong to induce him to want the well-being of others as much as his own, and to renounce those personal advantages, the achievement of which, would involve the sacrifice of others. If it were not so, why would he be the enemy of oppression and not seek to become himself an oppressor?

The anarchist knows that the individual cannot live outside society, indeed he would not exist as a human being but for the fact that he carries within him the sum total of the work of numberless generations, and profits during the whole of his life from the participation of his contemporaries.

He knows that the activity of each individual influences, directly or indirectly, the lives of every other being, and therefore recognizes the great law of solidarity, which predominates in society as in nature. And since he wants freedom for everyone, he must desire that the operation of this essential solidarity instead of being imposed and undergone, unconsciously and involuntarily, instead of being left to chance, and exploited for the advantage of a few to the detriment of the majority, should become conscious, and voluntary, and be applied for the equal benefit of all. The only possible alternative to being either the oppressed or the oppressor is voluntary cooperation for the greatest good of all; and anarchists are, of course, and they cannot but be, for cooperation which is free and desired.

We hope no one will want to "philosophise" and start hair-splitting about egoism and altruism. We agree: we are all egoists, we all seek our own satisfaction. But the anarchist finds his greatest satisfaction in struggling for the good of all, for the achievement of a society in which he can be a brother among brothers, and among healthy, intelligent, educated, happy people. But he who is adaptable, who is satisfied to live among slaves and draw profit from the labour of slaves, is not, and cannot be, an anarchist.[10]

To be an anarchist it is not enough to recognise that anarchism is a beautiful ideal—in theory everyone would agree, including sovereigns, leaders, capitalists, police and, I imagine, even Mussolini himself—but one must want to struggle to achieve anarchism, or at least to approximate to it, by seeking to reduce the power of the State and of privilege, and by demanding always greater freedom, greater justice.[11]

Why are we anarchists?

Apart from our ideas about the political State and government, that is on the coercive organisation of society, which are our specific characteristic, and those on the best way to ensure for everybody free access to the means of production and enjoyment of the good things of life, we are anarchists because of a feeling which is the driving force for all sincere social reformers, and without which our anarchism would be either a lie or just nonsense.

This feeling is the love of mankind, and the fact of sharing the sufferings of others. If I . . . eat I cannot enjoy what I am eating if I think that there are people dying of hunger; if I buy a toy for my child and am made happy by her pleasure, my happiness is soon embittered at seeing wide-eyed children standing by the shop window who could be made happy with a cheap toy but who cannot have it; if I am enjoying myself, my spirit is saddened as soon as I recall that there are unfortunate fellow beings languishing in jail; if I study, or do a job I enjoy doing, I feel remorse at the thought that there are so many brighter than I who are obliged to waste their lives on exhausting, often useless, or harmful tasks.

Clearly, pure egoism; others call it altruism, call it what you like; but without it, it is not possible to be real anarchists. Intolerance of oppression, the desire to be free and to be able to develop one's personality to its full limits, is not enough to make one an anarchist. That aspiration towards unlimited freedom, if not tempered by a love for mankind and by the desire that all should enjoy equal freedom, may well create rebels who, if they are strong enough, soon become exploiters and tyrants, but never anarchists.[12]

There are strong, intelligent, passionate individuals, with strong material or intellectual needs, who finding themselves, by chance, among the oppressed, seek, at all costs to emancipate themselves and do not resent becoming oppressors: individuals who, feeling imprisoned in existing society, come to despise and hate every society, and realising that it would be absurd to want to live isolated from the human community, seek to subject society and all men to their will and to the satisfaction of their desires. Sometimes, when they are well read, they think of themselves as *supermen*. They are unhampered by scruples; they want "to live their lives"; they poke fun at the revolution and at every forward-looking aspiration, they want to enjoy life in the present at any cost and at everybody's expense; they would sacrifice the whole of mankind for one hour's "intensive living" (there are those who have used these very words).

They are rebels, but not anarchists. They have the mentality and the feelings of unsuccessful bourgeois, and when they do succeed they not only become bourgeois in fact, but are not the least unpleasant among them.

We can sometimes, in the ever-changing circumstances of the struggle, find them alongside us; but we cannot, we must not, and we do not wish to be confused with them. And they know it only too well. But many of them like to call themselves anarchists. It is true—as well as deplorable.

We cannot prevent anyone from calling himself by whatever name he likes, nor can we, on the other hand, abandon the name that succinctly expresses our ideas and which, logically as well as historically, belongs to us. All we can do is to try to prevent any confusion, or at least seek to reduce it to a minimum.[13]

I am an anarchist because it seems to me that anarchy would correspond better than any other way of social life, to my desire for the good of all, to my aspirations towards a society which reconciles the liberty of everyone with cooperation and love among men, and not because anarchism is a scientific truth and a natural law. It is enough for me that it should not contradict any known law of nature to consider it possible and to struggle to win the support needed to achieve it.[14]

I am a communist (libertarian of course); I am for agreement and I believe that through an intelligent decentralisation, and a continuous exchange of ideas, it would be possible to arrive at the organisation of the necessary exchange of goods and satisfy the needs of all without having recourse to the money symbol, which is certainly fraught with problems and dangers. As every good communist does, I aspire to the abolition of money; and, as every good revolutionary,

I believe that it will be necessary to strip the bourgeoisie, invalidating all the symbols of wealth which permit people to live without working.[15]

We often find ourselves saying: "anarchism is the abolition of the *gendarme*" meaning by *gendarme* any armed force, any material force in the service of a man or of a class, to oblige others to do what they would otherwise not do voluntarily. Of course, that definition does not give even an approximate idea of what is meant by anarchy, which is a society founded on free agreement, in which every individual can achieve the maximum development, material and moral, as well as intellectual; in which he finds in social solidarity the guarantee for his freedom and well-being. The removal of physical constriction is not enough in itself to ensure that he will acquire the dignity of a free man, or learn to love his fellow men and to respect in them those rights which he wants others to respect for him, and to refuse both to command as well as to be commanded. One can be a willing slave for reasons of moral deficiency and a lack of faith in oneself, just as one can be a tyrant through wickedness or a lack of conscience when one does not meet adequate resistance. But this is not to say that "the abolition of the *gendarme*," that is the abolition of violence in social relations is not the basis, the indispensable condition without which anarchy could not flourish, and, indeed, could not be conceived.[16]

Since all the present ills of society have their origin in the struggle between men, in the seeking after well-being through one's own efforts and for oneself and against everybody, we want to make amends, replacing hatred by love, competition by solidarity, the individual search for personal well-being by the fraternal cooperation for the well-being of all, oppression and imposition by liberty, the religious and pseudo-scientific lie by truth, therefore:

1. Abolition of private property in land, in raw materials and the instruments of labour, so that no one shall have the means of living by the exploitation of the labour of others, and that everybody, being assured of the means to produce and to live, shall be truly independent and in a position to unite freely among themselves for a common objective and according to their personal sympathies.

2. Abolition of government and of every power which makes the law and imposes it on others: therefore abolition of monarchies, republics, parliaments, armies, police forces, magistratures, and any institution whatsoever endowed with coercive powers.
3. Organisation of social life by means of free association and federations of producers and consumers, created and modified according to the wishes of their members, guided by science and experience, and free from any kind of imposition which does not spring from natural needs, to which everyone, convinced by a feeling of overriding necessity, voluntarily submits.
4. The means of life, for development and well-being, will be guaranteed to children and all who are prevented from providing for themselves.
5. War on religions and all lies, even if they shelter under the cloak of science. Scientific instruction for all to advanced level.
6. War on rivalries and patriotic prejudices. Abolition of frontiers; brotherhood among all peoples.
7. Reconstruction of the family, as will emerge from the practice of love, freed from every legal tie, from every economic and physical oppression, from every religious prejudice.[17]

What we want, therefore, is the complete destruction of the domination and exploitation of man by man; we want men united as brothers by a conscious and desired solidarity, all cooperating voluntarily for the well-being of all; we want society to be constituted for the purpose of supplying everybody with the means for achieving the maximum well-being, the maximum possible moral and spiritual development; we want bread, freedom, love, and science—for everybody.[18]

I

1. Anarchist Schools of Thought

One can be an anarchist irrespective of the philosophic system one prefers. There are materialist-anarchists as there are others, like myself, who without prejudicing future developments of the human mind, prefer simply to declare their ignorance in these matters.

Certainly it is difficult to understand how certain theories can be reconciled with the practical aspects of life.

The mechanistic theory, no less than the theistic and pantheistic theories, would logically lead to indifference and inaction, to the supine acceptance of all that exists both in the moral and material fields.

Fortunately philosophic concepts have little influence on conduct. And materialists and "mechanicists" in the teeth of logic, often sacrifice themselves for an ideal. Just as, incidentally, do religious people, who believe in the eternal joys of paradise, but take good care to live as well as possible in this world, and when ill are afraid of dying and call in the doctor.[1]

There are those among the anarchists who like to call themselves communists, or collectivists, or individualists or what have you. Often it is a question of different interpretations of words which obscure and hide a fundamental identity of objectives; sometimes it is only a question of theories, hypotheses with which each person explains and justifies in different ways identical practical conclusions.[2]

Among the anarchists there are the revolutionists, who believe that the force which maintains the existing order must be overthrown by force in order to create a political climate in which the free development of individuals and of the community will be possible; and there are the educationists who think that social transformation can be achieved only by first changing people by means of education and propaganda. There are, too, the partisans of non-resistance, or of passive resistance who repudiate violence even when it serves to repel violence; and there are those who recognise the necessity for violence who, in their turn, are divided as to the nature, the extent and the limits of such violence. There are disagreements as to the anarchist attitude to the Trades Unions; disagreements on the need or otherwise of a specific anarchist organisation; permanent or temporary disagreement as to the relationship between anarchists and opposition parties.

And on these and other similar questions one must seek ways of reaching agreement; or if, as seems to be the case, agreement is not possible, we must know how to tolerate each other; by working together when in agreement and, leaving each one to do as he thinks fit without hampering each other when not. For, come to think about it, nobody can be absolutely certain of being in the right, and nobody is always right.[3]

Morally, anarchism is sufficient unto itself; but to be translated into facts it needs concrete forms of material life, and it is the preference for one or other form which differentiates the various anarchist schools of thought.

In the anarchist milieu, communism, individualism, collectivism, mutualism, and all the intermediate and eclectic programmes are simply the ways considered best for achieving freedom and solidarity in economic life; the ways believed to correspond most closely with justice and freedom for the distribution of the means of production and the products of labour among men.

Bakunin was an anarchist, and he was a collectivist, an outspoken enemy of communism because he saw in it the negation of freedom and, therefore, of human dignity. And with Bakunin, and for a long time after him, almost all the Spanish anarchists were collectivists, and yet they were among the most conscious and consistent anarchists.

Others for the same reason of defence and guarantee of liberty declare themselves to be individualists and they want each person to have as individual property the part that is due to him of the means of production and therefore the free disposal of the products of his labour.

Others invent more or less complicated systems of mutuality. But in the long run it is always the searching for a more secure guarantee of freedom which is the common factor among anarchists, and which divides them into different schools.[4]

The individualists assume, or speak as if they assumed, that (anarchist) communists want to impose communism, which of course would put them right outside the ranks of anarchism.

The communists assume, or speak as if they assumed, that the (anarchist) individualists reject every idea of association, want the struggle between men, the domination of the strongest—and this would put them not only outside the anarchist movement but outside humanity.

In reality those who are communists are such because they see in communism freely accepted the realisation of brotherhood, and the best guarantee for individual freedom. And individualists, those that are really anarchists, are anticommunist because they fear that communism would subject individuals nominally to the tyranny of the collectivity and in fact to that of the party or caste, which, with the excuse of administering things, would succeed in taking possession of the power to dispose of material things and thus of the people who need them. Therefore they want each individual, or each group, to be in a position to enjoy freely the product of their labour in conditions of equality with other individuals and groups, with whom they would maintain relations of justice and equity.

In which case it is clear that there is no basic difference between us. But, according to the communists, justice and equity are, under natural conditions, impossible of attainment in an individualistic society, and thus freedom too would not be attained.

If climatic conditions throughout the world were the same, if the land was everywhere equally fertile, if raw materials were evenly distributed and within reach of all who needed them, if social development were the same everywhere in the world, if the work of past generations had benefitted all countries to the same extent, if population were evenly distributed over the whole habitable area of the globe—then one could conceive of everyone (individuals or groups) finding the land, tools and raw materials needed to work and produce independently, without exploiting or being exploited. But natural and historical conditions being what they are, how is it possible to establish equality and justice between he who by chance finds himself with a piece of arid land which demands much labour for small returns with him who has a piece of fertile and well sited land? Or between the inhabitants of a village lost in the mountains or in the middle of a marshy area, with the inhabitant of a city which hundreds of generations of man have enriched with all the skill of human genius and labour?[5]

I warmly recommend Armand's book *l'Iniziazione individualista anarchica* which is a conscientious piece of work by one of the ablest individualist anarchists and which has received general approval among the individualists. But, in reading this book one asks oneself why on earth Armand continually talks of "anarchist individualism" as a body of doctrine when in general all he does is to expound principles common to anarchists of all tendencies. In fact Armand, who likes to call himself an amoralist, has actually produced a kind of manual or anarchist morality—not "individualist anarchist"—but anarchist in general, indeed more than anarchist, a deeply human morality, because it is based on those human feelings which make anarchy desirable and possible.[6]

Nettlau is mistaken, in my opinion, in believing that the differences between the anarchists who call themselves communists and those who call themselves individualists stem from their respective views on what forms economic life (production and distribution of goods) will take in an anarchist society. These after all are questions which concern the distant future; and if it is true that the ideal, the final aim, is the light that guides or should guide, man's behaviour, it is also even more true that what determines, above all else, agreement or disagreement is not what one aspires to do in the future, but what one does or wants to do in the present. In general, one reaches understanding, and there is a greater incentive to do so with those who are taking the same road as ourselves though they may be going somewhere else, than with those who, though declaring that their destination is the same as ours, take a road which runs in the opposite direction! Thus it has happened for anarchists of the different tendencies, in spite of the fact that fundamentally they wanted the same thing to find themselves, in fierce opposition on the practical questions of life and propaganda.

Admitted the basic principle of anarchism—which is that no-one should wish or have the opportunity to reduce others to a state of subjection and oblige them to work for him—it is clear that all, and only, those ways of life which respect freedom, and recognise that each individual has an equal right to the means of production and to the full enjoyment of the product of his own labour, have anything in common with anarchism.[7]

2. Anarchist—Communism

In 1876 we were, as we are still, anarchist communists; but this does not mean that we use communism as a panacea or dogma, and fail to see that to achieve communism certain moral and material conditions are needed which we must create.[1]

Luigi Galleani's "La Fine dell'Anarchismo" . . . is in essence a clear, serene, eloquent account of *anarchist communism* according to the Kropotkinian conception; a conception which I personally find too optimistic, too easy-going, too trusting in *natural harmonies*, but for all that, his is the most important contribution to anarchist propaganda that has been made so far.[2]

We too aspire to communism as the most perfect achievement of human solidarity, but it must be anarchist communism, that is, freely desired and accepted, and the means by which the freedom of everyone is guaranteed and can expand; for these reasons we maintain that State communism, which is authoritarian and imposed, is the most hateful tyranny that has ever afflicted, tormented and handicapped mankind.[3]

Those anarchists who call themselves communists (and I am one of them) do so not because they wish to impose their particular way of seeing things on others or because they believe that outside communism there can be no salvation, but because they are convinced, until proved wrong, that the more human beings are joined in brotherhood, and the more closely they cooperate in their efforts for the benefit of all concerned, the greater is the well-being and freedom which each can enjoy. They believe that Man, even if freed from oppression by his fellow men, still remains exposed to the hostile forces of Nature, which he cannot overcome alone, but which, in association with others, can be harnessed and transformed into the means for his own well-being. The man who would wish to provide for his material needs by working alone is a slave to his work . . . as well as not being always sure of producing enough to keep alive. It would be fantastic to think that some anarchists, who call themselves, and indeed are, communists, should desire to live as in a convent, subjected to common rules, uniform meals and clothes, etc.; but it would be equally absurd to think that they should want to do just as they like without taking into account the needs of others or of the right all have to equal freedom. Everybody knows that Kropotkin, for instance, who was one of the most active and eloquent anarchist propagandists of the communist idea was at the same time a staunch defender of the independence of the individual, and passionately desired that everybody should be able to develop and satisfy freely their artistic talents, engage in scientific research, and succeed in establishing a harmonious unity between manual and intellectual activity in order to become human beings in the noblest sense of the word. Furthermore communist-anarchists believe that because of the natural differences in fertility, salubrity, and location of the land masses, it would be impossible to ensure equal working conditions for everyone individually and so achieve, if not solidarity, at least, justice. But at the same time they are aware of the immense difficulties in the way of putting into practice that world wide, free-communism, which they look upon as the ultimate objective of a humanity emancipated and united, without a long period of free development. And for this reason they arrive at conclusions which could be perhaps expressed in the following formula: The achievement of the greatest measures of individualism is in direct ratio to the amount of communism that is possible; that is to say, a maximum of solidarity in order to enjoy a maximum of freedom.[4]

In theory communism is the ideal system which, so far as human relationships are concerned, would replace struggle by solidarity and would utilise natural energies and human labour to the best possible advantage and transform humanity into one big brotherhood intent on mutual aid and love.

But is this practical in the existing spiritual and material state of human affairs? And if so, within what limits?

Worldwide communism, that is a single community among all mankind, is an aspiration, an ideal goal at which one must aim, but which certainly could not be a possible form of economic organisation at present. We are, of course, speaking for our times and probably for some time to come; so far as the distant future is concerned we leave it to future generations to think about that.

For the present one can only think of multiple communities among people who are kindred spirits, and who would, besides, have dealings with each other of various kinds, communistic or commercial; and even within these limits there is always the problem of a possible antagonism between communism and freedom. Assuming the feeling exists that draws men towards brotherhood and a conscious and desired solidarity, and which will encourage us to propagate and put into effect as much communism as possible, I believe that, just as complete individualism would be uneconomic as well as impossible, so would complete communism be impossible as well as anti-libertarian, more so if applied over a large territory.

To organise a communist society on a large scale it would be necessary to transform all economic life radically, such as methods of production, of exchange and consumption; and this could not be achieved other than gradually, as the objective circumstances permitted and to the extent that the masses understood what advantages could be gained and were able to act for themselves. If, on the other hand, one wanted, and could, carry out in one sweep the wishes and the ambitions of a party, the masses, accustomed to obey and serve, would accept the new way of life as a new law imposed on them by a new government, and would wait for a new supreme power to tell them how to produce, and determine for them what they should consume. And the new power, not knowing, and being unable to satisfy a huge variety of often contradictory needs and desires, and not wanting to declare itself useless by leaving to the interested parties the freedom to act as they wish or as best they can, would reconstitute the State, based, as all States are, on military and police forces which, assuming it survived, would simply replace the old set of rules by new, and more fanatical ones. Under the pretext, and even perhaps with the honest and sincere intention of regenerating the world with a new Gospel, a new single rule would be imposed on everybody; all freedom would be suppressed and free initiative made impossible; and as a result there would be disillusionment, a paralyzing of production, black markets, and smuggling, increased power and corruption in the civil service, widespread misery and finally a more or less complete return to those conditions of oppression and exploitation which it was the aim of the revolution to abolish.

The Russian experiment must not have been in vain.

In conclusion, it seems to me, that no system can be vital and really serve to free mankind from the slavery of the remote past, if it is not the result of free development.

Human societies, if they are to be communities of free men working together for the greatest good of all, and no longer convents or despotisms held together by religious superstition or brute force, cannot be the artificial creation of an individual or of a sect. They must be the resultant of the needs and the competitive or divergent wills of all their members who by trial and error find the institutions which at any given time are the best possible, and who develop and change them as circumstances and wills change.

One may, therefore, prefer communism, or individualism or collectivism, or any other system, and work by example and propaganda for the achievement of one's personal preferences; but one must beware, at the risk of certain disaster, of supposing that one's own system is the only, and infallible one, good for all men, everywhere and for all times, and that its success must be ensured at all costs, by means other than those which depend on persuasion, which spring from the evidence of facts.

What is important and indispensable, the point of departure, is to ensure for everybody the means to be free.[5]

3. Anarchism and Science

> Science is a weapon which can be used for good or bad ends; but science ignores completely the idea of good and evil. We are therefore anarchists not because science tells us to be but because, among other reasons, we want everybody to be in a position to enjoy the advantages and pleasures which science procures.[1]

In science, theories are always hypothetical and provisional and are a convenient method for grouping and linking known facts, as well as a useful instrument for research, for the discovery and interpretation of new facts; but they are not the truth. In life—I mean social life—theories are for some people only the scientific guise in which they clothe their desires and their wills. The scientism (I am not saying science) which was prevalent in the second half of the 19th century produced that tendency to consider as scientific truth (namely, natural laws and therefore necessary and predestined) that which was no more than the concept, corresponding to different interests and to the various aspirations that each individual created for himself, of justice, progress, etc."Scientific socialism," as well as "scientific anarchism," were derived from this concept and, though professed by the most eminent among us, have always seemed to me grotesque concepts, a mixing up of things and concepts which are by their very nature quite distinct.

I may be right or wrong, but in any case I am pleased that I avoided the fashion of the period, and was therefore free of dogmatism and of any pretension of possessing the absolute "social truth."[2]

I do not believe in the infallibility of Science, neither in its ability to explain everything nor in its mission of regulating the conduct of Man, just as I do not believe in the infallibility of the Pope, in revealed Morality and the divine origins of the Holy Scriptures.

I only believe those things which can be proved; but I know full well that *proofs* are relative and can be, and are in fact, continually superseded and cancelled out by other proved facts; and therefore I believe that doubt should be the mental approach of all who aspire to get ever closer to the truth, or at least to that much of truth that it is possible to establish. . . .

To the *will to believe,* which cannot be other than the desire to invalidate one's own reason, I oppose the *will to know,* which leaves the immense field of research and discovery open to us. As I have already stated, I admit only that which can be proved in a way that satisfies my reason—and I admit it only *provisionally, relatively,* always in the expectation of new truths which are more true than those so far discovered. No *faith* then, in the religious sense of the word.

I sometimes say that faith is needed, or that in the struggle for the good, men of sure faith are needed. And there is even an anarchist newspaper which, presumably inspired by this need, bears the title *Fede!* (Faith). But in these cases the word is used in the sense of *determination, great hopes,* and has nothing in common with the blind belief in things which appear to be either incomprehensible or absurd.

But how, then, do I reconcile this incredulity in religion, and this, what I would call systematic doubt in the definitive results of science, with a moral rule and the determined will and hope of achieving my ideal of freedom, justice and human brotherhood? The fact is that I do not introduce science where science does not belong. The function of science is to discover and to state the fact and the conditions under which fact invariably is produced and is repeated; that is, to state that which is and which inevitably must be, and not that which men desire and want.

Science stops where inevitability ends and freedom begins. It serves man because it prevents him from getting lost in fanciful conceptions, and also supplies him with the means to increase the time available for the exercise of free will: a capacity of willing which distinguishes men, and perhaps to a different degree all animals, from inert matter and unconscious forces.

And it is in this ability to exercise willpower that one must seek for the sources of morality and the rules of behaviour.[3]

I protest against the charge of dogmatism, because, though I am unflinching and definite as to what I *want,* I am always doubtful about what I know, and I think that, in spite of all the efforts made to understand and explain the Universe, we have so far achieved neither certainty nor even the probability of certainty—and I wonder whether human intelligence will ever get there.

On the other hand to be told that I have a scientific mind does not displease me at all; I would be glad to deserve the term; for the scientific mind is one which seeks the truth by using positive, rational and experimental methods; which never cherishes illusions of having found the absolute Truth and is content with painstakingly approaching it, discovering partial truths, which it considers always as provisional and revisable. In my opinion, the scientist is he who examines facts and draws from them logical conclusions whatever they may be, as opposed to those who form a system for themselves and then seek confirmation in facts, and in so doing unconsciously select the facts which fit into their system and overlook the others; and perhaps even force and distort the facts to squeeze them into the framework of their concepts. The scientist makes use of hypotheses to work on, that is to say he makes certain assumptions which serve him as a guide and as a spur in his research, but he is not the victim of his imagination, nor does he allow familiarity with his assumptions to be hardened into a demonstrated truth, raising to a law, with arbitrary induction, every individual fact which serves his thesis.

The *scientism* which I reject and which, provoked and encouraged by the enthusiasm which followed the really marvellous discoveries made at that time in the fields of physical-chemistry and of natural history, dominated minds in the second half of the last century, is the belief that science is everything and is capable of everything; it is the acceptance as definitive truths, as dogmas, every partial discovery; it is the confusion of Science with Morals; of Force, in the mechanical sense of the word, with Thought; of natural Law with Will. Scientism logically leads to fatalism, that is, to the denial of free will and of freedom.[4]

In his attempt to fix the "place of Anarchism in Modern Science" Kropotkin finds that "Anarchism is a concept of the universe based on the mechanical interpretation of the phenomena which embrace all nature, not excluding the life of society."

This is philosophy, more or less acceptable, but it is certainly neither science nor Anarchism.

Science is the collection and systematisation of what we know or believe we know: it states the fact and seeks to discover the law of the fact, that is the conditions in which the fact inevitably occurs and repeats itself. It satisfies certain intellectual needs and is at the same time a most valid instrument of power. While, on the one hand, it indicates the limits of human power over natural laws, on the other it adds to the effective freedom of Man by giving him the means to turn these laws to his advantage. Science does not discriminate between men, and serves for good or evil, to liberate as well as to oppress.

Philosophy can be a hypothetical explanation of what is known, or an attempt to guess what is not known. It poses questions which, so far at least, go beyond the competence of science, and suggests answers which, in the present state of our knowledge, cannot be subjected to proof. Thus different philosophers offer divergent, and contradictory solutions. When philosophy is not simply a play on words and an illusionist's trick, it can be a spur and a guide to science, but it is not science.

Anarchy instead, is a human aspiration, which is not founded on any real or imagined natural necessity, but which can be achieved through the exercise of the human will. It takes advantage of the means that science offers to Man in his struggle against nature and between contrasting wills; it can profit from advances in philosophic thought when they serve to teach men to develop their reasoning powers and distinguish more clearly between reality and fantasy; but one leaves oneself open to ridicule by trying to confuse Anarchy with science or any given philosophical system. But let us see if "the mechanical conception of the universe" really explains known facts.

We will then see if it can at least be reconciled, and logically co-exist with anarchism or with any aspiration towards a state of things different from that which exists today.

The fundamental principle of mechanics is the conservation of energy: nothing is created and nothing can be destroyed.

A body cannot give up heat to another without cooling by a similar amount; one form of energy cannot be transformed into another (transference of heat, heat into electric current or vice versa, etc.) without that which is acquired in one way being lost by the other. Indeed, in all physical nature, the very common fact is verified that if someone has ten coppers and spends five, he is left with exactly five, neither more nor less.

Instead, if one has an idea it can be communicated to a million people without losing anything, and the more the idea is propagated the more it gains in strength and effectiveness. A teacher transmits to others what he knows, and does not, as a result become less knowledgeable; on the contrary in teaching others he learns new things and enriches his own mind. If a lead pellet released by a murderous hand cuts short the life of a man of genius, science may be able to explain what happens to all the material elements, (the physical energy of the man of genius when he was killed) and demonstrate that nothing remains of his physical characteristics once his corpse has decomposed, but that at the same time nothing has been lost materially because every atom of that corpse can be traced with all its energy in other combinations. But the ideas which that genius gave to the world, his inventions, remain and grow and can become a potent force; whereas, on the other hand, those ideas which were still developing in him and could have come to fruition, had he not been killed, are lost and cannot ever be found again.

Can mechanics explain this power, this specific quality of the products of the mind?

Please, do not ask me to explain in another way the fact which mechanics does not manage to explain.

I am not a philosopher; but one does not need to be a philosopher in order to see certain problems which more or less torment all thinking minds. And the fact of not knowing how to solve a problem does not oblige one to accept unconvincing solutions . . . the more so since the solutions the philosophers offer are so numerous as well as mutually contradictory.

And now let us see if "mechanicism" can be reconciled with anarchism.

In the mechanical concept (as, after all, in the theistic concept) everything is determined, inevitable, nothing can be other than what it is. Indeed if nothing is created and nothing is destroyed, if matter and energy (whatever they may be) are fixed quantities, subjected to mechanical laws, all phenomena are inalterably related.

Kropotkin says: Since man is a part of nature, since his personal and social life is also a phenomenon of nature—in the same way as in the growth of a flower, or in the evolution of life in the community of ants and bees—there is no reason why in passing from the flower to Man and from a colony of beavers to a human city, we should abandon the system which had hitherto served us so well, to seek another in the arsenal of metaphysics. And already at the end of the 18th century the great mathematician Laplace had said, "Given the forces animating nature and the respective situations of the beings that compose it, a sufficiently broad human intelligence would be able to know the past and the future as well as the present."

This is the purely mechanical concept; all that has been had to be, all that will be, must be *perforce*, inevitably, in every minute detail of time, place, and degree.

In such a concept, what meaning can the words "will, freedom, responsibility" have? And of what use would education, propaganda, revolt be? One can no more transform the predestined course of human affairs than one can change the course of the stars. What then?

What has Anarchy to do with this?[5]

Our desk is cluttered with manuscripts from good comrades who want to give "a scientific basis" to anarchism . . . and whose confused writings are accompanied by notes apologising for not being able to do better because . . . they have not had the opportunity to study.

But why then bother with the things one doesn't know about instead of doing good propaganda, based on needs and on human aspirations?

It is certainly not necessary to be a doctor to be a good and effective anarchist—indeed sometimes it is a disadvantage. But when it comes to talking about science perhaps it would not be a bad idea to know something about the subject!

And let no one accuse us, as one comrade did recently, of holding science in scant regard. On the contrary, we know what a beautiful, great, powerful and useful thing is science; we know how much it serves the emancipation of thought and the triumph of man in the struggle against adverse forces of nature, and for these reasons wish we all had the possibility of obtaining a general idea of *Science* as well as probing more deeply at least one of its innumerable branches.

In our programme it says not only "bread for all" but also "science for all." But it seems to us that to discuss science usefully it is first necessary to have clear ideas as to its scope and function. Science, like bread is not a free gift of Nature. It must be won by effort, and we struggle to create the conditions whereby all are in a position to make that effort.[6]

The aim of scientific research is to study nature, to discover the facts and the "laws" that govern it, that is the conditions in which the fact *invariably* occurs and *invariably* recurs. A science is established when it can foretell what will happen, whether it can or not explain why; if the prediction does not materialise, it means that there was error and it is needful to proceed further and do more thorough research. Chance, free-will, the exception, are concepts alien to science, which seeks that which is predestined, that which cannot be otherwise, that which is determined. That determination which interlinks in time and space all natural phenomena, and which it is the task of science to investigate and discover, does it embrace all that happens in the Universe, including psychic and social phenomena? The mechanists say it does, and think that everything is subjected to the same mechanical laws, everything is predetermined by physico-chemical antecedents: from the course of the stars, and the opening of a flower, to the heart throb of a lover and the unfolding of human history. And I concur willingly that the system appears grandiose and beautiful, and if it could be demonstrated to be true, would completely satisfy the spirit. But then, in spite of all the pseudo-logical efforts of the determinists to reconcile the System with life and moral sentiment, there just is no room, either conditioned or unconditioned, for will and for freedom. Our lives and the life of human society would all be predestined and foreseeable, *ab eterno* and for eternity, in each and every minute detail just as is every mechanical fact, and our will would be simply an illusion as in the case of the stone Spinoza talks about which when it falls is conscious of descent and believes that it falls because it wants to.

If this is admitted, which mechanists, cannot but admit without contradicting themselves, it becomes an absurdity to want to regulate one's own life, to want to educate oneself and others, to want to change, in one way or another, social organisation. All this bustle and activity to secure a better future, then, becomes the sterile fruit of an illusion, and could not last once one had discovered that it was an illusion. It is true that illusion and absurdity would be determined products of the mechanical functioning of the brain, and as such would be part of the system. But, once again, we ask what place is left for will and for freedom, for the effectiveness of human action on life and on the future of mankind? If Man is to have confidence, or at least the possibility of useful action, one must admit a creative force, a first cause, or first causes, independent of the physical world and the mechanical laws, and this force is what is called will.

To admit the existence of such a force, means of course, denying the general application of the principle of causality, and our logic is in difficulty. But is this not always the case when we try to seek the origins of things? We do not know what will is; but do we perhaps know what matter, or energy are? We know the facts, but not the reason for them, and however much we try we always arrive at an effect without a cause, to a first cause—and if to explain facts we need first causes to be ever present and ever active, we will accept their existence as a necessary, or at least convenient, hypothesis.

Viewed in this light, the function of science is to discover that which is determined (natural laws) and establish the limits where inevitability ends and freedom begins; and its great usefulness consists in freeing Man from the illusion of believing that he can do anything he likes and can always extend the radius of his effective freedom. So long as the forces which subject all bodies to the laws of gravitation were not known, Man might have thought it possible to fly at will, but remained on the ground; when science discovered the conditions required to float and to move in the atmosphere Man really acquired the freedom to fly.

In conclusion, all I am maintaining is that the existence of wills capable of producing new effects, independent of mechanical laws of nature, is *a necessary presupposition* for those who believe in the possibility of changing society.[7]

4. Anarchism and Freedom

In nature, outside human nature, force only rules, that is, brute force, ruthless, and limitless, because there does not yet exist that new force to which mankind owes its differentiation, and its superiority: the force of conscious will.

All specifically human life is a struggle against outside nature, and every forward step is adaptation, is the overcoming of a natural law.

Natural law is struggle, general slaughter, destruction, or oppression of the vanquished; and on the social plane the greater the tyranny the closer is one to the state of nature.

The concept of freedom for all, which inevitably involves the precept that one's freedom is limited by the equal freedom of others, is a human concept; it is probably mankind's greatest achievement and victory over nature.[1]

It is only too true that the interests, the passions and tastes of Man are not naturally harmonious, and that having to live together in society it is necessary that each individual should seek to adapt himself and reconcile his desires with those of others, in order to arrive at a *modus vivendi* which satisfies him as well as others. This involves a limitation on freedom, and shows that *freedom,* in its absolute sense, could not solve the question of a happy and voluntary co-existence.

The question can only be resolved by solidarity, brotherhood and love, as a result of which the sacrificing of desires which are irreconcilable with those of others, is voluntarily and willingly made.

But when one talks of freedom politically, and not philosophically, nobody thinks of the metaphysical bogy of abstract man who exists outside the cosmic and social environment and who, like some god, *could do what he wishes* in the absolute sense of the word.

When one talks of freedom one is speaking of a society in which no one could constrain his fellow beings without meeting with vigorous resistance, in which, above all, nobody could seize and use the collective force to impose his own wishes on others and on the very groups which are the source of power.

Man is not perfect, agreed. But this is one reason more, perhaps the strongest reason, for not giving anyone the means to "put the brakes on individual freedom."

Man is not perfect. But then where will one also find men who are not only good enough to live at peace with others, but also capable of controlling the lives of others in an authoritarian way? And assuming that there were, who would appoint them? Would they impose themselves? But who would protect them from the resistance and the violence of the "criminals"? Or would they be chosen by the "sovereign people," which is considered too ignorant and too wicked to live in peace, but which suddenly acquires all the necessary good qualities when it is a question of asking it to choose its rulers? . . .

The harmonious society cannot arise other than from free wills cooperating freely under the pressure of the necessities of life and in order to satisfy that need for brotherhood and love, which always flourishes among men once they are freed from the fear of being imposed upon and of lacking the necessities of life for themselves and their dependents.[2]

We pride ourselves with being, first and foremost, advocates of freedom; freedom not for us alone, but for everybody; freedom not only for that which seems to us to be the truth, but also for that which might be or appears to be error. . . .

Our demand is simply for what could be called social freedom, which is equal freedom for all, an equality of conditions such as to allow everybody to do as they wish, with the only limitation, imposed by inevitable natural necessities and the equal freedom of others. . . .

The freedom we want is not the abstract right, but the power, to do as one wishes; it therefore presupposes that everybody has the means to live and to act without being subjected to the wishes of others. And since to maintain life it is essential to produce, the prerequisite of freedom is that all land, raw materials and the means of production should be at the free disposal of all.[3]

Indeed it is not a question of right or wrong; it is a question of freedom for everybody, freedom for each individual so long as he respects the equal freedom of others.

None can judge with certainty who is right and who is wrong, who is nearest to the truth, or which is the best way to achieve the greatest good for each and everyone. Freedom coupled with experience, is the only way of discovering the truth and what is best; and there can be no freedom if there is a denial of the freedom to err.[4]

Who, in any case, is to tell us what is truth and what error? Shall we have to establish a ministry of public education with its qualified teachers, recognised textbooks, school inspectors, etc.? And all this in the name of the "people," just as with the social democrats, who want to get power in the name of the "proletariat"? And the corruption that is exercised by power, that is, the fact of thinking that one has the right, and is in a position, to impose one's own wishes on others?

With good reason we say that when the social democrats go to Parliament they virtually cease to be socialists. But this, surely, does not stem from the material action of taking a seat in an Assembly which is called Parliament; it is the power which goes with the title of member of parliament [which corrupts].

If we, in any way, dominate the lives of others and prevent them from doing what they wish to do, then for all practical purposes we cease to be anarchists.[5]

By all means let them go on calling us pure sentimentalists as long as they like but we cannot do otherwise than protest loudly against the reactionary, authoritarian, destructive theory which states that freedom is a good principle for a future society but not for the present. It is in the name of this theory that existing tyrannies have been established, and will be established, if the people allow themselves to be taken in.

Louis Blanc, the historian of the Great French Revolution, wanting to explain and justify the contradictions between the alleged humanitarian and liberal aspirations of the Jacobins, and the fierce tyranny they imposed once they were in power, in fact drew a distinction between the "republic" which was then an institution still to come, in which principles would be applied in full measure, with the "revolution" which was the present, and served to justify all tyrannies as a means to achieve the triumph of freedom and justice. What followed was the use of the guillotine upon the best revolutionaries as well as upon a vast number of unfortunates, consolidation of the bourgeois power, the Empire and the Restoration. . . .

To fight our enemies effectively, we do not need to deny the principle of freedom, not even for one moment: it is sufficient for us to want real freedom and to want it for all, for ourselves as well as for others.

We want to expropriate the property-owning class, and with violence, since it is with violence that they hold on to social wealth and use it to exploit the working class. Not because freedom is a good thing for the future, but because it is, at all times, a good thing, today as well as tomorrow, and the property owners by denying us the means for exercising our freedom, in effect, take it away from us.

We want to overthrow the government, all governments—and overthrow them with violence since it is by the use of violence that they force us into obeying—and once again, not because we sneer at freedom when it does not serve our interests but because governments are the negation of freedom and it is not possible to be free without being rid of them.

By force we want to deprive the priests of their privileges, because with these privileges, secured by the power of the State, they deny others the right, that is, the means, of equal freedom to propagate their ideas and beliefs.

The freedom to oppress, to exploit, to oblige people to take up arms, to pay taxes, etc., is the denial of freedom; and the fact that our enemies make irrelevant and hypocritical use of the word freedom is not enough to make us deny the principle of freedom which is the outstanding characteristic of our movement and a permanent, constant and necessary factor in the life and progress of humanity.

Equal freedom for all and the right, therefore, to resist every violation of freedom, and resist with brute force when the violation is maintained by brute force and there is no better way to oppose it successfully.

And this principle is true today and remains true at all times, since in any future society if anyone wished to oppress another human being, the latter would have the right to resist and to use force to resist force.

And furthermore, when does the present society cease to exist and the future society begin? When will it be possible to say that the revolution has definitely ended and the unopposed triumph of a free and equalitarian society started? If some people will have assumed the right to violate anybody's freedom on the pretext of preparing the triumph of freedom, they will always find that the people are not yet sufficiently mature, that the dangers of reaction are ever-present, that the education of the people has not yet been completed. And with these excuses they will seek to perpetuate their own power—which could begin as the strength of a people up in arms, but which, if not controlled by a profound feeling for the freedom of all, would soon become a real government, no different from the governments of today.

But, we shall be told, you therefore want the priests to go on brainwashing the young with their lies?

No, we believe it is necessary, and urgent, to destroy the harmful influence of the priest, but we also believe that the only means to achieve success is freedom—freedom for ourselves and for them. By the use of force we want to deprive the priests of all the privileges and advantages which they owe to the protection they receive from the State and to the conditions of poverty and subjection under which the workers live; but once this has been achieved, we rely and can only rely on the power of truth, that is, on argument. We are anarchists because we believe that no good comes from authority, or if some relative good could come from it, the consequent harm done would be a hundred times greater.

Some talk of the right to prevent the dissemination of error. But with which means?

If the strongest current of opinion supports the priests, then it is the priests who will obstruct our propaganda; and if, instead, opinion is on our side, what need is there to deny freedom in order to combat an influence on the wane, and run the risk that people will feel sympathy for it because it is being persecuted? All other considerations apart, it is in our interest always to be on the side of freedom, because, as a minority proclaiming freedom for all, we would be in a stronger position to demand that others should respect our freedom; and if we are a majority we will have no reason, if we really do not aspire to dominate, to violate the freedom of others. . . . So freedom for everybody and in everything, with the only limit of the equal freedom for others; which does *not* mean—it is almost ridiculous to have to point this out—that we recognise, and wish to respect, the "freedom" to exploit, to oppress, to command, which is oppression and certainly not freedom.[6]

5. Anarchism and Violence

Anarchists are opposed to violence; everyone knows that. The main plank of anarchism is the removal of violence from human relations. It is life based on the freedom of the individual, without the intervention of the *gendarme*. For this reason we are enemies of capitalism which depends on the protection of the *gendarme* to oblige workers to allow themselves to be exploited—or even to remain idle and go hungry when it is not in the interest of the bosses to exploit them. We are therefore enemies of the State which is the coercive, violent organisation of society.

But if a man of honour declares that he believes it stupid and barbarous to argue with a stick in his hand and that it is unjust and evil to oblige a person to obey the will of another at pistol point, is it, perhaps, reasonable to deduce that that gentleman intends to allow himself to be beaten up and be made to submit to the will of another without having recourse to more extreme means for his defence?

Violence is justifiable only when it is necessary to defend oneself and others from violence. It is where necessity ceases that crime begins....

The slave is always in a state of legitimate defence and consequently, his violence against the boss, against the oppressor, is always morally justifiable, and must be controlled only by such considerations as that the best and most economical use is being made of human effort and human sufferings.[1]

There are certainly other men, other parties and schools of thought which are as sincerely motivated by the general good as are the best among us. But what distinguishes the anarchists from all the others is in fact their horror of violence, their desire and intention to eliminate physical violence from human relations. . . . But why, then, it may be asked, have anarchists in the present struggle [against Fascism] advocated and used violence when it is in contradiction with their declared ends? So much so that many critics, some in good faith, and all who are in bad faith, have come to believe that the distinguishing characteristic of anarchism is, in fact, violence. The question may seem embarrassing, but it can be answered in a few words. For two people to live in peace they must both want peace; if one of them insists on using force to oblige the other to work for him and serve him, then the other, if he wishes to retain his dignity as a man and not be reduced to abject slavery, will be obliged, in spite of his love of peace, to resist force with adequate means.[2]

The struggle against government is, in the last analysis, physical, material.

Governments make the law. They must therefore dispose of the material forces (police and army) to impose the law, for otherwise only those who wanted to would obey it, and it would no longer be the law, but a simple series of suggestions which all would be free to accept or reject. Governments have this power, however, and use it through the law, to strengthen their power, as well as to serve the interests of the ruling classes, by oppressing and exploiting the workers.

The only limit to the oppression of government is the power with which the people show themselves capable of opposing it.

Conflict may be open or latent; but it always exists since the government does not pay attention to discontent and popular resistance except when it is faced with the danger of insurrection.

When the people meekly submit to the law, or their protests are feeble and confined to words, the government studies its own interests and ignores the needs of the people; when the protests are lively, insistent, threatening, the government, depending on whether it is more or less understanding, gives way or resorts to repression. But one always comes back to insurrection, for if the government does not give way, the people will end by rebelling; and if the government does give way, then the people gain confidence in themselves and make ever increasing demands, until such time as the incompatibility between freedom and authority becomes clear and the violent struggle is engaged.

It is therefore necessary to be prepared, morally and materially, so that when this does happen the people will emerge victorious.[3]

This revolution must of necessity be violent, even though violence is in itself an evil. It must be violent because it would be folly to hope that the privileged classes will recognise the injustice of, and harm caused by, their privileged status, and voluntarily renounce it. It must be violent because a transitional, revolutionary, violence is the only way to put an end to the far greater, and permanent, violence which keeps the majority of mankind in servitude.[4]

The bourgeoisie will not allow itself to be expropriated without a struggle, and one will always have to resort to the *coup de force*, to the violation of legal order by illegal means.[5]

We too are deeply unhappy at this need for violent struggle. We who preach love, and who struggle to achieve a state of society in which agreement and love are possible among men, suffer more than anybody by the necessity with which we are confronted of having to defend ourselves with violence against the violence of the ruling classes. However, to renounce a liberating violence, when it is the only way to end the daily sufferings and the savage carnage which afflict mankind, would be to connive at the class antagonisms we deplore and at the evils which arise from them.[6]

We neither seek to impose anything by force nor do we wish to submit to a violent imposition.

We intend to use force against government, because it is by force that we are kept in subjection by government.

We intend to expropriate the owners of property because it is by force that they withhold the raw materials and wealth, which is the fruit of human labour, and use it to oblige others to work in their interest.

We shall resist with force whoever would wish by force, to retain or regain the means to impose his will and exploit the labour of others.

We would resist with force any "dictatorship" or "constituent" which attempted to impose itself on the masses in revolt. And we will fight the republic as we fight the monarchy, if by republic is meant a government, however it may have come to power, which makes laws and disposes of military and penal powers to oblige the people to obey.

With the exception of these cases, in which the use of force is justified as a defence against force, we are always against violence, and for self-determination.[7]

I have repeated a thousand times that I believe that not to "actively" resist evil, adequately and by every possible way is, in theory absurd, because it is in contradiction with the aim of avoiding and destroying evil, and in practice immoral because it is a denial of human solidarity and the duty that stems from it to defend the weak and the oppressed I think that a regime which is born of violence and which continues to exist by violence cannot be overthrown except by a corresponding and proportionate violence, and that one is therefore either stupid or deceived in relying on legality where the oppressors can change the law to suit their own ends. But I believe that violence is, for us who aim at peace among men, and justice and freedom for all, an unpleasant necessity, which must cease the moment liberation is achieved—that is, at the point where defence and security are no longer threatened—or become a crime against humanity, and the harbinger of new oppression and injustice![8]

We are on principle opposed to violence and for this reason wish that the social struggle should be conducted as humanely as possible. But this does not mean that we would wish it to be less determined, less thoroughgoing; indeed we are of the opinion that in the long run half measures only indefinitely prolong the struggle, neutralising it as well as encouraging more of the kind of violence which one wishes to avoid. Neither does it mean that we limit the right of self-defence to resistance against actual or imminent attack. For us the oppressed are always in a state of legitimate defence and are fully justified in rising without waiting to be actually fired on; and we are fully aware of the fact that attack is often the best means of defence. . . .

Revenge, persistent hatred, cruelty to the vanquished when they have been overcome, are understandable reactions and can even be forgiven, in the heat of the struggle, in those whose dignity has been cruelly offended, and whose most intimate feelings have been outraged. But to condone ferocious anti-human feelings and raise them to the level of a principle, advocating them as a tactic for a movement, is both evil and counter-revolutionary.

For us revolution must not mean the substitution of one oppressor for another, of our domination for that of others. We want the material and spiritual elevation of man; the disappearance of every distinction between vanquished and conquerors; sincere brotherhood among all mankind—without which history would continue, as in the past, to be an alternation between oppression and rebellion, at the expense of real progress, and in the long term to the disadvantage of everybody, the conquerors no less than the vanquished.[9]

It is abundantly clear that violence is needed to resist the violence of the adversary, and we must advocate and prepare it, if we do not wish the present situation of slavery in disguise, in which most of humanity finds itself, to continue and worsen. But violence contains within itself the danger of transforming the revolution into a brutal struggle without the light of an ideal and without possibilities of a beneficial outcome; and for this reason one must stress the moral aims of the movement, and the need, and the duty, to contain violence within the limits of strict necessity.

We do not say that violence is good when we use it and harmful when others use it against us. We say that violence is justifiable, good and "moral," as well as a duty when it is used in one's own defence and that of others, against the demands of those who believe in violence; it is evil and "immoral" if it serves to violate the freedom of others. . . .

We are not "pacifists" because peace is not possible unless it is desired by both sides.

We consider violence a necessity and a duty for defence, but only for defence. And we mean not only for defence against direct, sudden, physical attack, but against all those institutions which use force to keep the people in a state of servitude.

We are against fascism and we would wish that it were weakened by opposing to its violence a greater violence. And we are, above all, against government, which is permanent violence.[10]

To my mind if violence is justifiable even beyond the needs of self-defence, then it is justified when it is used against us, and we would have no grounds for protest.[11]

To the alleged incapacity of the people we do not offer a solution by putting ourselves in the place of the former oppressors. Only freedom or the struggle for freedom can be the school for freedom.

But, you will say, to start a revolution and bring it to its conclusion one needs a force which is also armed. And who denies this? But this armed force, or rather the numerous armed revolutionary groups, will be performing a revolutionary task if they serve to free the people and prevent the reemergence of an authoritarian government. But they will be tools of reaction and destroy their own achievements if they are prepared to be used to impose a particular kind of social organisation or the programme of a particular party. . . .[12]

Revolution being, by the necessity of things, violent action, tends to develop, rather than remove, the spirit of violence. But the revolution as conceived by anarchists is the least violent of all and seeks to halt all violence as soon as the need to use force to oppose that of the government and the bourgeoisie, ceases.

Anarchists recognise violence only as a means of legitimate defence; and if today they are in favour of violence it is because they maintain that slaves are always in a state of legitimate defence. But the anarchist ideal is for a society in which the factor of violence has been eliminated, and their ideal serves to restrain, correct and destroy the spirit of revenge which revolution, as a physical act, would tend to develop.

In any case, the remedy would never be the organisation and consolidation of violence in the hands of a government or dictatorship, which cannot be founded on anything but brute force and recognition of the authority of police—and military—forces.[13]

. . . An error, the opposite of the one which the terrorists make, threatens the anarchist movement. Partly as a reaction to the abuse of violence during recent years, partly as a result of the survival of Christian ideas, and above all, as a result of the mystical preaching of Tolstoy, which owe their popularity and prestige to the genius and high moral qualities of their author, anarchists are beginning to pay serious attention to the party of passive resistance, whose basic principle is that the individual must allow himself and others to be persecuted and despised rather than harm the aggressor. It is what has been called *passive anarchy*.

Since there are some, upset by my aversion to useless and harmful violence, who have been suggesting that I displayed tolstoyanist tendencies, I take the opportunity to declare that, in my opinion, this doctrine however sublimely altruistic it may appear to be, is, in fact the negation of instinct and social duties. A man may, if he is a very good . . . Christian, suffer every kind of provocation without defending himself with every weapon at his disposal, and still remain a moral man. But would he not, in practice, even unconsciously, be a supreme egoist were he to allow others to be persecuted without making any effort to defend them? If, for instance, he were to prefer that a class should be reduced to abject misery, that a people should be downtrodden by an invader, that a man's life or liberty should be abused, rather than bruise the flesh of the oppressor?

There can be cases where passive resistance is an effective weapon, and it would then obviously be the best of weapons, since it would be the most economic in human suffering. But more often than not, to profess passive resistance only serves to reassure the oppressors against their fear of rebellion, and thus it betrays the cause of the oppressed.

It is interesting to observe how both the *terrorists* and the *tolstoyans*, just because both are mystics, arrive at practical results which are more or less similar. The former would not hesitate to destroy half mankind so long as the idea triumphed; the latter would be prepared to let all mankind remain under the yoke of great suffering rather than violate a principle.

For myself, I would violate every principle in the world in order to save a man: which would in fact be a question of respecting principle, since, in my opinion, all moral and sociological principles are reduced to this one principle: the good of mankind, the good of all mankind.[14]

6. Attentats

I remember that on the occasion of a much publicised anarchist *attentat* a socialist of the first rank just back from fighting in the Greco-Turkish war, shouted from the housetops with the approval of his comrades, that human life is always sacred and must not be threatened, not even in the cause of freedom. It appeared that he accepted the lives of Turks and the cause of Greek independence. Illogicality, or hypocrisy?[1]

Anarchist violence is the only violence that is justifiable, which is not criminal. I am of course speaking of violence which has truly anarchist characteristics, and not of this or that case of blind and unreasoning violence which has been attributed to anarchists, or which perhaps has been committed by real anarchists driven to fury by abominable persecutions, or blinded by oversensitiveness, uncontrolled by reason, at the sight of social injustices, of suffering for the sufferings of others.

Real anarchist violence is that which ceases when the necessity of defence and liberation ends. It is tempered by the awareness that individuals in isolation are hardly, if at all, responsible for the position they occupy through heredity and environment; real anarchist violence is not motivated by hatred but by love; and is noble because it aims at the liberation of all and not at the substitution of one's own domination for that of others.

There is a political party in Italy which, aiming at highly civilised ends, set itself the task of extinguishing all confidence in violence among the masses . . .

and has succeeded in rendering them incapable of any resistance against the rise of fascism. It seemed to me that Turati himself more or less clearly recognised and lamented the fact in his speech in Paris commemorating Jaurès.

The anarchists are without hypocrisy. Force must be resisted by force: today against the oppression of today; tomorrow against those who might replace that of today.[2]

McKinley, head of North American oligarchy, the instrument and defender of the capitalist giants, the betrayer of the Cubans and the Filipinos, the man who authorised the massacre of the strikers of Hazleton, the torturer of the workers in the "model republic"; McKinley who incarnated the militaristic, expansionist and imperialist policies on which the fat American bourgeoisie have embarked, has fallen foul of an anarchist's revolver.

If we feel at all distressed it is for the fate in store for the generous-hearted man, who opportunely or inopportunely, for good or tactically bad reasons, gave himself in wholesale sacrifice to the cause of equality and liberty. . . .

[It might be argued by those who have condemned Czolgosz's act] that the workers' cause and that of the revolution have not been advanced; that McKinley is succeeded by his equal, Roosevelt, and everything remains unchanged except that the situation for anarchists has become a little more difficult than before. And they may be right; indeed, from what I know of the American scene, this will most likely be the case.

What it means is that [as] in war there are brilliant as well as false moves, there are cautious combatants as well as others who are easily carried away by enthusiasm and allow themselves to be an easy target for the enemy, and may even compromise the position of their comrades. This means that each one must advise, defend and practice the methods which he thinks most suitable to achieve victory in the shortest time and with the least sacrifice possible; but it does not alter the fundamental and obvious fact that he who struggles, well or badly, against the common enemy and towards the same goal as us, is our friend and has a right to expect our warm sympathy even if we cannot accord him our unconditional approval.

Whether the fighting unit is a collectivity or a single individual cannot change the moral aspect of the problem. An armed insurrection carried out inopportunely can produce real or apparent harm to the social war we are fighting, just as an individual attentat which antagonises popular feeling; but if the insurrection was made to conquer freedom, no one will dare deny the socio-political characteristics of the defeated insurrectionists. Why should it be any different when the insurrectionist is a single individual? . . .

It is not a question of discussing tactics. If it were, I would say that in general I prefer collective action to individual action, also because collective action demands qualities which are fairly common and makes the allocation of tasks more or less possible, whereas one cannot count on heroism, which is exceptional and by its nature sporadic, calling for individual sacrifice. The problem here is of a higher order; it is a question of the revolutionary spirit, of that almost instinctive feeling of hatred of oppression, without which programmes remain dead letters however libertarian are the proposals they embody; it is a question of that combative spirit, without which even anarchists become domesticated and end up, by one road or another, in the slough of legalitarianism. . . .[3]

Gaetano Bresci, worker and anarchist, has killed Humbert, king. Two men: one dead prematurely, the other condemned to a life of torment which is a thousand times worse than death! Two families plunged into sadness!

Whose fault is it? . . .

It is true that if one takes into consideration such factors as heredity, education and social background, the personal responsibility of those in power is much reduced and perhaps even non-existent. But then if the king is not responsible for his commissions and omissions; if in spite of the oppression, the dispossession, and the massacre of the people carried out in his name, he should have continued to occupy the highest place in the country, why ever then should Bresci have to pay with a life of indescribable suffering, for an act which, however mistaken some may judge it, no one can deny was inspired by altruistic intentions?

But this business of seeking to place the responsibility where it belongs is only of secondary interest to us.

We do not believe in the right to punish; we reject the idea of revenge as a barbarous sentiment. We have no intention of being either executioners or avengers. It seems to us that the role of liberators and peacemakers is more noble and positive. To kings, oppressors and exploiters we would willingly extend our hand, if only they wished to become men among other men, equals among equals. But so long as they insist on profiting from the situation as it exists and to defend it with force, thus causing the martyrdom, the wretchedness and the death through hardships of millions of human beings, we are obliged, we have a duty to oppose force with force. . . .

We know that these attentats, with the people insufficiently prepared for them, are sterile and often, by provoking reactions which one is unable to control, produce much sorrow, and harm the very cause they were intended to serve.

We know that what is essential and undoubtedly useful is not just to kill a king, the man, but to kill all kings—those of the Courts, of parliaments and of the factories—in the hearts and minds of the people; that is, to uproot faith in the principle of authority to which most people owe allegiance.[4]

I do not need to repeat my disapproval and horror for attentats such as that of the Diana, which besides being bad in themselves are also stupid, because they inevitably harm the cause they would wish to serve. And I have never failed to protest strongly, whenever similar acts have taken place and especially when it has turned out that they have been committed by authentic anarchists. I have protested when it would have been better for me to remain silent, because my protest was inspired by superior reasons of principles and tactics, and because I had a duty to do so, since there are people gifted with little personal critical sense, who allow themselves to be guided by what I say. But now it is not a case of judging the fact, and discussing whether it was a good or bad thing to have done, or whether similar actions should or should not be repeated. Now it is a question of judging men threatened with a punishment a thousand times worse than the death penalty; and so one must examine who these men are, what were their intentions and the circumstances in which they acted.[5]

. . . I said that those assassins are *also* saints and heroes; and those of my friends who protest against my statement do so in homage to those whom they call the real saints and heroes, who, it would seem, never make mistakes.

I can do no more than confirm what I said. When I think of all that I have learned about Mariani and Aguggini; when I think what good sons and brothers they were, and what affectionate and devoted comrades they were in everyday life, always ready to take risks and to make sacrifices when there was urgent need, I bemoan their fate, I bemoan the destiny that has turned those fine and noble beings into assassins.

I said that one day they will be praised—I did not say that I would praise them; and they will be praised because, as has happened with so many others, the brutal action, the passion that misled them will be forgotten, and only the idea which inspired them and the martyrdom which made them sacrosanct will be remembered.

I don't want to get involved in historical examples; but I could if I wished find in the history of all conspiracies and revolutions, in that of the Italian Risorgimento as well as in our own, a thousand examples of men who have committed actions as bad and as stupid as that of the Diana and yet who are praised by their respective parties, because in fact one forgets the action and remembers the intention, and the individual becomes a symbol and the event is transformed into a legend.

Yes, there are saints and heroes who are assassins; there are assassins who are saints and heroes.

The human mind is really most complicated, and there is a disequilibrium between what one calls heart and what is called brain, between affective qualities and the intellectual faculties, which produces the most unpredictable results and makes possible the most striking contradictions in human behaviour. The war volunteer inebriated by patriotic propaganda, convinced of serving the cause of justice and civilisation, and prepared for the supreme sacrifice, who raged against the "enemy"—Italian against Austrian, or vice versa—and died in the act of killing, was undoubtedly a hero, but a hero who was unconsciously an assassin.

Torquemada who tortured others as well as himself to serve God and to save souls, was both a saint and an assassin. . . .

It could easily be argued that the saint and the hero are almost always unbalanced individuals. But then everything would be reduced to a question of words, to a question of definition. What is a saint? What is a hero?

Enough of hair-splitting.

What is important is to avoid confusing the act with the intentions, and in condemning the bad actions not to overlook doing justice to the good intentions. And not only on the grounds of respect for the truth, or human pity, but also for reasons of propaganda, for the practical repercussions that our judgment may have.

There are, and, so long as present conditions and the environment of violence in which we live last, there will always be generous men, who are rebellious and oversensitive, but who lack sufficient powers of reflection and who in certain situations allow themselves to be carried away by passion and strike out blindly. If we do not openly recognise the goodness of their intentions, if we do not distinguish between error and wickedness, we lose any moral influence over them and abandon them to their blind impulses. If instead, we pay homage to their goodness, their courage and sense of sacrifice, we can reach their minds through their hearts, and ensure that those valuable storehouses of energy shall be used in an intelligent and good, as well as useful, way in the interests of the [common] cause.[6]

II

7. Ends and Means

The end justifies the means. This saying has been much abused; yet it is in fact the universal guide to conduct. It would, however, be better to say: every end needs its means. Since morality must be sought in the aims, the means is determined.

Once the goal one is aiming at has been established, consciously or through necessity, the big problem of life is to find the means which, in the circumstances, leads to that end most surely and economically. In the way this problem is solved will depend, so far as it can depend on human will, whether the individual (or party) reaches or fails to achieve his ends, whether he is useful to his cause or unwittingly serves that of the enemy. To have found the right means, herein lies the whole secret of great men and parties that have left their mark on history.

For mystics, the aim of the Jesuits is the glory of God; for others it is the power of the Company of Jesus. They must therefore make every effort to brutalise, terrorise, and subject the masses.

The aim of the Jacobins, and all authoritarian parties who believe themselves to be in possession of absolute truth, is to impose their ideas on the ignorant masses. They must therefore make every effort to seize power, subject the masses, and fit humanity to the Procrustean bed of their concepts.

The problem for us is a different one; because our aims are so different, so also must be our means.

We do not carry on our struggle in order to put ourselves in the place of the exploiters and oppressors of today, nor do we even struggle for the triumph of an empty abstraction. We have nothing in common with that Italian patriot who declared: "What does it matter if all Italians die of hunger so long as Italy is great and glorious!"; nor even with that comrade who confessed to being indifferent to whether three quarters of humanity perished in making the world free and happy. . . .

In our opinion all action which is directed towards the destruction of economic and political oppression; which serves to raise the moral and intellectual level of the people; which gives them an awareness of their individual rights and their power, and persuades them themselves to act on their own behalf; [in a word] all activity that encourages a hatred of oppression and awakens love among Man, brings us closer to our ends and therefore is a good thing (subject only to a quantitative consideration: of obtaining the best results from the available forces at our disposal). On the other hand, all activity that tends to preserve the present state of affairs, that tends to sacrifice man against his will for the triumph of a principle, is bad because it is a denial of our ends. We seek the triumph of freedom and of love.

Should we, for this reason, renounce the use of violent means? Not at all. Our means are those that circumstances allow and impose.

Of course we do not wish to lay a finger on anyone; we would wish to dry all the tears of humanity and not be responsible for more tears. But we must either struggle in the world as it is or remain helpless dreamers. The day will come, we are convinced of this, when it will be possible to serve the cause of Mankind without hurting either oneself or others; but today this is not possible. Even the purest and gentlest of martyrs, those who would allow themselves to be dragged to the gallows for the triumph of good, without resisting, blessing their persecutors, as did the Christ of the legend, would be doing harm. Besides the harm to their own persons, which after all must be reckoned with too, they would cause bitter tears to be shed by all those who loved them. In all actions in life it is, therefore always a question of seeking to cause the least harm to achieve the greatest possible good. . . .

Obviously the revolution will be the cause of many tragedies and much suffering; but even if it produced a hundred times more, it would always be a blessing compared with the sufferings which now exist in the world as a result of the evil organisation of society.[1]

There are, and there always have been in all socio-political struggles, two kinds of hypnotisers.

There are those who consider that we are never mature enough, that we expect too much, that we must wait, and be satisfied to advance a little at a time with the aid of small reforms . . . which are periodically won and lost without ever solving anything. And there are those who affect contempt for the small things, and advocate all or nothing, and in putting forward schemes, probably excellent ones which cannot however be realised through lack of sufficient support, prevent, or seek to prevent, others from doing the little that can be done.

For us what is most important is not what we achieve . . . but how we achieve it.

If in order to secure an improvement in the situation one abandons one's basic programme and stops propagating it or struggling to realise it; if one induces the masses to pin their hopes on laws and the good-will of the rulers rather than in their own direct action; if one suffocates the revolutionary spirit, and ceases to foment discontent and resistance—then every advantage will prove illusory and ephemeral, and in all cases will bar the roads to the future society.

But if instead, one does not forget one's final objectives, and encourages the popular forces, as well as inciting to direct action and insurrection, very little may be achieved at the time, but one has made a step forward in the moral preparation of the mass of the people, and in the achievement of a more favourable social climate.

"The optimum is enemy of the good," says the proverb: let us do what we can, assuming we cannot do all we would wish; but do something we must.[2]

Another damaging argument sincerely advanced by many, but which for others is an excuse for doing nothing, is that the present social environment does not make morality possible; and that consequently it is useless to make efforts which cannot succeed, and it is therefore best to get all one can for oneself without bothering about others, except to change one's way of life when the social organisation will be changed. Obviously all anarchists and socialists understand the economic facts of life which today oblige man to struggle against man, and any observer will see the importance of a personal struggle against the overwhelming power of the present social environment. But it is also obvious that without revolt by the individual, who joins with others of like mind to offer resistance to the environment in order to change it, it will never change.

All of us, without exception, are obliged to live, more or less, in contradiction with our ideals; but we are anarchists and socialists because, and in so far as, we suffer by this contradiction, and seek to make it as small as possible. In the event of adapting ourselves to the environment, we would of course also lose the desire to change it, and would become ordinary bourgeois; bourgeois without money perhaps, but for all that bourgeois in our actions and intentions.[3]

8. Majorities and Minorities

We do not recognise the right of the majority to impose the law on the minority, even if the will of the majority in somewhat complicated issues could really be ascertained. The fact of having the majority on one's side does not in any way prove that one must be right. Indeed, humanity has always advanced through the initiative and efforts of individuals and minorities, whereas the majority, by its very nature, is slow, conservative, and submissive to superior force and to established privileges.

But if we do not for one moment recognise the right of majorities to dominate minorities, we are even more opposed to domination of the majority by a minority. It would be absurd to maintain that one is right because one is in a minority. If at all times there have been advanced and enlightened minorities, so too have there been minorities which were backward and reactionary; if there are human beings who are exceptional, and ahead of their times, there are also psychopaths, and especially are there apathetic individuals who allow themselves to be unconsciously carried on the tide of events.

In any case it is not a question of being right or wrong; it is a question of freedom, freedom for all, freedom for each individual so long as he does not violate the equal freedom of others. No one can judge with certainty who is right and who is wrong, who is closer to the truth and which is the best road to the greatest good for each and everyone. Experience through freedom is the only means to arrive at the truth and the best solutions; and there is no freedom if there is not the freedom to be wrong.

In our opinion, therefore, it is necessary that majority and minority should succeed in living together peacefully and profitably by mutual agreement and compromise, by the intelligent recognition of the practical necessities of communal life and of the usefulness of concessions which circumstances make necessary.[1]

As well as their reason and experience telling them that in spite of using all the alchemy of elections and parliament one always ends up by having laws which represent everything but the will of the majority, anarchists do not recognise that the majority as such, even if it were possible to establish beyond all doubt what it wanted, has the right to impose itself on the dissident minorities by the use of force.[2]

Apart from these considerations, there always exists the fact that in a capitalist regime, in which society is divided into rich and poor, into employers and employees whose next meal depends on the absolute power of the boss, there cannot be really free elections.[3]

9. Mutual Aid

Since it is a fact that man is a social animal whose existence depends on the continued physical and spiritual relations between human beings, these relations must be based either on affinity, solidarity and love, or on hostility and struggle. If each individual thinks only of his well-being, or perhaps that of his small consanguinary or territorial group, he will obviously find himself in conflict with others, and will emerge as victor or vanquished; as the oppressor if he wins, as the oppressed if he loses. Natural harmony, the natural marriage of the good of each with that of all, is the invention of human laziness, which rather than struggle to achieve what it wants assumes that it will be achieved spontaneously, by natural law. In reality, however, natural Man is in a state of continuous conflict with his fellows in his quest for the best, and healthiest site, the most fertile land, and in time, to exploit the many and varied opportunities that social life creates for some or for others. For this reason human history is full of violence, wars, carnage (besides the ruthless exploitation of the labour of others) and innumerable tyrannies and slavery.

If in the human spirit there had only existed this harsh instinct of wanting to predominate and to profit at the expense of others, humanity would have remained in its barbarous state and the development of order as recorded in history, or in our own times, would not have been possible. This order even at its worst, always represents a kind of tempering of the tyrannical spirit with a minimum of social solidarity, indispensable for a more civilised and progressive life.

But fortunately there exists in Man another feeling which draws him closer to his neighbour, the feeling of sympathy, tolerance, of love, and, thanks to it, mankind became more civilised, and from it grew our idea which aims at making society a true gathering of brothers and friends all working for the common good.

How the feeling arose which is expressed by the so-called moral precepts and which, as it develops, denies the existing morality and substitutes a higher morality, is a subject for research which may interest philosophers and sociologists, but it does not detract from the fact that it exists, independently of the explanations which may be advanced. It is of no importance that it may stem from the primitive, physiological fact of the sex act to perpetuate the human species; or the satisfaction to be derived from the company of one's fellow beings; or the advantages to be derived from union in the struggle against the common enemy and in revolt against the common tyrant; or from the desire for leisure, peace and security that even the victors feel a need for; or perhaps for these and a hundred other reasons combined. It *exists* and it is on its development and growth that we base our hopes for the future of humanity.

"The will of God," "natural laws," "moral laws," the "categorical imperative" of the Kantians, even the "interest clearly understood" of the Utilitarians are all metaphysical fantasies which get one nowhere. They represent the commendable desire of the human mind to want to explain everything, to want to get to the bottom of things, and could be accepted as provisional hypotheses for further research, were they not, in most cases, the human tendency of never wanting to admit ignorance and preferring wordy explanations devoid of factual content to simply saying "I don't know."

Whatever the explanations anyone may or may not choose to give, the problem remains intact: one must choose between love and hate, between brotherly cooperation and fratricidal struggle, between "altruism" and "egoism."[1]

The needs, tastes, aspirations, and interests of mankind are neither similar nor naturally harmonious; often they are diametrically opposed and antagonistic. On the other hand, the life of each individual is so conditioned by the life of others that it would be impossible, even assuming it were convenient to do so, to isolate oneself and live one's own life. Social solidarity is a fact from which no one can escape: it can be freely and consciously accepted and in consequence benefit all concerned, or it can be accepted willy-nilly, consciously or otherwise, in which case it manifests itself by the subjection of one to another, by the exploitation of some by others.

A whole host of practical problems arise in our day-to-day lives which can be solved in different ways, but not by all ways at the same time; yet each individual may prefer one solution to another. If an individual or group have the power to impose their preference on others, they will choose the solution which best suits their interests and tastes; the others will have to submit and sacrifice their wishes. But if no one has the possibility of obliging others to act against their will then, always assuming that it is not possible or considered convenient to adopt more than one solution, one must arrive by mutual concessions at an agreement which best suits everyone and least offends individual interests, tastes and wishes.

History teaches us, daily observation of life around us teaches, that where violence has no place [in human relations] everything is settled in the best possible way, in the best interests of all concerned. But where violence intervenes, injustice, oppression and exploitation invariably triumph.[2]

The fact is that human life is not possible without profiting by the labour of others, and that there are only two ways in which this can be done: either through a fraternal, equalitarian and libertarian association, in which solidarity, consciously and freely expressed unites all mankind; or the struggle of each against the other in which the victors overrule, oppress and exploit the rest....

We want to bring about a society in which men will consider each other as brothers and by mutual support will achieve the greatest well-being and freedom as well as physical and intellectual development for all....

The strongest man is the one who is the least isolated; the most independent is the one who has most contacts and friendships and thereby a wider field for choosing his close collaborators; the most developed man is he who best can, and knows how to, utilise Man's common inheritance as well as the achievements of his contemporaries.[3]

In spite of the rivers of human blood; in spite of the indescribable sufferings and humiliations inflicted; in spite of exploitation and tyranny at the expense of the weakest (by reason of personal, or social, inferiority); in a word, in spite of the struggle and all its consequences, that which in human society represents its vital and progressive characteristics, is the feeling of sympathy, the sense of a common humanity which in normal times, places a limit on the struggle beyond which one cannot venture without rousing deep disgust and widespread disapproval. For what intervenes is morality.

The professional historian of the old school may prefer to present the fruits of his research as sensational events, large-scale conflicts between nations and classes, wars, revolutions, the ins and outs of diplomacy and conspiracies; but what is really much more significant are the innumerable daily contacts between individuals and between groups which are the true substance of social life. And if one closely examines what happens deep down, in the intimate daily lives of the mass of humanity, one finds that as well as the struggle to snatch better working conditions, the thirst for domination, rivalry, envy and all the unhealthy passions which set man against man, is also valuable work, mutual aid, unceasing and voluntary exchange of services, affection, love, friendship and all that which draws people closer together in brotherhood. And human collectivities advance or decay, live or die, depending on whether solidarity and love, or hatred and struggle, predominate in the community's affairs; indeed, the very existence of any community would not be possible if the social feelings, which I would call the *good* passions, were not stronger than the bad.

The existence of sentiments of affection and sympathy among mankind, and the experience and awareness of the individual and social advantages which stem from the development of these sentiments, have produced and go on producing concepts of "justice" and "right" and "Morality" which, in spite of a thousand contradictions, lies and hypocrisy serving base interests, constitute a goal, an ideal towards which humanity advances.

This "morality" is fickle and relative; it varies with the times, with different peoples, classes and individuals; people use it to serve their own personal interests and that of their families, class or country. But discarding what, in official "morality," serves to defend the privilege and violence of the ruling class, there is always something left which is in the general interest and is the common achievement of all mankind, irrespective of class and race.[4]

The bourgeoisie in its heroic period, when it still felt itself a part of the people and fought for emancipation, had sublime gestures of love and self-abnegation; and the best among its thinkers and martyrs had the almost prophetic vision of that future of peace, brotherhood and well-being which socialists are struggling for today [1909]. But if altruism and solidarity were among the feelings of the best of them, the germ of individualism (in the sense of struggle between individuals), the principle of struggle (as opposed to solidarity) and the exploitation of man by man, were in the programme of the bourgeoisie and could not but give rise to baneful consequences. Individual property and the principle of authority, in the new disguises of capitalism and parliamentarism, were in that programme and had to lead, as has always been the case, to oppression, misery and the dehumanisation of the masses.

And now that the development of capitalism and parliamentarism has borne its fruits, and the bourgeoisie has exhausted every generous sentiment and progressive élan by the practice of political and economic competition, it is reduced to having to defend its privileges with force and deceit, while its philosophers cannot defend it against the socialist attacks except by bringing up, inopportunely, the law of vital competition.[5]

10. Reformism

The fundamental error of the reformists is that of dreaming of solidarity, a sincere collaboration, between masters and servants, between proprietors and workers which even if it might have existed here and there in periods of profound unconsciousness of the masses and of ingenuous faith in religion and rewards, is utterly impossible today.

Those who envisage a society of well stuffed pigs which waddle contentedly under the fertile of a small number of swineherd; who do not take into account the need for freedom and the sentiment of human dignity; who really believe in a God that orders, for his abstruse ends, the poor to be submissive and the rich to be good and charitable—can also imagine and aspire to a technical organisation of production which assures abundance to all and is at the same time materially advantageous both to the bosses and to the workers. But in reality "social peace" based on abundance for all will remain a dream, so long as society is divided into antagonistic classes, that is employers and employees. And there will be neither peace nor abundance.

The antagonism is spiritual rather than material. There will never be a sincere understanding between bosses and workers for the better exploitation of the forces of nature in the interests of mankind, because the bosses above all want to remain bosses and secure always more power at the expense of the workers, as well as by competition with other bosses, whereas the workers have had their fill of bosses and don't want more![1]

[Our good friends] are wasting their time when they tell us that a little freedom is better than a brutal and unbridled tyranny; that a reasonable working day, a wage that allows people to live better than animals, and protection of women and children, are preferable to the exploitation of human labour to the point of human exhaustion; or that the State school, bad as it is, is always better, from the point of view of the child's moral development, than schools run by priests and monks . . . for we are in complete agreement. And we also agree that there may be circumstances in which the Election results, national or local, can have good or bad consequences and that this vote might be determined by the anarchists' votes if the strength of the rival parties were equally balanced.

In most cases it is an illusion; when elections are tolerably free, the only value they have is symbolic: they indicate the state of public opinion, which would have imposed itself by more efficacious means, and with more far reaching results, if it had not been offered the outlet of elections. But no matter; even if some minor advances were the direct result of an electoral victory, anarchists should not flock to the polling booths or cease to preach their methods of struggle.

Since no one can do everything in this world, one must choose one's own line of conduct.

There is always an element of contradiction between minor improvements, the satisfaction of immediate needs and the struggle for a society which is really better than the existing one. Those who want to devote themselves to the erection of public lavatories and drinking fountains where there is a need for them, or who use their energies for the construction of a road, or the establishment of a municipal school, or for the passing of some minor law to protect workers or to get rid of a brutal policeman, do well, perhaps, to use their ballot paper in favour of this or that influential personage. But then—since one wants to be "practical" one must go the whole hog—so, rather than wait for the victory of the opposition party, rather than vote for the more kindred party, it is worth taking a short cut and support the dominant party, and serve the government already in office, and become the agent of the Prefect or the Mayor. And in fact the neo-converts we have in mind did not in fact propose voting for the most "progressive" party, but for the one that had the greater chance of being elected. . . . But in that case where does it all end? . . .[2]

In the course of human history it is generally the case that the malcontents, the oppressed, and the rebels, before being able to conceive and desire a radical change in the political and social institutions, restrict their demands to partial changes, to concessions by the rulers, and to improvements. Hopes of obtaining reforms as well as in their efficacy, precede the conviction that in order to destroy the power of a government or of a class, it is necessary to deny the reasons for that power, and therefore to make a revolution.

In the order of things, reforms are then introduced or they are not, and once introduced either consolidate the existing regime or undermine it; assist the advent of revolution or hamper it and benefit or harm progress in general, depending on their specific characteristic, the spirit in which they have been granted, and above all, the spirit in which they are asked for, claimed or seized by the people.

Governments and the privileged classes are naturally always guided by instincts of self-preservation, of consolidation and the development of their powers and privileges; and when they consent to reforms it is either because they consider that they will serve their ends or because they do not feel strong enough to resist, and give in, fearing what might otherwise be a worse alternative.

The oppressed, either ask for and welcome improvements as a benefit graciously conceded, recognise the legitimacy of the power which is over them, and so do more harm than good by helping to slow down, or divert and perhaps even stop the processes of emancipation. Or instead they demand and impose improvements by their action, and welcome them as partial victories over the class enemy, using them as a spur to greater achievements, and thus they are a valid help and a preparation to the total overthrow of privilege, that is, for the revolution. A point is reached when the demands of the dominated class cannot be acceded to by the ruling class without compromising their power. Then the violent conflict inevitably occurs.

It is not true to say therefore, that revolutionaries are systematically opposed to improvements, to reforms. They oppose the reformists on the one hand because their methods are less effective for securing reforms from governments and employers, who only give in through fear, and on the other hand because very often the reforms they prefer are those which not only bring doubtful immediate benefits, but also serve to consolidate the existing regime and to give the workers a vested interest in its continued existence. Thus, for instance, State pensions, insurance schemes, as well as profit sharing schemes in agricultural and industrial enterprises, etc.[3]

Apart from the unpleasantness of the word which has been abused and discredited by politicians, anarchism has always been, and can never be anything but, reformist. We prefer to say *reformative* in order to avoid any possible confusion with those who are officially classified as "reformists" and seek by means of small and often ephemeral improvements to make the present system more bearable (and as a result help to consolidate it); or who instead believe in good faith that it is possible to eliminate the existing social evils by recognising and respecting, in practice if not in theory, the basic political and economic institutions which are the cause of, as well as the prop that supports these evils. But in any case it is always a question of reforms, and the essential difference lies in the kind of reform one wants and the way one thinks of being able to achieve it. Revolution means, in the historical sense of the word, the radical reform of institutions, achieved rapidly by the violent insurrection of the people against existing power and privileges; and we are revolutionaries and insurrectionists because we do not just want to improve existing institutions but to destroy them completely, abolishing every form of domination by man over man, and every kind of parasitism on human labour; and because we want to achieve this as quickly as possible, and because we believe that institutions born of violence are maintained by violence and will not give way except to an equivalent violence. But the revolution cannot be made just when one likes. Should we remain inactive, waiting for the situation to mature with time?

And even after a successful insurrection, could we overnight realise all our desires and pass from a governmental and capitalist hell to a libertarian-communist heaven which is the complete freedom of man within the wished-for community of interests with all men?

These are illusions which can take root among authoritarians who look upon the masses as the raw material which those who have power can, by decrees, supported by bullets and handcuffs, mould to their will. But these illusions have not taken among anarchists. We need the people's consensus, and therefore we must persuade by means of propaganda and example, we must educate and seek to change the environment in such a way that this education may reach an ever increasing number of people. . . .

We are reformers today in so far as we seek to create the most favourable conditions and as large a body of enlightened militants so that an insurrection by the people would be brought to a satisfactory conclusion. We shall be reformers tomorrow, after a triumphant insurrection, and the achievement of freedom, in that we will seek with all the means that freedom permits, that is by propaganda, example and even violent resistance against anyone who should wish to restrict our freedom in order to win over to our ideas an ever greater number of people.

But we will never recognise the institutions; we will take or win all possible reforms with the same spirit that one tears occupied territory from the enemy's grasp in order to go on advancing, and we will always remain enemies of every government, whether it be that of the monarchy today, or the republican or Bolshevik governments of tomorrow.[4]

11. Organisation

Organisation which is, after all, only the practice of cooperation and solidarity, is a natural and necessary condition of social life; it is an inescapable fact which forces itself on everybody, as much on human society in general as on any group of people who are working towards a common objective. Since man neither wishes to, nor can, live in isolation—indeed being unable to develop his personality, and satisfy his physical and moral needs outside society and without the cooperation of his fellow beings—it is inevitable that those people who have neither the means nor a sufficiently developed social conscience to permit them to associate freely with those of a like mind and with common interests, are subjected to organisation by others, generally constituted in a class or as a ruling group, with the aim of exploiting the labour of others for their personal advantage. And the age-long oppression of the masses by a small privileged group has always been the result of the inability of most workers to agree among themselves to organise with others for production, for enjoyment and for the possible needs of defence against whoever might wish to exploit and oppress them. Anarchism exists to remedy this state of affairs. . . .[1]

There are two factions among those who call themselves anarchists, with or without adjectives: supporters and opponents of organisation. If we cannot succeed in agreeing, let us, at least, try to understand each other.

And first of all let us be clear about the distinctions, since the question is a triple one: organisation in general as a principle and condition of social life today and in a future society; the organisation of the anarchist movement; and the organisation of the popular forces and especially of the working masses for resistance to government and capitalism. . . .

The basic error committed by those opposed to organisation is in believing that organisation is not possible without authority.

Now, it seems to us that organisation, that is to say, association for a specific purpose and with the structure and means required to attain it, is a necessary aspect of social life. A man in isolation cannot even live the life of a beast, for he is unable to obtain nourishment for himself except in tropical regions or when the population is exceptionally sparse; and he is, without exception, unable to rise much above the level of the animals. Having therefore to join with other humans, or more accurately, finding himself united to them as a consequence of the evolutionary antecedents of the species, he must submit to the will of others (be enslaved) or subject others to his will (be in authority) or live with others in fraternal agreement in the interests of the greatest good of all (be an associate). Nobody can escape from this necessity; and the most extreme anti-organisers not only are subject to the general organisation of the society they live in, but also in the voluntary actions in their lives, and in their rebellion against organisation, they unite among themselves, they share out their tasks, they *organise* with whom they are in agreement, and use the means that society puts at their disposal. . . .[2]

Admitting as a possibility the existence of a community organised without authority, that is without compulsion—and anarchists must admit the possibility, or anarchy would have no meaning—let us pass on to discuss the organisation of the anarchist movement.

In this case too, organisation seems useful and necessary. If movement means the whole—individuals with a common objective which they exert themselves to attain—it is natural that they should agree among themselves, join forces, share out the tasks and take all those steps which they think will lead to the achievement of those objectives. To remain isolated, each individual acting or seeking to act on his own without coordination, without preparation, without joining his modest efforts to a strong group, means condemning oneself to impotence, wasting one's efforts in small ineffectual action, and to lose faith very soon in one's aims and possibly being reduced to complete inactivity. . . .

A mathematician, a chemist, a psychologist or a sociologist may say they have no programme or are concerned only with establishing the truth. They seek knowledge, they are not seeking *to do* something. But anarchy and socialism are not sciences; they are proposals, projects, that anarchists and socialists seek to realise and which, therefore need to be formulated as definite programmes. . . .

If it is true that [organisation creates leaders]; if it is true that anarchists are unable to come together and arrive at agreement without submitting themselves to an authority, this means that they are not yet very good anarchists, and before thinking of establishing anarchy in the world they must think of making themselves able to live anarchistically. The remedy does not lie in the abolition of organisation but in the growing consciousness of each individual member. . . . In small as well as large societies, apart from brute force, of which it cannot be a question for us, the origin and justification for authority lies in social disorganisation.

When a community has needs and its members do not know how to organise spontaneously to provide them, someone comes forward, an authority who satisfies those needs by utilising the services of all and directing them to his liking. If the roads are unsafe and the people do not know what measures to take, a police force emerges which in return for whatever services it renders expects to be supported and paid, as well as imposing itself and throwing its weight around; if some article is needed, and the community does not know how to arrange with the distant producers to supply it in exchange for goods produced locally, the merchant will appear who will profit by dealing with the needs of one section to sell and of the other to buy, and impose his own prices both on the producer and the consumer. This is what has happened in our midst; the less organised we have been the more prone are we to be imposed on by a few individuals. And this is understandable. . . .

So much so that organisation, far from creating authority, is the only cure for it and the only means whereby each one of us will get used to taking an active and conscious part in collective work, and cease being passive instruments in the hands of leaders....

But an organisation, it is argued, presupposes an obligation to coordinate one's own activities with those of others; thus it violates liberty and fetters initiative. As we see it, what really takes away liberty and makes initiative impossible is the isolation which renders one powerless. Freedom is not an abstract right but the possibility of acting: this is true among ourselves as well as in society as a whole. And it is by cooperation with his fellows that man finds the means to express his activity and his power of initiative.[3]

An anarchist organisation must, in my opinion [allow for] complete autonomy, and independence, and therefore full responsibility, to individuals and groups; free agreement between those who think it useful to come together for cooperative action, for common aims; a moral duty to fulfil one's pledges and to take no action which is contrary to the accepted programme. On such bases one then introduces practical forms and the suitable instruments to give real life to the organisation. Thus the groups, the federation of groups, the federations of federations, meetings, congresses, correspondence committees, and so on. But this also must be done freely, in such a way as not to restrict the thought and the initiative of individual members, but only to give greater scope to the efforts which in isolation would be impossible or ineffective. Thus for an anarchist organisation congresses, in spite of all the disadvantages from which they suffer as representative bodies . . . are free from authoritarianism in any shape or form because they do not legislate and do not impose their deliberations on others. They serve to maintain and increase personal contacts among the most active comrades, to summarise and encourage programmatic studies on the ways and means for action; to acquaint everybody with the situation in the regions and the kind of action most urgently needed; to summarise the various currents of anarchist opinions at the time and to prepare some kind of statistics therefrom. And their decisions are not binding but simply suggestions, advice and proposals to submit to all concerned, and they do not become binding and executive except for those who accept them and for as long as they accept them. The administrative organs they nominate—Correspondence Commissions, etc.—have no directive powers, do not take initiatives except for those who specifically solicit and approve of them, and have no authority to impose their own views, which they can certainly hold and propagate as groups of comrades, but which cannot be presented as the official views of the organisation. They publish the resolutions of the congresses and the opinions and proposals communicated to them by groups and individuals; and they act for those who want to make use of them, to facilitate relations between groups, and cooperation between those who are in agreement on various initiatives; each is free to correspond with whoever he likes direct, or to make use of other committees nominated by specific groupings.

In an anarchist organisation individual members can express any opinion and use every tactic which is not in contradiction with the accepted principles and does not interfere with the activities of others. In every case a particular organisation lasts so long as the reasons for union are superior to those for dissension: otherwise it disbands and makes way for other, more homogenous groupings.

Certainly the life and permanence of an organisation is a condition for success in the long struggle before us, and besides, it is natural that every institution should by instinct aim at lasting indefinitely. But the duration of a libertarian organisation must be the result of the spiritual affinity of its members and of the adaptability of its constitution to the continually changing circumstances. When it can no longer serve a useful purpose it is better that it should die.[4]

We would certainly be happy if we could all get along well together and unite all the forces of anarchism in a strong movement; but we do not believe in the solidity of organisations which are built up on concessions and assumptions and in which there is no real agreement and sympathy between members.

Better disunited than badly united. But we would wish that each individual joined his friends and that there should be no isolated forces, or lost forces.[5]

It remains for us to speak of the organisation of the working masses for resistance against both the government and the employers.

. . .Workers will never be able to emancipate themselves so long as they do not find in union the moral, economic and physical strength that is needed to subdue the organised might of the oppressors.

There have been anarchists, and there are still some, who while recognising the need to organise today for propaganda and action, are hostile to all organisations which do not have anarchism as their goal or which do not follow anarchist methods of struggle. . . . To those comrades it seemed that all organised forces for an objective less than radically revolutionary, were forces that the revolution was being deprived of. It seems to us instead, and experience has surely already confirmed our view, that their approach would condemn the anarchist movement to a state of perpetual sterility. To make propaganda we must be among the people, and it is in the workers' associations that workers find their comrades and especially those who are most disposed to understand and accept our ideas. But even when it were possible to do as much propaganda as we wished outside the associations, this could not have a noticeable effect on the working masses. Apart from a small number of individuals more educated and capable of abstract thought and theoretical enthusiasms, the worker cannot arrive at anarchism in one leap. To become a convinced anarchist, and not in name only, he must begin to feel the solidarity that joins him to his comrades, and to learn to cooperate with others in the defence of common interests and that, by struggling against the bosses and against the government which supports them, should realise that bosses and governments are useless parasites and that the workers could manage the domestic economy by their own efforts. And when the worker has understood this, he is an anarchist even if he does not call himself such.

Furthermore, to encourage popular organisations of all kinds is the logical consequence of our basic ideas, and should therefore be an integral part of our programme.

An authoritarian party, which aims at capturing power to impose its ideas, has an interest in the people remaining an amorphous mass, unable to act for themselves and therefore always easily dominated. And it follows, logically, that it cannot desire more than that much organisation, and of the kind it needs to attain power: Electoral organisations if it hopes to achieve it by legal means; Military organisation if it relies on violent action.

But we anarchists do not want to *emancipate* the people; we want the people to *emancipate themselves*. We do not believe in the good that comes from above and imposed by force; we want the new way of life to emerge from the body of the people and correspond to the state of their development and advance as they advance. It matters to us therefore that all interests and opinions should find their expression in a conscious organisation and should influence communal life in proportion to their importance.

We have undertaken the task of struggling against existing social organisation, and of overcoming the obstacles to the advent of a new society in which freedom and well-being would be assured to everybody. To achieve this objective we organise ourselves in a party and seek to become as numerous and as strong as possible. But if it were only our party that was organised; if the workers were to remain isolated like so many units unconcerned about each other and only linked by the common chain; if we ourselves besides being organised as anarchists in a party, were not as workers organised with other workers, we could achieve nothing at all, or at most, we might be able to impose ourselves . . . and then it would not be the triumph of anarchy but our triumph. We could then go on calling ourselves anarchists, but in reality we should simply be rulers, and as impotent as all rulers are where the general good is concerned.[6]

III

12. Production and Distribution

One must produce, say the government and the bourgeoisie.

One must produce, say the reformists.

One must produce, we (anarchists) also say.

But produce for whom? Produce what? And what are the reasons that not enough is produced?

They say, the revolution cannot take place because production is insufficient, and that we would run the risk of dying of hunger.

We say, the revolution must take place so as to be able to produce and stop the greater part of the population from living in a state of chronic hunger.[1]

... Arturo Labriola, the well known Italian intransigent socialist, maintained at a public meeting some time ago that "the urgent problem which needs solving is not that of the distribution of wealth, but the rational organisation of production."

This is a major error which should be examined, because it compromises the very bases of socialist doctrine, and leads to conclusions which are anything but socialist.

From Malthus onwards, the conservatives of all schools have maintained that poverty does not result from unjust distribution of wealth, but from limited productivity or deficient human industry.

Socialism, in its historic origins and in its basic essence, is the negation of this thesis; it is a clear statement that the social problem is above all a matter of social justice, a question of distribution.

If the thesis sustained by Labriola were true, it would be false to maintain that the antagonisms between bosses and workers cannot be solved, since the workers would find a solution by reason of the interest both bosses and salaried classes have in increasing the quantity of goods; socialism would therefore be false, at least as a practical means for solving the social problem.[2]

Our comrade and friend, Rudolf Rocker says: "The internationalization of raw materials (coal, minerals, oil, etc.) is one of the most important conditions for the realization of socialism and the freeing of humanity from economic, political and social bondage."

In my opinion this is a mistake, a grave error which could serve the enemies of the revolution to paralyze popular movements in those countries which, while lacking particular raw materials, can find themselves, in a given historical situation, better able than others to overthrow the capitalist system.

Such was the case in Italy in 1920. The happy concourse of circumstances made a revolution of a socialist character (using socialist in its widest sense) possible as well as relatively easy. We anarchists and the syndicalists of the Unione Sindacale, strained every nerve to push the masses to act for themselves; but the socialist party, which was then led by the communists, and the General Confederation of labour, (much stronger numerically, organisationally and materially than we were), were determined to prevent any kind of action, and made great use of the argument that we lacked raw materials in Italy. I remember that in Milan, during a heated discussion, a socialist, secretary of the Chemical workers, exclaimed: "How do you expect to make a revolution; don't you know that there are no stocks of rubber in Italy and that in the event of a revolution none would reach us from abroad?" Obviously that good socialist wanted to postpone the advent of socialism until either rubber plantations had been established in Italy or foreign governments had given an undertaking to send us rubber in spite of the revolution!

These raw materials are obviously very useful but they are certainly not indispensable. Humanity lived for innumerable centuries without carbonised vegetable matter, without oil, without rubber, without such an abundance of minerals—and *could* live without all this stuff in conditions of justice and liberty, that is under socialism, given human understanding and a desire for them.

The question of the distribution of raw materials has assumed such large proportions because of capitalist interests which have been built up around them. It is the capitalists of the various countries who get rich by the exploitation of raw materials and who fight among themselves for the rights; and rival governments find the means of power and revenue in the monopolies enjoyed by their co-nationals.

For the workers, the availability of materials which make work lighter and satisfy certain special needs is as important as you like, but comes after the overriding question of equality and freedom.

Certainly, as Rocker says, the earth will have to be an economic domain available to everybody, the riches of which will be enjoyed by all human beings. But this will happen after, not before, socialism has triumphed everywhere. For the time being, governments, in their own interests and on behalf of their respective financiers and capitalists, defend the monopolies which they have secured in the struggle, and will probably go to war rather than give them up. Briefly then, the internationalisation of natural wealth is not the condition for, but the consequence of, socialism.[3]

The artificial scarcity of goods is a characteristic of the capitalist system and it is the task of the revolution to make rational use of the land and the tools of production in order to increase production to the point where it amply satisfies the needs of all.[4]

Since the means of production (land, tools, etc.) belong to a small number of people who use them to make others work for their profit, it follows that production increases so long as the employers' profits increase, and is artificially held back, when increased production results in smaller profits. In other words, the employer limits production to what he can sell at a profit, and halts production as soon as he stops making profits, or when the prospects of so doing seem remote. And thus, the whole economic life of society, stems not from the necessity of satisfying the needs of everybody, but from the interests of the employers and by the competition in which they are engaged among themselves. Hence limited production to keep prices high; hence the phenomenon of unemployment even when the needs are urgent; hence uncultivated or badly cultivated land; hence poverty and the subjection of the majority of workers.

Under such conditions, how is it possible to produce in abundance for everybody?[5]

There have been many anarchists, and among them some of the most eminent, who have propagated the idea that the quantity of goods produced and stored in the warehouses and granaries is so over-abundant that it would only be necessary to draw on these stores to fully satisfy the needs and wishes of all without having to worry ourselves about the problems of work and production for a long time to come. And, of course, they found people who were willing to believe them. Human beings are only too liable to succumb to a tendency to avoid toil and dangers. Just as the social democrats found a considerable measure of support among the masses when they tried to make out that it was sufficient to put a piece of paper in the ballot box in order to emancipate oneself, so some anarchists attracted other masses by assuring them all that was needed was a one-day epic struggle in order to enjoy, without effort, or with a minimum of effort, the paradise of abundance in a state of freedom.

Now, this is precisely the contrary of the truth. Capitalists make others produce to sell for profit, and therefore stop production as soon as they see that profits would diminish or disappear. They generally find it more advantageous to keep markets in a situation of relative shortage; and this is shown by the fact that one bad harvest can result in goods being in short supply or even not available at all. It can be said therefore, that the greatest harm wrought by the capitalist system is not so much the army of parasites that it feeds, as the obstacles it places in the way of the production of useful commodities. The hungry and the badly clothed are dazzled when they pass shops bulging with goods of every kind; but try to distribute this wealth among all the needy and you will see how small would be each one's share!

Socialism, the aspiration to socialism, in the broad sense of the word, appears as a problem of distribution in so far as it is the spectacle of the poverty of workers compared with the comfort and luxury of the parasites, and the moral revolt against the blatant social injustices which have driven the victims, and all men of feeling, to seek and to advocate better ways of living together in society. But the achievement of socialism—be it anarchist or authoritarian, mutualist or individualist, etc.—is above all a problem of production. When the goods do not exist, it is useless to seek the best way of distributing them, and if men are reduced to fighting over their crust of bread, the sentiments of love and brotherhood are in danger of being overwhelmed by the brutal struggle for existence.

Fortunately today the means of production abound. Mechanisation, science, and technology have centupled the productive potential of human labour. But one has to work, and to do so usefully one must have the know-how: how to do the work and how to organise it in the most economical way.

If anarchists want to act effectively in competition with the various political parties, they must study in depth—each one the branch with which he is most familiar—all the theoretical and practical problems related to useful work.[6]

We must bear in mind that on the morrow of the revolution we shall be faced with the danger of hunger. This is not a reason for delaying the revolution, because the state of production will, with minor variations, remain the same, so long as the capitalist system lasts.

But it is a reason for us to pay attention to the problem and of how in a revolutionary situation, to avoid all waste, to preach the need for reducing consumption to a minimum, and to take immediate steps to increase production, especially of food.[7]

At the very moment of the revolution, as soon as the defeat of bourgeois military power makes it possible, we should put into effect, by means of the free initiative of all workers' organisations, by all militant groups, and all volunteers of the revolutionary movement, the expropriation and the placing of all existing wealth in common and, without delay, proceed to the organisation of distribution and the reorganisation of production according to the needs and wishes of the different regions, communes, and groups, and thus arrive, under the impetus of the idea and of needs, at the understandings, agreements, and decisions needed to carry on the life of society.[8]

Production and distribution must be controlled, that is one must ascertain which commodities are needed and in what quantities; where they are needed and what means are available to produce them and distribute them. Colomer says that "under anarchy it is the individual who determines production and consumption in relation to his needs and his capabilities"; but a moment's reflection should make him realise that he is talking nonsense. Since an individual cannot alone produce all he needs and must exchange his products with those of others, it is necessary that each should know not only what he can produce and what he requires, but be aware of the needs and capabilities of others as well.[9]

Liberty and labour are the prerequisites of socialism (anarchist, communist, etc.) just as they also are the prerequisites of all human progress.[10]

13. The Land

The problem of the land is perhaps the most serious, and dangerous problem which the revolution will have to solve. In justice (abstract justice which is contained in the saying *to each his own*) the land belongs to everybody and must be at the disposal of whoever wants to work it, by whatever means he prefers, whether individually, or in small or large groups, for his own benefit or on behalf of the community.

But justice does not suffice to ensure civilised life, and if it is not tempered, almost cancelled out, by the spirit of brotherhood, by the consciousness of human solidarity, it leads, through the struggle of each against all, to subjection and the exploitation of the vanquished, and that is, to injustice in all social relations.

To each his own. The *own* of each should be the part share due to him of the natural wealth and the accumulated wealth of past generations on top of what he produces by his own efforts. But how to divide justly the natural wealth, and determine in the complexity of civilised life and in the complex process of production, what is an individual's production? And how is one to measure the value of the products for the purposes of exchange?

If one starts from the principle, of each for himself, it is utopian to hope for justice, and to claim it, is hypocrisy, maybe unconscious, which serves to cover up the meanest egoism, the desire for domination and the avidity of each individual.

Communism then appears to be the only possible solution; the only system, based on natural solidarity, which links all mankind; and only a desired solidarity linking them in brotherhood, can reconcile the interests of all and serve as the basis for a society in which everyone is guaranteed the greatest possible well-being and freedom.

On the question of possession and utilisation of the land it is even clearer. If all the cultivable landmasses were equally fertile, equally healthy, and equally well situated for the purpose of barter, one could visualise a division of the land in equal parts among all the workers, who would then work, in association if they wished, and how they wished, in the interests of production.

But the conditions of fertility, the health and situation of the land are so different that it is impossible to think in terms of an equable distribution. A government by nationalising the land and renting it to land workers could, in theory, resolve the problem by a tax, which would go to the State, what economists call the economic return (that is, whatever a piece of land, given equal work, produces in excess over the worse piece). It is the system advocated by the American Henry George. But one sees immediately that such a system presupposes the continuation of the bourgeois order, apart from the growing power of the State and the governmental and bureaucratic powers with which one would have to contend. So, for us, who neither want government nor believe that individual possession of agricultural land is possible or desirable—economically or morally—the only solution is communism. And for this reason we are communists.

But communism must be voluntary, freely desired, and accepted; for were it instead to be imposed, it would produce the most monstrous tyranny which would result in a return to bourgeois individualism.

Now, while waiting for communism to demonstrate, by the example of the collectives so organised from the outset, its advantages and be desired by all, what is our practical agrarian programme, to be put into operation as soon as the revolution takes place?

Once legal protection has been removed from property, the workers will have to take possession of all land which is not being directly cultivated, by existing owners with their own hands; they will have to establish themselves into associations and organise production, making use of the ability and all the technical skills of those who have always been workers, as well as of the former bourgeoisie who having been expropriated and, being no longer able to live by the work of others, will by the necessity of things have become workers as well. Agreements will be promptly reached with the associations of industrial workers for the exchange of goods, either on a communistic basis or in accordance with the different criteria prevailing in different localities.

Meanwhile all food stocks would be expropriated by the people in revolt and distribution to the different localities and individuals organised through the initiative of the revolutionary groups. Seeds, fertilisers and farm machinery, and working animals will be supplied to the land workers; free access to the land for whoever wants to work it.

There remains the question of peasant proprietors. Should they refuse to join forces with the others there would be no reason to harass them so long as they do the work themselves and do not exploit the labour of others. . . . The disadvantages, the virtual impossibility of isolated work, would soon attract them into the orbit of the collectivity. . . .[1]

14. Money and Banks

It is a mistake to believe as some do that the banks are, or are in the main, a means to facilitate exchange; they are a means to speculate on exchange and currencies, to invest capital and make it produce interest, and to fulfil other typically capitalist operations, which will disappear as soon as the principle that no one has the right or the possibility of exploiting the labour of others, triumphs.

That in the post-revolutionary period, in the period of reorganisation and transition, there might be "offices for the concentration and distribution of the capital of collective enterprises," that there might or not be titles recording the work done and the quantity of goods to which one is entitled, is something we shall have to wait and see about, or rather, it is a problem which will have many and varied solutions according to the system of production and distribution which will prevail in the different localities and among the many natural and artificial groupings that will exist. What seems essential to me is that all money actually in circulation, industrial shares, title deeds, government securities, and all other securities which represent the right and the means for living on the labour of others should immediately be considered valueless and also, in so far as it is possible to do so, destroyed.[1]

It is customary in [anarchist] circles to offer a simplicist solution to the problem [of money] by saying that it must be abolished. And this would be the solution if it were a question of an anarchist society, or of a hypothetical revolution to take place in the next hundred years, always assuming that the masses could become anarchist and communist before the conditions under which we live had been radically changed by a revolution.

But today the problem is complicated in quite a different way. Money is a powerful means of exploitation and oppression; but it is also the only means (apart from the most tyrannical dictatorship or the most idyllic accord) so far devised by human intelligence to regulate production and distribution automatically.

For the moment, rather than concerning oneself with the abolition of money one should seek a way to ensure that money truly represents the useful work performed by its possessors. . . .

Let us assume that a successful insurrection takes place tomorrow. Anarchy or no anarchy, the people must go on eating and providing for all their basic needs. The large cities must be supplied with necessities more or less as usual.

If the peasants and carriers, etc. refuse to supply goods and services for nothing, and demand payment in money which they are accustomed to considering as real wealth, what does one do? Oblige them by force? In which case we might as well wave goodbye to anarchism and to any possible change for the better. Let the Russian experience serve as a lesson.

And so?

The comrades generally reply: But the peasants will understand the advantages of communism or at least of the direct exchange of goods for goods.

This is all very well; but certainly not in a day, and the people cannot stay without eating for even a day. I did not mean to propose solutions [at the Bienne meeting]. What I do want to do is to draw the comrades' attention to the most important questions which we shall be faced with in the reality of a revolutionary morrow.[2]

15. Property

OUR OPPONENTS, INTERESTED DEFENDERS OF THE EXISTING system are in the habit of saying, to justify the right to private property, that it is the condition and guarantee of freedom.

And we agree with them. Are we not always repeating that he who is poor is a slave? Then why are they our opponents?

The reason is clear and is that in fact the property they defend is capitalist property, that is, property which allows some to live by the work of others and which therefore presupposes a class of dispossessed, propertyless people, obliged to sell their labour power to the property-owners for less than its value. . . .[1]

The principal reason for the bad exploitation of nature, and of the miseries of the workers, of the antagonisms and the social struggles, is the *right to property* which confers on the owners of the land, the raw materials and of all the means of production, the possibility to exploit the labour of others, and to organise production not for the well-being of all, but in order to guarantee a maximum profit for the owners of property. It is necessary therefore to abolish property.[2]

The principle for which we must fight and on which we cannot compromise, whether we win or lose is that all should possess the means of production in order to work without subjection to capitalist exploitation, large or small. The abolition of individual property, in the literal sense of the word, will come, if it comes, by the force of circumstances, by the demonstrable advantages of communistic management, and by the growing spirit of brotherhood. But what has to be destroyed at once, even with violence if necessary, is *capitalistic property*, that is, the fact that a few control the natural wealth and the instruments of production and can thus oblige others to work for them.

Imposed communism would be the most detestable tyranny that the human mind could conceive. And free and voluntary communism is ironical if one has not the right and the possibility to live in a different regime, collectivist, mutualist, individualist—as one wishes, always on condition that there is no oppression or exploitation of others.

Free then is the peasant to cultivate his piece of land, alone if he wishes; free is the shoe maker to remain at his last, or the blacksmith in his small forge. It remains to be seen whether not being able to obtain assistance or people to exploit—and he would find none because nobody, having a right to the means of production and being free to work on his own or as an equal with others in the large organisations of production would want to be exploited by a small employer—I was saying, it remains to be seen whether these isolated workers would not find it more convenient to combine with others and voluntarily join one of the existing communities.

The destruction of title deeds would not harm the independent worker whose real title is possession and the work done.

What we are concerned with is the destruction of the titles of the proprietors who exploit the labour of others and, above all, of expropriating them in fact in order to put the land, houses, factories, and all the means of production at the disposal of those who do the work.

It goes without saying that former owners would only have to take part in production in whatever way they can, to be considered equals with all other workers.[3]

Will property [in the revolutionary period] have to be individual or collective? And will the collective holding the undivided goods be the local group, the functional group, the group based on political affinity, the family group—will it comprise all the inhabitants of a nation *en bloc* and eventually all humanity?

What forms will production and exchange assume? Will it be the triumph of *communism* (production in association and free consumption for all) or *collectivism* (production in common and the distribution of goods on the basis of the work done by each individual), or *individualism* (to each the individual ownership of the means of production and the enjoyment of the full product of his labour), or other composite forms that individual interest and social instinct, illuminated by experience, will suggest?

Probably every possible form of possession and utilisation of the means of production and all ways of distribution of produce will be tried out at the same time in one or many regions, and they will combine and be modified in various ways until experience will indicate which form, or forms, is or are, the most suitable.

In the meantime . . . the need for not interrupting production, and the impossibility of suspending consumption of the necessities of life, will make it necessary to take decisions for the continuation of daily life at the same time as expropriation proceeds. One will have to do the best one can, and so long as one prevents the constitution and consolidation of new privilege, there will be time to find the best solutions.

But what is the solution that seems best to me and to which one should try to approximate?

I call myself a communist, because communism, it seems to me, is the ideal to which mankind will aspire as love between men, and an abundance of production, will free them from the fear of hunger and will thus destroy the major obstacle to brotherhood between them. But really, even more than the practical forms of organisation which must inevitably be adjusted according to the circumstances, and will always be in a constant state of change, what is important is the spirit which informs those organisations, and the method used to bring them about; what I believe important is that they should be guided by the spirit of justice and the desire of the general good, and that they should always achieve their objectives through freedom, and voluntarily. If freedom and a spirit of brotherhood truly exist, all solutions aim at the same objective of emancipation and human enlightenment and will end by being reconciled by fusion. If, on the contrary, there is no freedom and the desire for the good of all is lacking, all forms of organisation can result in injustice, exploitation, and despotism.[4]

16. Crime and Punishment

Every anarchist propagandist is familiar with the key objections: who will keep criminals in check [in the anarchist society]? To my mind their concern is exaggerated since delinquency is a phenomenon of little importance compared with the vastness of ever present and general social realities. And one can believe in its automatic disappearance as a result of an increase in material well-being and education, not to mention advances in pedagogy and medicine. But however optimistic may be our hopes, and rosy the future, the fact remains that delinquency and the fear of crime today prevents peaceful social relations, and it will certainly not disappear from one moment to the next following a revolution, however radical and thoroughgoing it may turn out to be. It could even be the cause of upheaval and disintegration in a society of free men, just as an insignificant grain of sand can stop the most perfect machine.

It is worthwhile and indeed necessary that anarchists should consider the problem in greater detail than they normally do, not only in order the better to deal with a popular "objection" but in order not to expose themselves to unpleasant surprises and dangerous contradictions.

Naturally the crimes we are talking about are anti-social acts, that is those which offend human feelings and which infringe the right of others to equality in freedom, and not the many actions which the penal code punishes simply because they offend against the privileges of the dominant classes.[1]

Crime, in our opinion, is any action which tends to consciously increase human suffering; it is the violation of the right of all to equal freedom and to the greatest possible enjoyment of material and moral well-being.

We know that having thus defined delinquency, it is always difficult even for those who accept the definition, to determine in fact what actions are criminal and which are not; for Man's views differ as to what causes pain or happiness, what is good and what is bad, except in those bestial crimes which offend fundamental human feelings and are therefore universally condemned.[2]

I imagine that no one would be prepared, theoretically, to deny that freedom understood in the sense of reciprocity, is the basic prerequisite of any civilisation, of "humanity"; but only anarchy represents its logical and complete realisation. On this assumption, he is a criminal—not against nature or the result of a metaphysical law, but against his fellow men and because the interests and feelings of others have been offended—whoever violates the equal freedom of others. And so long as such people exist, we must defend ourselves.[3]

This necessary defence against those who violate not the *status quo* but the deepest feelings which distinguish men from beasts, is one of the pretexts by which governments justify their existence. One must eliminate all the social causes of crime, one must develop in man brotherly feelings, and mutual respect; one must, as Fourier put it, seek useful alternatives to crime. But if, and so long as, there are criminals, either the people will find the means, and have the energy, to directly defend themselves against them, or the police and the magistrature will reappear and with them, government.

It is not by denying a problem that one solves it.[4]

One can, with justification, fear that this necessary defence against crime could be the beginning of and the pretext for, a new system of oppression and privilege. It is the anarchists' mission to see that this does not happen. By seeking the causes of each crime and making every effort to eliminate them; by making it impossible for anybody to derive personal advantage out of the detection of crime, and leaving it to the interested groups themselves to take whatever steps they deem necessary for their defence; by accustoming oneself to consider criminals as brothers who have strayed, as sick people needing loving treatment, as one would for any hydrophobe or dangerous lunatic—it will be possible to reconcile the complete freedom of all with defence against those who obviously and dangerously threaten it.

Obviously this is possible, when crime will be reduced to sporadic, individual, and truly pathological cases. If it were a fact that criminals were too numerous and powerful; if, for example, they were what the bourgeoisie and fascism are today [1922], then it is not a question of discussing what we will do in an anarchist society.[5]

With the growth of civilisation, and of social relations; with the growing awareness of human solidarity which unites mankind; with the development of intelligence and a refinement of feelings there is certainly a corresponding growth of social duties, and many actions which were considered as strictly individual rights and independent of any collective control will be considered, indeed they already are, matters affecting everybody, and must therefore be carried out in conformity with the general interest. For instance, even in our times parents are not allowed to keep their children in ignorance and bring them up in a way which is harmful to their development and future well-being. A person is not allowed to live in filthy conditions and neglect those rules of hygiene which can affect the health of others; one is not allowed to have an infectious disease and not have it treated. In a future society it will be considered a duty to seek to ensure the good of all, just as it will be considered blameworthy to procreate if there are reasons to believe that the progeny will be unhealthy and unhappy. But this sense of our duties to others, and of theirs to us must, according to our social concepts, develop without any other outside sanction than the esteem or the disapproval of our fellow citizens. Respect, the desire for the well-being of others, must enter into the customs, and manifest themselves not as duties but as a normal satisfaction of social instincts.

There are those who would improve the morality of people by force, who would wish to introduce an Article into the penal code for every possible human action, who would place a *gendarme* alongside every nuptial bed and by every table. But these people if they lack the coercive powers to impose their ideas, only succeed in making a mockery of the best things; and if they have the power to command, make what is good hateful, and encourage reaction. . . . For us the carrying out of social duties must be a voluntary act, and one has the right to intervene with material force only against those who offend against others *violently* and prevent them from living in peace. Force, physical restraint, must only be used against attacks of violence and for no other reason than that of self-defence.

But who will judge? Who will provide the necessary defence? Who will establish what measures of restraint are to be used? We do not see any other way than that of leaving it to the interested parties, to the people, that is the mass of citizens, who will act in different ways according to the circumstances and according to their different degrees of social development. One must, above all, avoid the creation of bodies specialising in police work; perhaps something will be lost in repressive efficiency but one will also avoid the creation of the instrument of every tyranny.

We do not believe in the infallibility, nor even in the general goodness of the masses; on the contrary. But we believe even less in the infallibility and goodness of those who seize power and legislate, who consolidate and perpetuate the ideas and interests which prevail at any given moment.

In every respect the injustice, and transitory violence of the people is preferable to the leaden-rule, the legalised State violence of the judiciary and police.

We are, in any case, only one of the forces acting in society, and history will advance, as always, in the direction of the resultant of all the [social] forces.[6]

We must reckon with a residue of delinquency . . . which we hope will be eliminated more or less rapidly, but which in the meantime will oblige the mass of workers to take defensive action. Discarding every concept of punishment and revenge, which still dominate penal law, and guided only by the need for self-defence and the desire to rehabilitate, we must seek the means to achieve our goal, without falling into the dangers of authoritarianism and consequently finding ourselves in contradiction with the system of liberty and free-will on which we seek to build the new society.[7]

For authoritarians and statesmen, the question is a simple one: a legislative body to list the crimes and prescribe the punishments; a police force to hunt out the delinquents; a magistrature to judge them; and a prison service to make them suffer. And, as is understandable, the legislative body seeks through its penal laws to defend, above all, established interest, which it represents, and to protect the State from those who seek to "subvert" it. The police force exists to suppress crime, and having therefore an interest in the continued existence of crime becomes provocative, and develops in its officers aggressive and perverse instincts; the magistrature also lives and prospers thanks to crime and delinquents, and serves the interests of the government and the ruling classes, and acquires, in the course of exercising its function, a special way of reasoning, which makes it into a machine for awarding a maximum number of people the longest sentences it can. The warders are, or become, insensitive to the suffering of prisoners and at best, passively observe the rules without a spark of human feeling. One sees the results in statistics on delinquency. The penal laws are changed, the police force and the magistrature are reorganised, the prison system is reformed . . . and delinquency persists and resists all attempts to destroy, or reduce it. It is true of the past and the present, and we think it will apply in the future too, if the whole concept of crime is not changed, and all the organisms which live on the prevention and repression of delinquency are not abolished.[8]

There are in France stringent laws against the traffic in drugs and against those who take them. And as always happens, the scourge grows and spreads in spite, and perhaps because of, the laws. The same is happening in the rest of Europe and in America. Doctor Courtois-Suffit, of the French Academy of Medicine, who, already last year [1921], had sounded the alarm against the dangers of cocaine, noting the failure of penal legislation, now demands . . . new and more stringent laws.

It is the old mistake of legislators, in spite of experience invariably showing that laws, however barbarous they may be, have never served to suppress vice or to discourage delinquency. The more severe the penalties imposed on the consumers and traffickers of cocaine, the greater will be the attraction of forbidden fruits and the fascination of the risks incurred by the consumer, and the greater will be the profits made by the speculators, avid for money.

It is useless, therefore to hope for anything from the law. We must suggest another solution. Make the use and sale of cocaine free [from restrictions], and open kiosks where it would be sold at cost price or even under cost. And then launch a great propaganda campaign to explain to the public, and let them see for themselves, the evils of cocaine; no one would engage in counter-propaganda because nobody could exploit the misfortunes of cocaine addicts.

Certainly the harmful use of cocaine would not disappear completely, because the social causes which create and drive those poor devils to the use of drugs would still exist. But in any case the evil would decrease, because nobody could make profits out of its sale, and nobody could speculate on the hunt for speculators. And for this reason our suggestion either will not be taken into account, or it will be considered impractical and mad.

Yet intelligent and disinterested people might say to themselves: Since the penal laws have proved to be impotent, would it not be a good thing, as an experiment, to try out the anarchist method?[9]

We will not repeat the classical arguments against the death penalty. They seem lies, when we hear them used by those who then come out in favour of life imprisonment and other inhuman substitutes for the death penalty. Nor will we speak of the "sanctity of life" which all affirm but violate when it suits them, either by actually taking life or treating others in such a way as to torment or shorten their lives.

Fortunately only few men are born, or become, moral bloodthirsty and sadistic monsters whose death we would not know how to mourn. If these poor devils were to be a continuous threat to everybody and there were no other way of defending ourselves other than by killing them, one could also admit the death penalty.

But the trouble is that in order to carry out the death penalty one needs an executioner. The executioner is, or becomes, a monster; and on balance it is better to let the monsters that there are go on living, rather than to create others.

And this applies to real delinquents, anti-social beings who arouse no sympathy and provoke no commiseration. When it comes to the death penalty as a means of political struggle, then . . . well history teaches us what can be the consequences.[10]

IV

17. Anarchists and the Working Class Movements

Today the most powerful force for social transformation is the working-class movement (the trade-union movement), and on its intentions depends to a large degree the course that events will take and the objectives of any future revolution. Through the organisations established for the defence of their interests, workers acquire an awareness of the oppression under which they live and of the antagonisms which divide them from their employers, and so begin to aspire to a better life, get used to collective struggle and to solidarity, and can succeed in winning those improvements which are compatible with the continued existence of the capitalist and statist regime. Later, when the conflict is beyond solution, there is either revolution or reaction.

Anarchists must recognise the usefulness and the importance of the workers' movement, must favour its development, and make it one of the levers for their action, doing all they can so that it, in conjunction with all existing progressive forces, will culminate in a social revolution which leads to the suppression of classes and to complete freedom, equality, peace, and solidarity among all human beings. But it would be a great and fatal illusion to believe, as many do, that the workers' movement can and must on its own, by its very nature, lead to such a revolution. On the contrary, all movements founded on material and immediate interests (and a mass working-class movement cannot be founded on anything else), if the ferment, the drive and the unremitting efforts of men of ideas struggling and making sacrifices for an ideal future are lacking, tend to adapt themselves to circumstances, foster a conservative spirit, and the fear of change in those who manage to improve their conditions, and often end up by creating new privileged classes and serving to support and consolidate the system which one would want to destroy.

Hence the impelling need for strictly anarchist organisations which struggle both inside and outside the trade unions for the achievement of anarchism and which seek to sterilise all the germs of degeneration and reaction.

But it is obvious that to achieve their ends anarchist organisations must be, in their constitution and in their operation, in harmony with anarchist principles, that is, they must not in any way be marked by an authoritarian spirit, and that they should know how to reconcile the free action of individuals with the need for, and the pleasures to be derived from, cooperation, which serve to develop the consciences of their members as well as their abilities to take initiative. Anarchist organisations should also be an educative force in the circle in which they operate and a moral and material preparation for the future we desire.[1]

The task of anarchists is to work to strengthen the revolutionary conscience of organised workers and to remain in the Unions as anarchists.

It is true that the Unions, for pressing reasons, are often obliged to engage in negotiations and accept compromises. I do not criticise them for that, but it is for this very reason that I have to consider the Unions as essentially reformist.

The Unions perform a function of bringing together the proletarian masses and of eliminating conflicts which could otherwise arise between worker and worker. While the Unions must engage in the struggle to obtain immediate benefits, and after all it is just and only human that workers should demand better conditions, revolutionaries go beyond this. They struggle for the revolution which will expropriate capital and destroy the State, every State by whatever name it is called.

Since economic slavery is the product of political servitude, to eliminate one it is necessary to eliminate the other, even if Marx said otherwise.

Why does the peasant bring the corn to the boss?

Because the gendarme is there to oblige him to do so. Thus, Trade Unionism cannot be an end in itself, since the struggle must also be waged at a political level to distinguish the role of the State.

The anarchists do not want to dominate the U.S.I. (Unione Sindacale Italiana); they would not wish to even if all the workers in its ranks were anarchists, neither do they wish to assume the responsibility for its negotiations. We who do not seek power, only want the consciences of men; only those whose wish is to dominate prefer sheep the better to lead them.

We prefer intelligent workers, even if they are our opponents, to anarchists who are such only in order to follow us like sheep. We want freedom for everybody; we want the masses to make the revolution for the masses.

The person who thinks with his own brain is to be preferred to the one who blindly approves everything. For this reason, as anarchists, we support the U.S.I. because this organisation does develop the consciences of the masses. Better an error consciously committed and in good faith, than a good action performed in a servile manner.[2]

Just because I am convinced that the Unions can and must play a most useful, and perhaps necessary, role in the transition from present society to the equalitarian society, I would wish them to be judged at their true worth and by never forgetting that they have a natural tendency to become closed corporations limited to making narrow, sectional demands, or worse still, for their members only; we will thus be in a better position to combat this tendency and prevent them from becoming conservative organisms. Just as, in fact, I recognise the extreme usefulness that cooperatives, by accustoming workers to manage their own affairs, the organisation of their work and other activities, can have at the beginning of a revolution as experienced organisations capable of dealing with the distribution of goods and serving as nerve centres for the mass of the population, I combat the shopkeeper spirit which seems to develop naturally in their midst. I would wish that they were open to all, that they conferred no privileges on their members and, above all, that they did not transform themselves, as often happens, into real capitalistic Liability Companies, which employ and exploit wage earners as well as speculating on the needs of the public.

In my opinion, cooperatives and Trades Unions, under the capitalist regime, do not naturally, or by reason of their intrinsic value, lead to human emancipation (and this is the controversial point), but can be producers of good and evil, today organs of conservation or social transformation, tomorrow, serving the forces of reaction or revolution. All depends on whether they limit themselves to their real function as defenders of the immediate interests of their members or are animated and influenced by the anarchist spirit, which makes the ideals stronger than sectional interests. And by anarchist spirit I mean that deeply human sentiment, which aims at the good of all, freedom and justice for all, solidarity and love among the people; which is not an exclusive characteristic only of self-declared anarchists, but inspires all people who have a generous heart and an open mind. . . .[3]

The working class movement, in spite of all its merits and its potentialities, cannot be, in itself, a revolutionary movement in the sense of being a negation of the juridical and moral bases of present society.

It can, every new organisation can, in the spirit of its founders and according to the letter of its rules, have the highest aspirations and the most radical intentions, but if it wants to exercise its function as a workers' Union, that is, the present defence of its members' interests, it must recognise *de facto* the institutions which it has denied in theory, adapt itself to circumstances, and attempt to obtain, step by step, as much as it can, by negotiating and compromising with the bosses and the government.

In a word, the Trade Unions are, by their very nature reformist and never revolutionary. The revolutionary spirit must be introduced, developed, and maintained by the constant actions of revolutionaries who work from within their ranks as well as from outside, but it cannot be the normal, natural definition of the Trade Unions function. On the contrary, the real and immediate interests of organised workers, which it is the Unions' role to defend, are very often in conflict with their ideals and forward-looking objectives; and the Union can only act in a revolutionary way if permeated by a spirit of sacrifice and to the extent that the ideal is given precedence over the interest, that is, only if, and to the extent that, it ceases to be an economic Union and becomes a political and idealistic group. And this is not possible in the large Trade

Unions which in order to act need the approval of the masses always more or less egotistic, timorous, and backward.

Nor is this the worst aspect of the situation.

Capitalist society is so constituted that, generally speaking, the interests of each class, of each category, of each individual are in conflict with those of all other classes, categories, and individuals. And in daily life one sees the most complicated alignments of harmony and clashes of interests between classes and between individuals who, from the point of view of social justice should always be friends or always enemies. And it often happens, in spite of the much vaunted solidarity of the proletariat, that the interests of one category of workers are antagonistic to those of others and favourable to those of a category of employers; as also happens, that in spite of the desired international brotherhood, the present interests of the workers of any one country ties them to their native capitalists and puts them in a position of hostility to foreign workers. As an example we would refer to the situation of the various workers' organisations to the question of Tariffs, and Customs barriers, and the voluntary role played by the working masses in wars between capitalist States.

The list is unending—antagonism between employed and unemployed, between men and women, between native workers and foreign workers in their midst, between workers who use a public service and those who work in that service, between those who have a trade and those who want to learn it. But I would here draw special attention to the interest that workers engaged in the luxury trades have in the prosperity of the wealthy classes and that of a whole number of categories of workers in different localities that "business" should come their way, even if at the expense of other localities and to the detriment of production which is useful to the community as a whole. And what should be said of those who work in industries harmful to society and to individuals, when they have no other way of earning a living? In normal times, when there is no faith in an imminent revolution, just go and try to persuade workers at the Arsenals who are threatened with unemployment not to demand that the government should build new battleships! And try, with Trade Union means, and doing justice to all, to solve the conflicts between dock labourers, who have no other way of ensuring the means of livelihood for themselves than by monopolising all the available work for those who have been working there a long time, and the new arrivals, the "casuals" who demand their right to work and life! All this, and much else that could be said, shows that the workers' movement, in itself, without the ferment of revolutionary imagination contrasting with the short term interests of the workers, without the criticism and the impulse of the revolutionaries, far from leading to the transformation of society to the advantage of all, tends to encourage group egoism and to create a class of privileged workers living on the backs of the great mass of the "disinherited."

And this explains the general phenomenon that in all countries workers' organisations as they have grown and become strong, have become conservative and reactionary, and those who have served the workers' movement honestly and with dreams of a society based on well-being and justice for all, are condemned, like Sisyphus, to having to start all over again every so often.[4]

This need not happen if there is a spirit of rebellion among the masses, and if idealism inspires and influences those more skillful and favoured by circumstances, who are in a position to constitute the new privileged class. But there is no doubt that if we remain at the level of the defence of present-day interests, which is that of the Trade Unions (and since there is no harmony of interests, nor can they be harmonised in a capitalistic regime), the struggle between workers is a normal occurrence which can, in certain circumstances, and among certain sections become more bitter than the struggle between workers and exploiters.

To convince oneself, one only needs to observe what are the largest workers' organisations in the countries in which there is much organisation and little propaganda or revolutionary tradition. Let us take the American Federation of labour in the United States. It does not carry on a struggle against the bosses except in the sense that two business men struggle when they are discussing the details of a contract. The real struggle is conducted against the newcomers, the foreigners, or natives who seek to be allowed to work in any industrial job; against the forced blacklegs who cannot obtain work in the factories recognised by the Federation because the members are against them, and are obliged to offer their services to the "open shops" . . . Those American Unions when they have reached the membership which they think sufficient to be able to deal with the employers as equals, immediately seek to prevent the admission of new members by imposing prohibitive entrance fees or quite blatantly simply refusing all new applications for membership. They impose rigorous limitations on the work that members in each Union can undertake, and prohibit workers in one Union from invading the territory "of the others." Skilled workers look down on manual workers; whites despise and oppress blacks; the "real Americans" consider Chinese, Italians, and other foreign workers as inferiors. If a revolution were to come in the United States, the strong and wealthy Unions would inevitably be against the Movement, because they would be worried about their investments and the privileged position they have assured for themselves. And the same would probably happen in Britain and elsewhere.

This is not Trade Unionism, I know; and trade unionists who unceasingly fight this tendency of the Unions to become the instrument of base egoism, are performing a most useful task. But the tendency is there and cannot be corrected except by transcending trade union methods.

The Unions will be most valuable in a revolutionary situation, but on condition that they are . . . as little like Trade Unions as possible.[5]

It is not true, whatever the syndicalists may say, that the workers' organisations of today will serve as the framework for the future society and will facilitate the transition from the bourgeois to the equalitarian regime. This is an idea which met with favour among the members of the First International; and if I am not mistaken, one will find in Bakunin's writings that the new society would be achieved by all workers joining the Sections of the International.

To my mind this is a mistake.

The structure of existing workers' organisations corresponds to present-day conditions of economic life, which is the result of historic developments and capitalist domination. And the new society cannot be achieved without breaking up those structures and creating new organisms corresponding to the new conditions and the new social objectives.

Workers today are grouped according to the trades they practice, the industries in which they work, the employers against whom they must struggle, or the business to which they are tied. What will be the use of these groupings when, without the employers and with business relations turned upside down, a large number of existing trades and industries will have to disappear, some permanently because they are useless and harmful, others temporarily because, though useful in the future, will have no *raison d'être* or possibility of existence in the period of social upheaval? Of what use, just to quote one of a thousand examples that come to mind, will be the organisations of the marble quarrymen of Carrara when what will be needed is that they should go and cultivate the land and increase the production of foodstuffs, leaving to the future the construction of monuments and marble palaces?

Certainly workers' organisations, especially in their cooperative forms (which incidentally, under the capitalist system, tend to curb workers' resistance) can serve to develop among workers technical and administrative capacities, but in a revolutionary period and for social reorganisation they must disappear and be absorbed in the new popular groupings as circumstances demand. And it is the task of revolutionaries to seek to prevent the development of an *esprit de corps* in these existing organisations which would be an obstacle to satisfying the new Social needs.

Therefore, in my opinion, the workers' movement is an instrument to be used today for raising and educating, the masses, and tomorrow for the inevitable official clash. But it is an instrument which has its disadvantages and its dangers. And we anarchists must make every effort to neutralise the disadvantages, parry the dangers, and use the movement as much as we can for our ends. This does not mean, as has been suggested, that we would wish the workers' movement to be the tool of the anarchists. Of course we would be happy if *all* workers, if everybody were anarchists . . . but in that case anarchy would be a fact and there would be no need for such discussions.

In the present state of affairs, what we would wish is that the workers' movements were open to all forward-looking, imaginative propaganda and that they participated in all the economic, political, and moral activities of society, living and developing free from all outside control, from us no less than from the political parties.[6]

There are many comrades who aim at making the working class movement and the anarchist movement all one, and where they can, as for example in Spain,

Argentina, and to a lesser extent in Italy, France, Germany, etc., they try to give the workers' organisations a frankly anarchist programme. There are those who call themselves "anarcho-syndicalists"; or when they link up with others who are really not anarchists, they take the name of "revolutionary syndicalists." It is necessary to explain what is meant by "syndicalism."

If it is a question of the sought-after future, if, that is, by syndicalism is meant the form of social organisation which should replace the capitalistic and statal organisation, then either it is the same as anarchy, and is therefore a term which only serves to confuse matters, or it is different from anarchy and cannot therefore be accepted by anarchists. Indeed, among the ideas and plans for the future put forward by this or that syndicalist, there are some which are genuinely anarchist, but there are others which present, under different names, and in different guises, the authoritarian structure which is the cause of the evils which today we complain of, and therefore can have nothing in common with anarchy. But it is not syndicalism as a social system that I wish to deal with, since it is not this which can determine the present activity of anarchists in regard to the working-class movement. What we are interested in are all workers' organisations, all the Unions constituted to resist the oppression of the employers and to reduce or destroy the exploitation of human labour by those who control the sources of wealth and the means of production.

Now I say that these cannot be anarchist organisations, and it is not a good thing to wish that they should be, because if they were they would neither manage to do their job nor serve the ends which anarchists aim at in joining them.

The Unions are created to defend today the present interests of workers and improve their conditions as much as possible until such time as they are in a position to carry through a revolution which will make the existing wage earners into free workers, freely associated for the benefit of all.

For the Union to serve its own end and at the same time be a means for education and the terrain for propaganda aimed at a future radical social transformation, it is necessary that it should bring together all workers, or at least all those workers who aim at improving their conditions and whom one succeeds in rendering capable of some kind of resistance against the bosses. Does one perhaps want to wait for workers to be anarchists before inviting them to organise themselves and before admitting them to the organisations of resistance, when it would no longer be required because the masses would already be capable of making the revolution? In this case the Trade Union would be duplicating the role of the anarchist group and would remain impotent both in obtaining improvements and in making the revolution. Alternatively one has an anarchist programme on paper and is satisfied with formal, unconscious support, and so brings together people who follow the organisers sheep like, and who will disappear, or go over to the enemy, at the first opportunity in which it is really necessary to act as anarchists.

Trade Unionism is in its nature reformist. All that can be hoped from it is that the reforms which it demands and pursues are such and obtained in ways which serve revolutionary education and preparation and leave the way free to ever greater demands.

Every fusion or confusion between the anarchist movement and the trade union movement ends, either in rendering the latter unable to carry out its specific task or by weakening, distorting, or extinguishing the anarchist spirit.

The Union can emerge with a socialist, revolutionary, or anarchist programme, and indeed it is with such programmes that many workers' organisations were originally launched. But they remain faithful to the programme so long as they are weak and impotent, that is so long as they are propaganda groups, initiated and sustained by a few enthusiastic and convinced individuals rather than organisms capable of effective action; but then as they manage to attract the masses to their ranks, and acquire the strength to demand and impose improvements, the original programme becomes an empty slogan which no one bothers about, tactics are readjusted to contingent needs, and the enthusiasts of the first hour either adapt themselves or must make way for the "practical" men, who pay attention to the present without worrying about the future.

There certainly are comrades who in spite of being in the front rank of the trade union movement remain sincere and enthusiastic anarchists, as there are workers' groupings which seek their inspiration in anarchist ideas. But it would be a too easy way of criticising, to seek the thousand examples in which these men and these groups in the reality of their day to day actions are in contradiction with anarchist ideas. I agree that these are the hard facts of life.

One cannot act in an anarchist way when one is obliged to deal with employers and the authorities; one cannot let the masses act for themselves when they refuse to act and ask for, or demand, leaders. But why confuse anarchism with what anarchism is not, and why should we, as anarchists, shoulder the responsibility for transactions and compromises made necessary because the masses are not anarchist, not even if they belong to an organisation which has written the anarchist programme into its Constitution?

In my opinion anarchists must not want the Trade Unions to be anarchist, but they must act within their ranks in favour of anarchist aims, as individuals, as groups and as federations of groups. Just as there are, or there should be, study and discussion groups, propaganda groups working among the public with the written and spoken word, cooperative groups, factory groups, groups among the land workers, in the barracks as well the schools, so special groups should be formed in the different organisations which engage in the class struggle.

Of course, it would be ideal if everyone was anarchist and that organisations functioned in an anarchist way; but in that case, it is clear that there would be no need to organise for the struggle against the employers, for there would no longer be bosses. But in the situation as it is, and recognising that the social development of one's workmates is what it is, the anarchist groups should not expect the workers' organisations to act as if they were anarchist, but should make every effort to induce them to approximate as much as possible to the anarchist method. If for the life of the organisation and for the needs and wishes of its members it is absolutely necessary to negotiate, to compromise, and establish doubtful contacts with the authorities, so be it; but this must be done by others, not by anarchists whose role is that of pointing to the insufficiency and precariousness of all improvements which can be obtained under a capitalist regime, and of pushing the struggle always towards more radical solutions. Anarchists in the Unions should struggle for them to be open to all workers whatever their views or party affiliations on the one condition: of solidarity in the struggle against the bosses; they should be opposed to the corporative spirit and any ambitions to a monopoly of organisation or work. They should prevent the Unions from serving as an instrument to be manipulated by politicians for electoral or other authoritarian ends; they should advocate and practice direct action, decentralisation, autonomy, and individual initiative; they should make special efforts to help members learn how to participate directly in the life of the organisation and to dispense with leaders and full-time functionaries.

In other words, they should remain anarchists, always in close touch with anarchists, and remembering that the workers' organisation is not the end, but just one of the means, however important, in preparing the way for the achievement of anarchism.[7]

One must not confuse "syndicalism," which is intended to be a doctrine and a method for solving the social problem, with the promotion, the existence and the activities of the workers' Unions. . . .

For us it is not all that important that the workers should want more or less; what is important is that they should try to get what they want, by their own efforts, by their *direct action* against the capitalists and the government.

A small improvement achieved by one's own effort is worth more, in its effect on morale—materially too, in the long term—than a large scale reform granted by government or capitalists for doubtful ends or even out of the "kindness of their hearts."[8]

We have always understood the vital importance of the workers' movement and the need for anarchists to play an active and forceful part in it. And often it has been as a result of the initiative of our comrades that workers' groups have been formed which are more lively and more progressive. We have always thought that the Trade Union is, today, a means whereby workers can begin to understand their position as slaves, to want their emancipation and to accustom themselves to the solidarity of all the oppressed in the struggle against the oppressors—and that tomorrow it will serve as the first necessary nucleus for the continuation of social life and the reorganisation of production without bosses and parasites.

But we have always discussed, and often disagreed, on the ways anarchist action had to be carried out in relation to the workers' organisation.

Should one join the Unions or stay out though taking part in all the struggles, seeking to make them as radical as possible, and always remaining in the forefront of action and danger?

And above all, whether anarchists should accept executive posts within the Unions, and thus lend themselves to those negotiations, compromises, adjustments, and contacts with the authorities and the employers, which the workers themselves demand of them and which are part and parcel of the day to day demands for better conditions or for the defence of concessions already won?

In the two years that followed the peace and up to the eve of the triumph of fascist reaction we found ourselves in a unique situation.

The revolution seemed imminent, and the material and spiritual conditions were, in fact, present to make a revolution possible as well as necessary.

But we anarchists lacked by a long chalk the necessary strength to make the revolution with our methods and relying exclusively on our numbers; we needed the masses, and they were quite prepared to take action, but they were not anarchist. In any case, a revolution without the support of the masses, even had it been possible, could have only resulted in a new domination, which even if exercised by anarchists would have always been the negation of anarchism, would have corrupted the new rulers and would have ended in the return of the Statist, capitalistic order.

To have withdrawn from the struggle, and abstained because we could not do just what we would have wished to do, would have been a renunciation of every present or future possibility, of every hope of developing the movement in the direction we wished it to go. It would have been renunciation for all time because there will never be anarchist masses until society has been economically and politically transformed, and the same problem will present itself each time circumstances create a situation with revolutionary possibilities.

It will therefore be necessary at all costs to win the confidence of the masses, and be in a position to "push" them when they are in the mood for action, and for this it seemed useful to secure executive posts in the workers' organisations. All the dangers of reformism, corruption were pushed into the background, and in any case it was assumed that there wouldn't be time for them to take effect.

So it was decided to leave everybody free to act according to the circumstances and as they thought best, conditional on their not forgetting that they were anarchists guided at all times by the overriding interest of the anarchist cause.

But now bearing in mind recent experience, and in view of the present situation . . . it seems to me that it would be useful to return to the question and see whether it is a case of modifying our tactic on this most important aspect of our activity.

In my opinion, we must join the Unions, because by remaining outside we appear inimical to them, our criticisms are viewed with suspicion and at a time of agitation we shall appear as intruders and our participation coldly received. . . .

And so far as soliciting and accepting posts as leaders I believe that in general, and in calm periods, it is better to avoid doing so. But I believe that the damage and the danger lie not so much in the fact of occupying an executive post—which in certain circumstances can be useful and also necessary—but where the post becomes a permanent one. In my opinion, the executive personnel should be renewed as often as possible, both in order to give as many workers as possible experience of administrative jobs, as well as to prevent organisational work from becoming a profession and inducing those who do it from introducing into the workers' struggle concern about losing their jobs.

And all this not only in the interests of the present struggle and the education of the workers, but also, and what is more important, with an eye on the development of the revolution once it has started.

Anarchists are justifiably opposed to authoritarian communism, which presupposes a government wanting to direct every aspect of social life, and placing the organisation of production and the distribution of wealth under the orders of its nominees, which cannot but create the most hateful tyranny and the crippling of all the living forces in society.

The Unions, apparently in agreement with the anarchists in their aversion for State centralisation, want to dispense with the government putting the Unions in its place; and they say that it is the Unions which must take over the wealth, requisition all foodstuffs, and be responsible for their distribution as well as organise production and barter. And I would see nothing to object to in this if the Unions opened their doors wide to all the population, and left the dissidents free to act and to have their share.

But in practice this expropriation and this distribution cannot be effected impulsively, by the mass, even if in possession of a Union card, without producing a harmful waste of natural wealth and the sacrificing of the weaker to the stronger; and even more difficult would it be to establish by mass meetings, agreements between the different regions, and the barter arrangements between the various corporations of producers. Provision therefore would have to be made through decisions taken at popular assemblies and carried out by groups and individuals who have volunteered or are duly delegated.

Now, if there are a limited number of people who through long tenure of office are considered trade union leaders; if there are permanent secretaries and official organisers, it will be they who will automatically find themselves charged with organising the revolution, and they will tend to consider as intruders and irresponsible elements, those who want to take independent action, and will want to impose their will, even with the best of intentions—even by the use of force.

And then the "syndicalist regime" would soon become the same lie, the same tyranny which the so-called "dictatorship of the proletariat" has become. The remedy for this danger and the condition for the success of the revolution as a progressive force, is the "formation" of a large number of individuals with initiative and the ability to tackle practical tasks: by accustoming the masses not to leave the common cause in the hands of a few, and to delegate, when delegation is necessary, only for specific missions and for limited duration. And the syndicate, if organised and acting in a truly libertarian manner, is the most effective means to create just such a situation and just such a spirit.[9]

The workers' Union was born out of the necessity to provide for present needs, out of the desire to improve personal conditions, and to protect oneself from a possible worsening of conditions, and is the Union of those who, deprived of the means of production and thus obliged by the exigencies of life to allow themselves to be exploited by those who possess the means, seek, through solidarity with their companions in misery, the strength to struggle against the exploiters. And at this level of the economic struggle, that is, against capitalist exploitation, it would have been possible and easy to achieve the unity of the working class against the owning class.

It was not achieved because the political parties, which incidentally have often been the founders and the first animators of the Trade Union movement, wished to use the workers' associations as a recruiting centre as well as weapons for their particular ends, whether of revolution or conservatism. Hence the divisions within the working class, organised into many groupings under the influence of the political parties, and the concern, of those who want workers' unity, to remove the Unions from the tutelage of political parties. Buried under these intentions is an error and a lie.

If by politics is meant that which concerns the organisation of human relations, and more specifically, the free or limited relations between people and the existence or nonexistence of a "government" which assumes public powers and uses force to impose its will and defend its own interests and those of the class from which it springs, it is clear that politics enters into every expression of social existence, and that a workers' organisation cannot be truly independent of the parties except by itself becoming a party. . . .

It is idle to hope, and in my opinion it would be a bad thing to wish, that politics should be excluded from the Unions, since every economic question of some importance automatically becomes a political question, and it is in the political field, that is, by the struggle between governors and governed, that the question of the emancipation of the workers and of human liberty will have to be finally resolved.

And it is natural, and clear, that it should be so. . . .

The capitalists can maintain the struggle in the economic field so long as workers demand small, and generally illusory improvements; but as soon as they see their profits seriously diminished and the very existence of their privileges threatened, they appeal to government and if it is not sufficiently understanding and not strong enough to defend them, as in the recent cases of Italy and Spain, they use their own wealth to finance new repressive forces and to set up a new government which will serve them better.

Workers' organisations must therefore, of necessity, adopt a line of action in face of present as well as possible future government action.

One can accept the *status quo*, recognise the legitimacy of economic privilege and the government that defends it, and be content to manoeuvre between the different bourgeois factions and obtain some improvements—as happens with the huge organisations which are inspired by no ideal, such as the American Federation of labour and a large part of the British Unions—and then one becomes in practice the tool of the oppressors and gives up the task of freeing oneself from servitude.

But if one aspires to complete emancipation or even if one only wants specific improvements which do not depend on the will of the boss or the whims of the Markets, there are but two ways of freeing oneself from the threat of government. Either by seizing the reins of government and using the public powers, and the collective force captured and held down by the rulers, to get rid of the capitalist system—or by weakening and destroying government by leaving to the workers and to all who in one way or another, by manual and intellectual work, cooperate in keeping social life going, the freedom to provide for individual and social needs in the way they consider best, but without the right or the possibility of imposing their will on others by the use of force. Now, how is it possible to maintain unity when there are some who would wish to use the strength of the organisation to get a seat in the government, while others believe that every government is of necessity oppressive and iniquitous, and would therefore wish to lead the organisation in the direction of struggle against every authoritarian institution now or in the future? How can social democrats, State communists and anarchists be held together?

This is the problem, and one which can be overlooked at certain moments, such as in a clearly defined struggle, when all are unanimous, but which always reemerges and is not easy to solve so long as conditions of violence, and a diversity of opinion as to the means for resisting violence, exist. The democratic method, that is, of leaving the majority to decide and of "maintaining discipline" does not solve the question, since it too is a lie and is not sincerely supported except by those who have or believe they have the majority on their side. Apart from the fact that the "majority" always means a majority among the leaders and not of the masses, one cannot expect, or even wish, that someone who is firmly convinced that the course taken by the majority leads to disaster, should sacrifice his own convictions and passively look on, or even worse, support a policy he considers wrong.

To say: let the others get on with it and you try in your turn to win over the majority to your point of view is rather similar to the argument used in the, army: "accept your punishment and then put in your complaint"—and it is an unacceptable system when what one does today destroys the possibility of doing otherwise tomorrow. There are matters over which it is worth accepting the will of the majority because the damage caused by a split would be greater than that caused by the error; there are circumstances in which discipline becomes a duty because to fail in it would be to fail in the solidarity between the oppressed and would mean betrayal in face of the enemy. But when one is convinced that the organisation is pursuing a course which threatens the future and makes it difficult to remedy the harm done, then it is a duty to rebel and to resist even at the risk of providing a split.

But then, what is the way out of this difficulty, and what should be the conduct of anarchists in the circumstances?

In my view the solution would be: general agreement and solidarity in the purely economic struggle; complete autonomy of individuals and groups in the political struggle.

But is it possible to see in time where the economic struggle becomes a political struggle? And are there any important economic struggles which do not become political right from the start as a result of government intervention?

In any case we anarchists should extend our activities into all organisations to preach unity among all workers, decentralisation, freedom of initiative, within the common framework of solidarity and not worry over much if the mania for centralisation and authoritarianism of some, or the intolerance to all, even reasonable, discipline by others, leads to new splits. For, if organisation of the workers is a fundamental necessity in the struggles of today and for the achievements of tomorrow, the existence, or the longevity of this or that particular organisation is not all that important. What is essential is that individuals should develop a sense of organisation and solidarity, and the conviction that fraternal cooperation is necessary to fight oppression and to achieve a society in which everybody will be able to enjoy his own life.[10]

18. The Occupation of the Factories

General strikes of protest no longer upset anybody; neither those who take part in them nor those against whom they are directed. If only the police had the intelligence to avoid being provocative, they would pass off as any public holiday.

One must seek something else. We put forward an idea: the take-over of factories. For the first attempt probably only a few will take part and the effect will be slight; but the method certainly has a future, because it corresponds to the ultimate ends of the workers' movement and constitutes an exercise preparing one for the ultimate general act of expropriation.[1]

The metal workers started the movement over wage rates. It was a strike of a new kind. Instead of abandoning the factories, the idea was to remain inside without working, and maintain a night and day guard to ensure that the bosses could not operate the night shift. But this was in 1920. Throughout Italy there was revolutionary fervour among the workers and soon the demands changed their character. Workers thought that the moment was ripe to take possession once for all of the means of production. They armed themselves for defence, they transformed many factories into veritable fortresses, and began to organise production on their own. Bosses were either thrown out or held in a state of arrest.... It was the right of property abolished in fact, and the law violated in so far as it served to defend capitalist exploitation; it was a new regime, a new form of social life which was being ushered in. And the government stood by because it felt impotent to offer opposition: it admitted it later when apologising to Parliament for its failure to take repressive action.

The movement grew and showed signs of drawing in other categories of workers; here and there peasants occupied the land. It was the beginning of a revolution which was developing, I would say, almost in an ideal way.

The reformists naturally frowned on the movement, and sought to bring it down. The [socialist daily] *Avanti!* not knowing which way to turn, tried to make out that we were pacifists, because in *Umanità Nova* we had said that if the movement spread to all sectors of industry, that if workers and peasants had followed the example of the metallurgists, of getting rid of the bosses and taking over the means of production, the revolution would succeed without shedding a single drop of blood.

But this was of no avail. The masses were with us; we were called to the factories to speak, to encourage, and to advise the workers, and would have needed to be in a thousand places at once to satisfy all their requests. Wherever we went it was the anarchists' speeches which were applauded while the reformists had to withdraw or make themselves scarce.

The masses were with us because we were the best interpreters of their instincts, their needs, and interests.

Yet, the underhand work of the CGL[2] and the agreements entered into with the Giolitti government to create the impression of a kind of victory through the sham of *workers control* was sufficient to induce the workers to abandon the factories, at the very moment when their chances of success were greatest.[3]

The occupation of the factories and the land suited perfectly our programme of action.

We did all we could, through our paper (*Umanità Nova* daily, and the various anarchist and syndicalist weeklies) and by personal action in the factories, for the movement to grow and spread. We warned the workers of what would happen to them if they abandoned the factories; we helped in the preparation of armed resistance, and explored the possibilities of making the revolution without hardly a shot being fired if only the decision had been taken to use the arms that had been accumulated.

We did not succeed, and the movement collapsed because there were too few of us and the masses were insufficiently prepared.

When D'Aragona [the secretary of the CGL] and Giolitti [the Prime Minister] concocted the farce of workers control with the acquiescence of the socialist party, which was at the time under communist leadership, we put the workers on their guard against the wicked betrayal. But as soon as the order to leave the factories was issued by the CGL, the workers, who though they had always received us and called for us with enthusiasm and who had applauded our incitement to all-out resistance, docilely obeyed the order, though they disposed of powerful military means for resistance.

The fear in each factory of remaining alone in the struggle, as well as the difficulty of laying-in food supplies for the various strong points induced everybody to give in, in spite of the opposition of individual anarchists dispersed among the factories.

The movement could not last and triumph without growing and spreading, and in the circumstances it could not grow without the support of the leaders of the CGL and the Socialist Party which disposed of the large majority of organised workers. Both Confederation and Socialist Party (including the communists) lined up against the movement and it all had to end in a victory for the bosses.[4]

19. Workers and Intellectuals

The origin of this division of men into "intellectuals" (who often are simply idle people without any intellectuality) and "workers" can be found in the fact that at times and in circumstances when to produce enough to amply satisfy one's needs demanded excessive and unpleasant effort, and when one ignored the advantages of solidarity and cooperation, the strongest or the more fortunate, found a way of obliging others to work for them. This manual work, apart from being more or less exhausting, also became a symbol of social inferiority; and thus the seigneurs willingly tired themselves and killed each other in equestrian exercises, dangerous and exhausting hunts, and wore themselves out in competitions, but would feel dishonoured at having to dirty their hands doing even the lightest productive job. Work was something for slaves to do; and such is still the case today in spite of greater knowledge and the advances in applied mechanics and science, which make it easy to provide in abundance for the needs of all by pleasant work, reasonable in its duration and in the physical effort demanded.

When everybody will have the free use of the means of production and no man will be able to oblige others to work for him, then it will be in the interests of all to organise work so that it is as productive and pleasant as possible—and then everybody will be able to pursue their studies, useful or useless, without thereby becoming parasites. There would be no parasites, firstly because no one would want to keep parasites and then because everybody would find that by giving their share of manual labour towards production they would at the same time satisfy their body's need for physical activity.

All would work, including the poets and the transcendental philosophers, without any ill effects to poetry or philosophy. On the contrary. . . .[1]

We have no "working class" prejudices, no preferences for the manual worker because he is a manual worker, and above all no admiration for the uneducated and the illiterates, who, nevertheless, have the valid excuse, that their condition is not their fault.

We are revolutionaries, and know that a revolution made without the participation of forces and values which cannot be acquired without an intellectual background, could well appear to be radical, but in fact would be no more than an explosion of anger without significance and without a future. And for this reason we always welcome with open arms the support of writers, artists, scientists, engineers, technicians, and others who can offer the concourse of intellects rich in ideas and informed by facts.

But on the other hand we know that most of the so-called intellectuals are, by reason of their education, their family background, their class prejudices, tied to the Establishment, and tend to want the subjection of the mass of the people to their will. Whereas the mass of workers, even if they are ignorant or illiterate, constitute, because of their needs and their passion for justice which comes to them from the injustice to which they are subjected, the principal force behind the revolution and the guarantee that it will not resolve itself into a simple change of masters.

Therefore we accept the intellectuals with pleasure and without suspicion when they fuse with the working class, when they join the people without pretensions to command; without a patronising air of condescension, but with the open mind of someone who comes in the midst of brothers to repay them the debt he has contracted in educating himself and cultivating his intellect which, in most cases, is at the expense of the children of those whose manual work has produced the means.[2]

Emma Goldman [in "My further Disillusionment in Russia"] gives as among the main causes for the failure of the Russian revolution the hostility, the hatred that workers felt for the intellectuals, and their contempt for science and the things of the mind.

This doesn't seem to me to be quite correct.

Workers have even too much respect and admiration for educated people . . . who very often have very little education. And this attitude is both a good thing as well as bad. For there are all kinds of intellectuals, revolutionary and reactionary, good ones and bad ones, and above all harmful ones as well as useful ones, depending on the subject to which they have directed their studies and their activities. There are scientists, doctors, engineers, artists, and teachers, but there are also priests, lawyers, politicians, and militarists.

Thus it is in Italy, and I imagine it must be the same in Russia, since one observes that all, or at least almost all, the leaders of the Russian revolution, are intellectuals; indeed one can say that the struggle has taken place between intellectuals while the mass, as is usual, has served as the instrument [in their struggle].

Surely so long as science and higher education will be a privilege of the few (and it will be so so long as existing economic conditions prevail) it is inevitable that those who have knowledge will predominate over those who haven't; but to prevent this preponderance from being a reason and a means to perpetuate present evils or to create new privileges and new tyrannies, one must at the same time stress the glory of science and the usefulness and the need for technical direction, and inspire those who are ignorant with the desire to educate and raise themselves, but one must also make them feel and understand that ignorance is not a reason for being oppressed and ill-treated, but rather gives one a right to greater consideration by way of compensation for being deprived of those things that are among the best in human civilisation.

And "intellectuals," who have had the good fortune of receiving an education, if they take part in a revolution through a sincere love for the good of others, must put themselves at the level of the least fortunate to help them to raise themselves, and not look upon the mass as a flock to lead . . . and to fleece, depriving them thereby of the chance of educating themselves in responsibility and freedom, and even worse, obliging them to obedience by recourse to the *gendarmes*.[3]

What we would call the natural tendency of intellectuals, is to keep apart from the people, and to form themselves into coteries; to give themselves airs and end up by believing themselves protectors and saviours who the masses should worship . . . and maintain. To separate them from the masses, to give them the illusion of fighting for the general good while they enjoy advantages and different standards of life, will encourage just what the drafters of the Appeal [for an International of Intellectuals] so rightly deprecate: the formation of "a harmful and dangerous caste" inside the working-class movement.

And in any case, what could be the activity and the mission of this special International?

If it were a question of an association, such as already exist, to help in the study of science, history and literature, or in order to disseminate a general culture among the people, the project might be possible and useful. And all enlightened people irrespective of party and class could play a part in such a venture. The truth, science, is neither bourgeois nor proletarian, neither revolutionary nor conservative, and everybody can feel interested in its progress.

But what is proposed is an organisation for struggle, an organisation which wants to take its place in the social struggle. And in that case how could men be held together and work usefully, who, even if they more or less share equal final objectives, pursue different means, belong to rival political parties and who in every practical issue would find themselves lined up against each other? How can pacifists and war supporters, revolutionaries and legalitarians, democrats and totalitarians, authoritarians and anarchists be made to agree?

In practice this is what must happen to every Intellectual International, which is neither a purely scientific and a political institution nor an organisation closely linked to one party. A few pompous manifestoes, the decorative support of a few "big names," of those who through vanity or laziness always say yes . . . followed by a fictitious, rickety and useless existence. And even this mere preteens of life would not continue without creating a bureaucracy interested in the continuation of the organisation . . . and in its salaries. This bureaucracy, once the founders tire and withdraw, would manage for a long time to fill the members lists with the names of thousands who knowing how to read and write more or less well, enjoy giving themselves airs of being writers.

But in what way would this be useful to the cause?

For these reasons I believe that our friends who have got caught up in this venture would do well to repeat, at a distance of fifty years, Michael Bakunin's gesture when having declared at a Congress of the Association for Peace and Liberty, that peace and liberty could not be secured except by struggle among the workers for social justice, he abandoned that Association, which was also a kind of International of intellectuals, and, with the revolutionary socialist minority attending the Congress, joined the International Workers' Association. . . .[4]

20. Anarchism, Socialism, and Communism

It is true that anarchists and socialists have always profoundly disagreed in their concepts of historic evolution and the revolutionary crises that this evolution creates, and consequently they have hardly ever been in agreement on the means to adopt, or the opportunities that have existed from time to time to open up the way towards human emancipation.

But this is only an incidental and minor disagreement.

There have always been socialists who have been in a hurry, just as there are also anarchists who want to advance with leaden feet, and even some who do not believe at all in revolution. The important, fundamental dissension is quite another: socialists are authoritarians, anarchists are libertarians.

Socialists want power, whether by peaceful means or by force is of no consequence to them, and once in office, wish to impose their programme on the people by dictatorial or democratic means. Anarchists instead maintain, that government cannot be other than harmful, and by its nature it defends either an existing privileged class or creates a new one; and instead of aspiring to take the place of the existing government anarchists seek to destroy every organism which empowers some to impose their own ideas and interests on others, for they want to free the way for development towards better forms of human fellowship which will emerge from experience, by everybody being free and, having, of course, the economic means to make freedom possible as well as a reality.

It seems unbelievable that even today, after what has happened and is happening in Russia [1921], there are still people who imagine that the differences between socialists and anarchists is only that of wanting the revolution slowly or in a hurry.[1]

The democratic socialist party . . . was born in Italy as a consequence of our mistakes and of the degeneration of the revolutionary spirit among the people; and it will fall, or be reduced to a party of mere politicians, when we, having learned from past failures, are able to be active among the masses, and create a revolutionary spirit in the Italian people.

In any case the democratic socialists would be wrong if they were to seek to draw profit from these "confessions of an anarchist," since we owe our mistakes, common to all the old revolutionary schools, in large measure to Marxist theories, which we anarchists have all shared at some time, in a more logical if less orthodox manner than those professing to be Marxists (not excluding Marx himself possibly) but we have been shedding these theories as we have freed ourselves from the errors of Marxism.[2]

From 1871, when we began our propaganda in Italy, we have always been, and have always called ourselves *socialist-anarchists*. In conversation, we would also call ourselves just anarchists, because it was understood that the anarchists were socialists, just as in earlier days, when we were the only socialists in Italy, we often called ourselves simply socialists, since it was generally understood that socialists were also anarchists. We have always been of the opinion that socialism and anarchy are two words which basically have the same meaning, since it is not possible to have economic emancipation (abolition of property) without political emancipation (abolition of government) and vice versa.[3]

Social democrats start off from the principle that the State, government, is none other than the political organ of the dominant class. In a capitalistic society, they say, the State necessarily serves the interests of the capitalists and ensures for them the right to exploit the workers; but that in a socialist society, when private property were to be abolished, and with the destruction of economic privilege class distinctions would disappear, then the State would represent everybody and become the impartial organ representing the social interests of all members of society.

Here a difficulty immediately arises. If it be true that Government is necessarily, and always, the instrument of those who possess the means of production, how can this miracle of a socialist government arising in the middle of a capitalist regime with the aim of abolishing capitalism, come about? Will it be as Marx and Blanqui wished by means of a dictatorship imposed by revolutionary means, by a *coup de force*, which by revolution decrees and imposes the confiscation of private property in favour of the state, as representative of the interests of the collectivity? Or will it be, as apparently all Marxists, and most modern Blanquists believe, by means of a socialist majority elected to Parliament by universal suffrage? Will one proceed in one step to the expropriation of the ruling class by the economically subjected class, or will one proceed gradually in obliging property owners and capitalists to allow themselves to be deprived of all their privileges a bit at a time?

All this seems strangely in contradiction with the theory of "historic materialism" which is a fundamental dogma for Marxists. . . .[4]

"Communism is the road that leads in the direction of anarchism." This is the theory of the Bolsheviks; the theory of Marxists and authoritarian socialists of all schools. All recognise that anarchy is a sublime ideal, that it is the goal towards which mankind is, or should, be moving, but they all want to become the government, to oblige the people to take the right road. Anarchists say instead, that anarchy is the way that leads to communism . . . or elsewhere.

To achieve communism before anarchy, that is before having conquered complete political and economic liberty, would mean (as it has meant in Russia) stabilising the most hateful tyranny, to the point where people long for the bourgeois regime, and to return later (as will happen in Russia) to a capitalistic system as a result of the impossibility of organising a social life which is bearable and as a reaction of the spirit of liberty which is not a privilege of the "latin spirit" as the *Communist* foolishly accuses me of saying, but a necessity of the human spirit for action in Russia no less than in Italy.

However much we detest the democratic lie, which in the name of the "people" oppresses the people in the interests of a class, we detest even more, if that is possible, the dictatorship which, in the name of the "proletariat" places all the strength and the very lives of the workers in the hands of the creatures of a so-called communist party, who will perpetuate their power and in the end reconstruct the capitalist system for their own advantage.[5]

When F. Engels, perhaps to counter anarchist criticisms, said that once classes disappear the State as such has no *raison d'être* and transforms itself from a government over men into an administration of things, he was merely playing with words. Whoever has power over things has power over men; whoever governs production also governs the producers; who determines consumption is master over the consumer.

This is the question; either things are administered on the basis of free agreement among the interested parties, and this is anarchy; or they are administered according to laws made by administrators and this is government, it is the State, and inevitably it turns out to be tyrannical.

It is not a question of the good intentions or the good will of this or that man, but of the inevitability of the situation, and of the tendencies which man generally develops in given circumstances.[6]

What is the true basis of the differences between anarchists and State communists? We are for freedom, for the widest and most complete freedom of thought, organisation, and action. We are for the freedom of all, and it is therefore obvious, and not necessary to continually say so, that everyone in exercising his right to freedom must respect the equal freedom of everybody else: otherwise there is oppression on one side and the right to resist and to rebel on the other.

But State communists, to an even greater extent than all other authoritarians, are incapable of conceiving freedom and of respecting for all human beings the dignity that they expect, or should expect, from others. If one speaks to them of freedom they immediately accuse one of wanting to respect, or at least tolerate, the freedom to oppress and exploit one's fellow beings. And if you say that you reject violence when it exceeds the limits imposed by the needs of defence, they accuse you of . . . pacifism, without understanding that violence is the whole essence of authoritarianism, just as the repudiation of violence is the whole essence of anarchism.[7]

Monarchy is the most suitable political form to impose respect for the privileges of a closed caste; and thus every aristocracy, whatever the circumstance by which it has come into being, tends to establish a monarchical regime, openly or disguised; just as every monarchy, tends to create and perpetuate an all-powerful aristocracy. The Parliamentary system, that is the republic (since constitutional monarchy is in fact only a half-way system in which the function of parliament is still cluttered up with monarchical and aristocratic hangovers) is the most convenient system for the bourgeoisie; and every republic tends in the direction of the constitution of a bourgeois class, just as, on the other hand, at heart, if not in appearances, the bourgeoisie is always republican.

But which is the political form most readily adaptable to the realisation of the principle of solidarity in human relations? What is the method which most surely can lead us to the complete and definite triumph of socialism?

Of course it is not possible to answer this question with absolute certainty because one is dealing with things that have not yet taken place, and logical deductions necessarily lack the evidence of experience. One must therefore be satisfied with the solution which seems to offer the greatest possibilities of success. But that element of doubt, which always remains in the human spirit when it is a question of historical prediction, and which is like a door which has been left open in the human brain to receive new truths, must make us more tolerant and more disposed to be cordially sympathetic towards those who seek the same goals but by other roads, without, however, paralyzing our action or preventing us from choosing our way and following it resolutely.

The basic characteristic of socialism is its equal application to all members of society. For this reason no one must be in a position to exploit the labour of another by capturing the means of production, and no one must be able to impose his will on others by means of brute force, or, which is the same thing, by capturing political power: economic exploitation and political domination being two continually interacting aspects of the same thing—the subjection of man by man.

To attain to, and consolidate socialism it would seem that a means is needed which cannot at the same time be a source of exploitation and domination and lead to a form of organisation which is most readily adaptable to the different and varied interests and preferences of individuals and human groups. This means it cannot be *dictatorship* (*monarchy, caesarism, etc.*) since it replaces the will and intelligence of all by that of one or a few; it tends to impose on everybody universal rules in spite of a difference in conditions; it creates the necessity for an armed force to impose obedience on recalcitrants; it gives rise to rival interests among the masses and those who are closest to power; and it ends either with successful rebellion or in the consolidation of a ruling class, which, of course, also becomes the owning class. Neither does *parliamentarism* (*democracy, republic*) appear to be a good means since it too substitutes the will of a few for that of all, and if on the one hand it allows a little more freedom than dictatorship, on the other it creates greater illusions, and in the name of a fictitious collective interest, rides roughshod over every real interest, and by means of elections and the vote, disregards the wishes of each and everyone.

There remains free organisation, from below upwards, from the simple to the complex, through free agreement and the federation of associations of production and consumption, that is *anarchy*. And this is the means we prefer.

For us, then, *socialism* and anarchy are neither antagonistic nor equivalent terms; but they are terms which are closely linked, just as the ends is linked to its necessary means, just as the substance is linked to the form it embodies.

Socialism without anarchy, that is State socialism, seems impossible to us, since it would be destroyed by the very organism destined to support it. Anarchy without socialism seems equally impossible to us, for in such a case it could not be other than the domination of the strongest, and would therefore set in motion right away the organisation and consolidation of this dominion, that is to the constitution of government.[8]

21. Anarchists and the Limits of Political Co-Existence

"Everywhere and at all times, especially since my return to Italy [1919] I have repeatedly stated that a union of intent is possible, in spite of our disagreements, to bring about real and lasting results which will really allow the workers to conquer well-being and freedom. Not only have I repeatedly declared that it is possible; I also believe it to be necessary."

"You mean to say that it is necessary for the revolution . . ."

"Certainly! If we anarchists could achieve the revolution on our own, or if the socialists could on their own, we could enjoy the luxury of each acting independently and of perhaps quarrelling. But the revolution will be made by all the proletariat, all the people, whereas the socialists and anarchists are a numerical minority, though they appear to enjoy the sympathy of the people as a whole. For us to be divided even where there are grounds for unity, would mean dividing the workers, or rather, cooling off their sympathies, as well as making them less likely to follow the socialistic line common to both socialists and anarchists and which is at the heart of the revolution. It is up to the revolutionaries, especially the anarchists and socialists, to see to this by not exaggerating the differences and paying attention above all to the realities and objectives which can unite us and assist us to draw the greatest possible revolutionary advantage from the [present] situation."[1]

Sandomirsky is for the United Front. I am too when it can be achieved in the interests of a liberating revolution.

Meantime, though having no faith left in the revolutionary capacity of the Bolsheviks, I again urge and hope that they will not descend to the level of, or even lower than, the American executioner, the Spanish torturer or the Italian jailer, and will understand that the least they can do is to put an end to the persecutions and set free anarchists and other political prisoners.[2]

Alone we cannot subdue fascism, even less destroy existing institutions. So either we must unite with those who, though not anarchists, share short term, common objectives with us, or allow that the fascists, with the connivance of the government, should be free to terrorise the country, or that the monarchy should go on ruling undisturbed.

But in "revolutionary alliances" one is always "betrayed." Possibly one is. But we prefer to run the risk of being betrayed by others, than betray ourselves to the point of extinction through inaction.

Even the betrayals will not be entirely useless, since they will show the workers who is on their side, and show the revolutionaries who among them really wants to make the revolution.[3]

In recent years we have approached the different avant-garde parties with a view to joint action, and we have always been disappointed. Must we for this reason isolate ourselves, or take refuge from "impure" contacts and stand still trying to move only when we have the necessary strength and in the name of our complete programme? I think not.

Since we cannot make the revolution by ourselves . . . we should be prepared to support those who are prepared to act, even if it carries with it the risk of later finding ourselves alone and betrayed.

But in giving others our support, that is, in always trying to use the forces at the disposal of others, and taking advantage of every opportunity for action, we must always be ourselves and seek to be in a position to make our influence felt and count at least in direct proportion to our strength.

To this end it is necessary that we should be agreed among ourselves and seek to coordinate and organise our efforts as effectively as possible.[4]

Certainly, it is very difficult to distinguish clearly in practice where useful cooperation against the common enemy ends and where a fusion begins which would lead the weakest party to renounce its specific aims. . . .

We should find ourselves on the one hand alongside the republicans in the revolutionary act and on the other in agreement with the communists in expropriating the bourgeoisie, assuming they were prepared to carry it out in a revolutionary way without first waiting to establish their state, their dictatorship. But not for these reasons would we become republicans or State communists.[5]

We can have relations of cooperation with non-anarchist parties so long as we share a need to fight a common enemy and are unable to destroy him unaided; but as soon as a party takes power and becomes the government, the only relations we can have with it are those between enemies.

Of course it is in our interest that so long as government exists it should be as unoppressive as possible, the less it is a government the better.

But freedom, even a relative freedom, is not won by helping government but by making it feel the danger of squeezing the people too far.[6]

We have always sought to achieve the alliance of all who want to make a revolution in order to destroy the material power of the common enemy, but we have always made it crystal clear that such an affiance should last only for the duration of the insurrectionary act itself, and that immediately after and, if possible or necessary, during the insurrection itself, we would seek to realise our ideas by resisting the formation of a new government or of any centralised authority, and by seeking to urge the masses to take immediate possession of all the means of production and the social wealth, and themselves organise the day to day affairs of the community on the basis of its state of development and the wishes of the people in the different regions.[7]

For my part, I do not believe there is "one solution" to the social problems, but a thousand different and changing solutions in the same way as social existence is different and varied in time and space.

After all, every institution, project or utopia would be equally good to solve the problem of human contentedness, if everybody had the same needs, the same opinions or lived under the same conditions. But since such unanimity of thought and identical conditions are impossible (as well as, in my opinion, undesirable) we must in our daily conduct as well as in our projects for the future, always bear in mind that we are not, and will not in the foreseeable future, be living in a world populated only by anarchists. For a long time to come we shall be a relatively small minority. To isolate ourselves is virtually impossible, but even if we could it would be at the expense of the social task we have undertaken, as well as of our own personal well-being. One must therefore find ways of living among non-anarchists, as anarchistically as possible, and which will further our propaganda and offer possibilities of applying our ideas.[8]

V

22. The Anarchist Revolution

The Revolution is the creation of new living institutions, new groupings, new social relationships; it is the destruction of privileges and monopolies; it is the new spirit of justice, of brotherhood, of freedom which must renew the whole of social life, raise the moral level and the material conditions of the masses by calling on them to provide, through their direct and conscious action, for their own futures. Revolution is the organisation of all public services by those who work in them in their own interest as well as the public's; Revolution is the destruction of all coercive ties; it is the autonomy of groups, of communes, of regions; Revolution is the free federation brought about by a desire for brotherhood, by individual and collective interests, by the needs of production and defence; Revolution is the constitution of innumerable free groupings based on ideas, wishes, and tastes of all kinds that exist among the people; Revolution is the forming and disbanding of thousands of representative, district, communal, regional, national bodies which, without having any legislative power, serve to make known and to coordinate the desires and interests of people near and far and which act through information, advice and example. Revolution is freedom proved in the crucible of facts—and lasts so long as freedom lasts, that is until others, taking advantage of the weariness that overtakes the masses, of the inevitable disappointments that follow exaggerated hopes, of the probable errors and human faults, succeed in constituting a power, which supported by an army of conscripts or mercenaries, lays down the law, arrests the movement at the point it has reached, and then begins the reaction.[1]

The great majority of anarchists, if I am not mistaken, hold the view that human perfectibility and anarchy would not be achieved even in a few thousand years, if first one did not create by the revolution, made by a conscious minority, the necessary environment for freedom and well-being. For this reason we want to make the revolution as soon as possible, and to do so we need to take advantage of all positive forces and every favourable situation that arises.[2]

The task of the conscious minority is to profit from every situation to change the environment in a way that will make possible the education and spiritual elevation of the people, without which there is no real way out.

And since the environment today, which obliges the masses to live in misery, is maintained by violence, we advocate and prepare for violence. That is why we are revolutionaries, and not because "we are desperate men, thirsting for revenge and filled with hate."[3]

We are revolutionaries because we believe that only the revolution, the violent revolution, can solve the social question. . . . We believe furthermore that the revolution is an act of will—the will of individuals and of the masses; that it needs for its success certain objective conditions, but that it does not happen of necessity, inevitably, through the single action of economic and political forces.[4]

I told the jury [at my trial] in Milan that I am a revolutionary not only in the philosophical meaning of the word but also in the popular and insurrectionalist sense; and I said so in order to clearly distinguish between my views and those of others who call themselves revolutionaries, but who interpret the world even astronomically so as not to have to bring in the fact of violence, the insurrection, which must open the way to revolutionary achievements. I declared that I had not sought to provoke revolution because at the time there was no need to provoke it; what was urgently needed instead was to bend all our efforts for the generally desired revolution to succeed and not lead to new tyrannies; but I insisted that I would have provoked it if the situation demanded then, just as I would in a similar situation in the future.[5]

I had said "we want to make the revolution as soon as possible"; Colomer replies that it would be wiser to say "We want to make anarchy as soon as possible." A poor polemical expedient! Since we are convinced that anarchy cannot be achieved until after the revolution which will sweep away the first material obstacles, it is clear that our efforts must in the first instance be directed to making the revolution and in such a way that it is in the direction of anarchy.... I have repeated thousands of times that we would have to provoke the revolution with all the means at our disposal and act in it as anarchists, that is to say, opposing the constitution of any authoritarian regime and putting into operation as much as we can of our programme. And I would wish that, to take advantage of the increased freedom that we would have won, anarchists were morally and technically prepared to realise within the limits of their numbers, those forms of social life and cooperation which they consider best and most suitable for paving the way for the future.[6]

We do not want to "wait for the masses to become anarchist before making the revolution," the more so since we are convinced that they will never become anarchist if the institutions which keep them enslaved are not first violently destroyed. And since we need the support of the masses to build up a force of sufficient strength and to achieve our specific task of radical change of the social organism by the direct action of the masses, we must get closer to them, accept them as they are, and from within their ranks seek to "push" them forward as much as possible. That is, of course, if we really intend to work for the practical achievement of our ideals, and are not content with preaching in the desert for the simple satisfaction of our intellectual pride.

We are accused of a "reconstructive mania"; we are told that to speak of the "morrow of the revolution" as we do, is a meaningless phrase because the revolution is a profound change in the whole of social life, which has already started and will go on for centuries to come.

All this is simply a misuse of words. If one takes revolution in that sense, it is synonymous with progress, with a historic view of life, which through a thousand and one vicissitudes will end, if our wishes come true, in the total triumph of anarchy throughout the world. In that sense all kinds of people are revolutionary. When you introduce the centuries into the argument, everyone will agree with everything you say.

But when we speak of revolution, when the masses speak of it, as when one refers to it in history, one simply means the *insurrection triumphant*. Insurrections will be necessary as long as there are power groups which use their material force to exact obedience from the masses. And it is only too clear that there will be many more insurrections before the people win that minimum of indispensable conditions for free and peaceful development, when humanity will be able to advance towards its noblest objectives without cruel struggles and useless suffering.[7]

By revolution we do not mean just the insurrectionary act, which is nevertheless indispensable (except in the most unlikely event that the existing regime collapses without the need for a push from outside), but would be sterile if it served to replace one state of coercion by another.[8]

One must clearly distinguish between the revolutionary act which destroys as much as it can of the old regime and puts in its place new institutions, and government which comes afterwards to halt the revolution and suppress as many of the revolutionary conquests as it can.

History teaches us that all advances that are the result of revolutions were secured in the period of popular enthusiasm, when either a recognised government did not exist or was too weak to make a stand against the revolution. But once the government was formed, so reaction started which served the interest of the old and the new privileged classes and took back from the masses all that it could.

Our task then is to make, and to help others make, the revolution by taking advantage of every opportunity and all available forces: advancing the revolution as much as possible in its constructive as well as destructive role, and always remaining opposed to the formation of any government, either ignoring it or combating it to the limits of our capacities.

We will no more recognise a republican Constituent than we now recognise the parliamentary monarchy. We cannot stop it if the people want it; we might even occasionally be with them in fighting attempts to bring about a restoration [of the monarchy]; but we will want and will demand complete freedom for those who think as we do and who wish to live outside the tutelage and oppression of the State, to propagate their ideas by word and deed. Revolutionaries, yes; but above all anarchists.[9]

1. Destruction of all political power is the first duty of the proletariat.
2. Any organisation of an allegedly provisional revolutionary political power to achieve this destruction cannot be other than one trick more, and would be as dangerous to the proletariat as are all present governments.
3. In refusing every compromise for the achievement of the social revolution, workers of the world must establish solidarity in revolutionary action outside the framework of bourgeois politics.

These [anarchist] principles [as formulated in 1872 at the Congress of St. Imier under the inspiration of Bakunin] continue to point to the right road for us. Those who have tried to act in contradiction to them have disappeared, because however defined, State, dictatorship, and parliament can only lead the masses back to slavery. All experience so far bears this out. Needless to say, for the delegates of St. Imier as for us and all anarchists, the abolition of political power is not possible without the simultaneous destruction of economic privilege.[10]

The conviction, which I share, of those who see the need for a revolution to eliminate the material forces which exist to defend privilege and to prevent every real social progress, has led many of them to believe that the only important thing is the insurrection, and to overlook what has to be done to prevent an insurrection from remaining a sterile act of violence against which an act of reactionary violence would be the eventual reply. For these comrades all practical questions, of organisation, of how to make provisions for the distribution of food, are today idle questions: for them these are matters which will solve themselves, or will be solved by those who come after us. . . . Yet the conclusion we come to is: Social reorganisation is something we must all think about right now, and as the old is destroyed we shall have a more human and just society as well as one more receptive to future advances. The alternative is that "the leaders" will think about these problems, and we shall have a new government, which will do exactly as all previous governments have done, in making the people pay for the scant and poor services they render, by taking away their freedom and allowing them to be oppressed by every kind of parasite and exploiter.[11]

I say that in order to abolish the "gendarme" and all the harmful social institutions we must know what to put in their place, not in a more or less distant future but immediately, the very day we start demolishing. One only destroys, effectively and permanently, that which one replaces by something else; and to put off to a later date the solution of problems which present themselves with the urgency of necessity, would be to give time to the institutions one is intending to abolish to recover from the shock and reassert themselves, perhaps under other names, but certainly with the same structure.

Our solutions may be accepted by a sufficiently large section of the population and we shall have achieved anarchy, or taken a step towards anarchy; or they may not be understood or accepted and then our efforts will serve as propaganda and place before the public at large the programme for a not distant future. But in any case we must have our solutions: provisional, subject to correction and revision in the light of experience, but we must have our solutions if we do not wish to submit passively to those of others, and limit ourselves to the unprofitable role of useless and impotent grumblers.[12]

I believe that we anarchists, convinced of the validity of our programme, must make special efforts to acquire a predominating influence in order to be able to swing the movement towards the realisation of our ideals; but we must acquire this influence by being more active and more effective than the others. Only in this way will it be worth acquiring. Today, we must examine thoroughly, develop and propagate our ideas and coordinate our efforts for common action. We must act inside the workers' movement to prevent it from limiting itself to, and being corrupted by, the exclusive demand for the small improvements possible under the capitalist system, and seek to make it serve for the preparation of the complete social transformation. We must work among the mass of unorganised, and possibly unorganisable, workers, to awaken in them the spirit of revolt and the desire and hope for a free and happy existence. We must initiate and support every possible kind of movement which tends to weaken the power of the State and of the capitalists and to raise the moral level and material conditions of the workers. We must, in a word, get ready and prepare, morally and materially, for the revolutionary act which has to open the way to the future.

And tomorrow, in the revolution, we must play an active part (if possible before, and more effectively, than the others) in the necessary physical struggle, seeking to make it as radical as possible, in order to destroy all the repressive forces of the State and to induce the workers to take possession of the means of production (land, mines, factories, transport, etc.) and of all existing goods, and themselves organise, immediately, a just distribution of food products. At the same time we must arrange for the exchange of goods between communes and regions and continue and intensify production and all those services which are of use to the public.

We must, in every way possible, and in accord with local conditions and possibilities, encourage action by workers' associations, cooperatives, groups of volunteers—in order to prevent the emergence of new authoritarian groups, new governments, combating them with violence if necessary, but above all, by rendering them useless.

And if there were not sufficient support among the people to prevent the reconstitution of the State, its authoritarian institutions and its organs of repression, we should refuse to cooperate or recognise it, and rebel against its demands, claiming full autonomy for ourselves and for all dissident minorities. In short we should remain in a state of open rebellion if possible, and prepare the way to convert present defeat into a future success. . . .

I do not think that what matters is the triumph of our plans, our projects and our utopias, which in any case will need the confirmation of experiment, and may as a result have to be modified, developed or adapted to the true moral and material conditions in time and place. What matters most of all is that the people, all people, should lose their sheeplike instincts and habits with which their minds have been inculcated by an age-long slavery, and that they should learn to think and act freely. It is to this great task of spiritual liberation that anarchists must especially devote their attention.[13]

Once the government has been overthrown, or at least neutralised, it will be the task of the people, and especially of those among them who have initiative and organising ability, to provide for the satisfaction of immediate needs and to prepare for the future by destroying privileges and harmful institutions and in the meantime seeing to it that those useful institutions which today serve the ruling class either exclusively or principally, shall operate in favour of all.

Anarchists will have the special mission of being the vigilant custodians of freedom, against all aspirants to power and against the possible tyranny of the majority.[14]

We are agreed in thinking that apart from the problem of assuring victory against the material forces of the adversary there is also the problem of giving life to the revolution after victory.

We are in agreement that a revolution which were to result in chaos would not be a vital revolution.

But one must not exaggerate; it should not be thought that we must, and can, find, here and now, a perfect solution for every possible problem. One should not want to foresee and determine too much, because instead of preparing for anarchy we might find ourselves indulging in unattainable dreams or even becoming authoritarians, and consciously or otherwise, proposing to act like a government which in the name of freedom and the popular will subject people to its domination. . . . The fact is that one cannot educate the masses if they are not in a position, or obliged by necessity, to act for themselves, and that the revolutionary organisation of the workers, useful and necessary as it is, cannot be stretched indefinitely: at a certain point if it does not erupt in revolutionary action, either the government strangles it or the organisation itself degenerates and breaks up—and one has to start all over again from the beginning.[15]

I would be unable to accept the view that all past revolutions though they were not anarchist revolutions were useless, nor that future ones which will still not be anarchist will be useless. Indeed, I incline to the view that the complete triumph of anarchy will come by evolution, gradually, rather than by violent revolution: when an earlier or several earlier revolutions will have destroyed the major military and economic obstacles which are opposed to the spiritual development of the people, to increasing production to the level of needs and desires, and to the harmonising of contrasting interests.

In any case, if we take into account our sparse numbers and the prevalent attitudes among the masses, and if we do not wish to confuse our wishes with the reality, we must expect that the next revolution will not be an anarchist one, and therefore what is more pressing, is to think of what we can and must do in a revolution in which we will be a relatively small and badly armed minority. . . . But we must, however, beware of ourselves becoming less anarchist because the masses are not ready for anarchy. If they want a government, it is unlikely that we will be able to prevent a new government being formed, but this is no reason for our not trying to persuade the people that government is useless and harmful or of preventing the government from also imposing on us and others like us who don't want it. We will have to exert ourselves to ensure that social life and especially economic standards improve without the intervention of government, and thus we must be as ready as possible to deal with the practical problems of production and distribution, remembering, incidentally, that those most suited to organise work are those who now do it, each in his own trade. . . . If we are unable to prevent the constitution of a new government, if we are unable to destroy it immediately, we should in either case refuse to support it in any shape or form. We should reject military conscription and refuse to pay taxes. Disobedience on principle, resistance to the bitter end against every imposition by the authorities, and an absolute refusal to accept any position of command.

If we are unable to overthrow capitalism, we shall have to demand for ourselves and for all who want it, the right of free access to the necessary means of production to maintain an independent existence.

Advise when we have suggestions to offer; teach if we know more than others; set the example for a life based on free agreement between individuals; defend even with force if necessary and possible, our autonomy against any government provocation . . . but command—never.

In this way we shall not achieve anarchy, which cannot be imposed against the wishes of the people, but at least we shall be preparing the way for it.[16]

23. The Insurrection

But how will this revolution be achieved?

Naturally one must begin with the insurrectionary act which sweeps away the material obstacles, the armed forces of the government which are opposed to any social transformation.

For the insurrection it is desirable, and it may well be indispensable, that all the anti-monarchical forces, since we are living under a monarchist regime, should be united. It is necessary to be as prepared as possible, morally and materially; and it is above all necessary to profit by all agitations and to seek to extend them and transform them into resolutive movements, to avoid the danger that while the organisations are getting ready the popular forces exhaust themselves in isolated actions.[1]

The masses will make the insurrection, but cannot prepare it technically. Men, groups, and parties are needed who are joined by free agreement, under oath of secrecy, and provided with the necessary means to create the network of speedy communications to keep those concerned informed of all incidents likely to provoke a widespread popular movement.

And when we say that the specific task of organisation must be carried outside the official parties it is because the latter have other tasks which exclude the secrecy needed for the preparation of illegal activities; but it is above all because we have no faith in the revolutionary fervour of the progressive parties as constituted today.[2]

Every new idea and institution, all progress and every revolution have always been the work of minorities. It is our aspiration and our aim that everybody should become socially conscious and effective; but to achieve this end, it is necessary to provide all with the means of life and for development, and it is therefore necessary to destroy with violence, since one cannot do otherwise, the violence which denies these means to the workers.

Naturally, the "small numbers," the minority, must be sufficient, and those who imagine that we want to have an insurrection a day without taking into account the forces opposing us, or whether circumstances are in our favour or against us, misjudge us. In the, now remote, past, we were able, and did, carry out a number of minute insurrectionary acts which had no probability of success. But in those days we were indeed only a handful, and wanted the public to talk about us, and our attempts were simply means of propaganda.

Now it is no longer a question of uprisings to make propaganda; now we can win, and so we want to win, and only take such action when we think we can win. Of course we can be mistaken, and on the grounds of temperament may be led into believing that the fruit is ripe when it is still green; but we must confess our preference for those who err on the side of haste as opposed to those who always play a waiting game and let the best opportunities slip through their fingers for they, through fear of picking a green fruit then let the whole crop go rotten![3]

We must seek to play an active, and if possible a preponderant role in the insurrectionary act. But with the defeat of the forces of repression which serve to keep the people in slavery; with the demobilisation of the army, the dissolution of the police and the magistrature, etc.; having armed the people so that it can resist any armed attempt by reaction to reestablish itself; having called on willing hands to undertake the organisation of public services and to provide, with concepts of just distribution, for the most urgent needs, using with care existing stocks in the various localities—having done all this, we shall have to see to it that there must be no wasted effort and that those institutions, those traditions and habits, those methods of production, exchange and aid should be respected and utilised, if they perform, even insufficiently or badly, necessary services, seeking by all means to destroy every trace of privilege, but being chary of destroying anything that cannot be replaced by something which serves the general good more effectively. We must push the workers to take possession of the factories, to federate among themselves and work for the community, and similarly the peasants should take over the land and the produce usurped by the landlords, and come to an agreement with the industrial workers on the necessary exchange of goods.[4]

We will see to it that all empty and under-occupied houses are used so that no one will be without a roof over his head. We will hasten to abolish banks and destroy title deeds and all that represents and guarantees the power of the State and capitalist privilege. And we will try to reorganise things in such a way that it will be impossible for bourgeois society to be reconstituted. And all this, and whatever else would be required to satisfy public needs and the development of the revolution would be the task of volunteers, by all kinds of committees, local, intercommunal, regional, and national congresses which would attend to the coordination of social activity; would take necessary decisions, advising and carrying out what they considered useful, but without having any right, or the means, to impose their wishes by force, and relying for approval only on the services they rendered and on the demands of the situation as recognised by all concerned. Above all no *gendarmes*, by whatever name they might be called. The creation of voluntary militia, without powers to interfere as militia in the life of the community, but only to deal with any armed attacks by the forces of reaction to reestablish themselves, or to resist outside intervention by countries as yet not in a state of revolution.[5]

A successful insurrection is the most potent factor in the emancipation of the people, for once the yoke has been shaken off, the people are free to provide themselves with those institutions which they think best, and the time lag between passing the law and the degree of civilisation which the mass of the population has attained, is breached in one leap. The insurrection determines the revolution, that is, the speedy emergence of the latent forces built up during the "evolutionary" period.

Everything depends on what the people are capable of wanting. In past insurrections the people unaware of the real reasons for their misery, have always wanted very little, and have achieved very little. What will they want from the next insurrection?

The answer in part, depends on our propaganda and what efforts we put into it.[6]

24. Expropriation

To destroy radically this oppression without any danger of it reemerging, all people must be convinced of their right to the means of production, and be prepared to exercise this basic right by expropriating the landowners, the industrialists and financiers, and putting all social wealth at the disposal of the people.[1]

[In Teramo] at a meeting of peasants the local secretary of the Trade Unions, the president of the socialist cooperative and two socialist MPs told the peasants: "Keep yourselves ready; when your leaders will tell you to strike, abandon the fields, and if on the other hand they tell you to gather in only your share, obey them and leave the other half unharvested."

This is the advice of good reformists. For in fact when the crop is lost one can more easily tell the people that the revolution cannot be made because one would die of hunger.

When will these bad shepherds make up their minds to tell the peasants: "harvest everything and give nothing to the bosses? And after the harvest get the land ready and sow for the coming year with the firm conviction that the bosses must never get anything again."[2]

If one really wants to change the system in fact and not just superficially, it will be necessary to destroy capitalism de facto, expropriating those who now control all social wealth, and immediately set about organising, on a local basis, and without passing through legal channels, a new social life. Which means to say that in order to create the "social republic" one must first bring about . . . Anarchy![3]

One of the basic tenets of anarchism is the abolition of monopoly, whether of the land, raw materials, or the means of production, and consequently the abolition of exploitation of the labour of others by those who possess the means of production. The appropriation of the labour of others, of all that permits a man to live without contributing his share to society, is from the anarchist and socialist point of view, theft.

Landowners, capitalists have robbed the people, with violence and dishonesty, of the land and all the means of production, and in consequence of this initial theft can each day take away from the workers the product of their labour. But they have been lucky thieves, they have become strong, have made laws to legitimate their situation, and have organised a whole system of repression to defend themselves both from the demands of the workers as well as from those who would want to replace them by the same means. And now the theft of the former is called property, commerce, industry, etc.; whereas the term robbers in common parlance, is reserved for those who would wish to follow the example of capitalists but who, having arrived too late, and in unfavourable circumstances, cannot do so without rebelling against the law.

But a difference in the names by which they are usually referred to, cannot cancel out the moral and social identity of the two situations. The capitalist is a thief who has succeeded through his efforts or those of his ancestors; the common thief is a would-be capitalist, who is simply waiting to become one in fact, to live, without working, on the proceeds of his hauls, that is on the work of others.

As enemies of the capitalists, we cannot have sympathy for the thief who aspires to become a capitalist. As partisans of expropriation by the people for the benefit of everybody, we cannot, as anarchists, have anything in common with actions, the purpose of which, is simply to transfer wealth from the hands of one boss into the hands of another.

Of course I am speaking of the professional thief, the person who does not want to work and seeks the means to live parasitically on the work of others.

It is quite another matter when a man denied the means of working robs in order that he or his family shall not die of hunger. In such a case, theft (if it can thus be called) is a revolt against social injustice, and can become the most sacred right and also the most urgent of duties. . . .

It is true that the professional thief is also a victim of the social environment. The example set by his superiors, his educational background, and the disgusting conditions in which many people are obliged to work, easily explain why some men, who are not morally better than their contemporaries, finding themselves with the choice of being exploiters or exploited choose to be the former and seek to become exploiters with the means they are capable of. But these extenuating circumstances could equally be applied to the capitalists, but in so doing one only demonstrates more clearly the basic identity between the two professions.

Since anarchist ideas cannot be used to push people into becoming capitalists, neither can they be used to make people into thieves. On the contrary, by giving discontented people ideas about a better life and the hope of general emancipation, anarchist ideas if anything advocate withdrawal from all legal or illegal actions which encourage adaptation to the capitalist system and tend to perpetuate it.

In spite of all this, the social environment is so powerful and personal temperaments so diverse, that there is no reason why some anarchists should not become thieves, just as there are some who become business men or industrialists; but in that case both the former and the latter act not because of any anarchist ideas but in spite of them.

25. Defence of the Revolution

The revolution we want consists in depriving the present holders of their power and wealth and in putting the land and the means of production and all existing wealth at the disposal of the workers, that is of everybody, since those who are not, will have to become, workers. And the revolutionaries must defend this revolution by seeing to it that no individual, party or class finds the means to constitute a government and restore privilege in favour of new or old bosses. . . .

To defend, to save the revolution there is only one means: that of pushing the revolution as far as it will go. So long as there are those who will be in a position to oblige others to work for them; so long as there are those who are in a position to violate the freedom of others, the revolution will not be complete, and we will be still in a state of legitimate defence and to the violence which oppresses we will oppose the violence that liberates.

Do you fear that the dispossessed bourgeoisie may hire soldiers of fortune to restore the old regime? Dispossess them completely and you will see that without money you can employ no one.

Do you fear a military coup? Arm all the population, ensure that they really are in possession of all wealth so that every person will have to defend his own freedom and the means which can ensure his well-being, and you will see whether the generals seeking adventures will find who to follow them. But if after that, the people in arms, in possession of the land, the factories, and all the natural wealth were incapable of defending themselves, and allowed themselves once again to be brought under the yoke, it would mean that they were still not capable of enjoying freedom. The revolution would have failed and the work of education and preparation would have to be resumed for another attempt which would have greater chances of success because it would benefit from the seeds that had been sown at the previous attempt.[1]

The dangers with which a revolution is faced do not come solely or principally from the reactionaries conspiring for a restoration and calling for foreign intervention; they also come from the possibility of degeneration of the revolution itself; and from the *arrivistes* who, though revolutionaries, nevertheless retain a mentality and sympathies which are bourgeois and seek to direct the revolution towards ends which are anything but equalitarian and libertarian.[2]

Once the situation is reached whereby no one could impose his wishes on others by force, nor take away from any man the product of his labour, anarchists could then only act through propaganda and by example.

Destroy the institutions and the machinery of existing social organisations? Yes, certainly, if it is a question of repressive institutions; but these are, after all, only a small part of the complex of social life. The police, the army, the prisons, and the judiciary are potent institutions for evil, which exercise a parasitic function. Other institutions and organisations manage, for better or for worse, to guarantee life to mankind; and these institutions cannot be usefully destroyed without replacing them by something better.

The exchange of raw materials and goods, the distribution of foodstuffs, the railways, postal services, and all public services administered by the State or by private companies, have been organised to serve monopolistic and capitalist interests, but they also serve real needs of the population. We cannot disrupt them (and in any case the people would not in their own interests allow us to) without reorganising them in a better way. And this cannot be achieved in a day; nor as things stand, have we the necessary abilities to do so. We are delighted therefore if in the meantime, others act, even with different criteria from our own.

Social life does not admit of interruptions, and the people want to live on the day of the revolution, on the morrow, and always.[3]

There are still many people who are fascinated by the idea of "terror." For them it seems that the guillotine, firing squads, massacres, deportations, and jails are powerful and indispensable arms of the revolution, and observe that if so many revolutions have been defeated and have not produced the results hoped for, it is the fault of the goodness, and "weakness" of the revolutionaries, who have not persecuted, repressed and killed on a large enough scale.

It is a prejudice current in some revolutionary circles which had its origins in the rhetoric and historic falsification of the apologists of the Great French Revolution and has been revived in recent years by the Bolsheviks in their propaganda. But the truth is just the opposite; Terror has always been the instrument of tyranny. In France it served the grim tyranny of Robespierre and paved the way for Napoleon and the subsequent reaction. In Russia it persecuted and killed anarchists and socialists, and massacred rebellious workers and peasants, and has halted the development of a revolution which really might have ushered in a new era for mankind. Those who believe in the liberating and revolutionary efficacy of repression and savagery have the same kind of backward mentality as the jurists who believe that crimes can be prevented and the world morally improved by the imposition of stiff punishments.

The Terror, like war, awakens atavistic and bellicose sentiments, still barely covered by a cloak of civilisation, and raises to the highest posts the worse elements of the population. And far from serving to defend the revolution it discredits it, makes it repellent to the masses and after a period of fierce struggles, gives rise, of necessity, to what they would today call "a return to normality," that is, to the legalisation and perpetuation of tyranny. Whichever side wins, one always arrives at the creation of a strong government, which assures peace to some at the price of freedom, and to others domination without too many risks....

Certainly the revolution must be defended and developed with an inexorable logic; but one must not and cannot defend it with means which contradict its ends.

The most powerful means for defending the revolution remains always that of taking away from the bourgeoisie the economic means on which their power is based, and of arming everybody (until such time as one will have managed to persuade everybody to throw away their arms as useless and dangerous toys), and of interesting the mass of the population in the victory of the revolution.

If in order to win it were necessary to erect the gallows in the public square, then I would prefer to lose.[4]

And after the revolution, that is, after the defeat of the existing powers and the overwhelming victory of the forces of insurrection, what then?

It is then that gradualism really comes into operation. We shall have to study all the practical problems of life: production, exchange, the means of communication, relations between anarchist groupings and those living under some kind of authority, between communist collectives and those living in an individualistic way; relations between town and country, the utilisation for the benefit of everybody of all natural sources of power and of raw materials; distribution of industries and, cultivation according to the natural resources of the different regions; public education, care of children and the aged, health services, protection against common criminals and the more dangerous ones who might again try to suppress the freedom of others for the benefit of individuals or parties—and so on. And in every problem [anarchists] should prefer the solutions which not only are economically superior but which satisfy the need for justice and freedom and leave the way open for future improvements, which other solutions might not.

In the event justice, liberty and solidarity should override economic advantages. One must not think of destroying everything in the belief that later things will look after themselves. Present civilisation is the result of development extending over thousands of years, and has solved, in a way, the problem of large concentrations of population, often crowded into small territories, and of satisfying their ever-increasing and complex needs. Its benefits have decreased—because development has been taking place under the pressure of authority in the interests of the ruling classes; but even if one takes away authority and privilege, the advantages acquired, the triumphs of man over the adverse forces of nature, the accumulated experience of past generations, sociability learned through cohabitation throughout the ages and by the proven benefits of mutual aid—all these advantages will remain, and it would be foolish, and in any case impossible, to give up all these things.

We must therefore fight authority and privilege, but take advantage of all the benefits of civilisation; and nothing must be destroyed which satisfies, even badly, a human need until we have something better to put in its place. We must be intransigent in our opposition to all capitalist imposition and exploitation, and tolerant of all social concepts which prevail in different human groupings, so long as they do not threaten the equal rights and freedom of others; and content ourselves with advancing gradually in step with the moral development of the people and as the available material and intellectual means increase—doing all we can, of course, by study, work, and propaganda to hasten the development towards ever more advanced ideals.[5]

But after the successful insurrection, when the government has fallen, what must be done?

We anarchists would wish that in every district the workers, or, more accurately, those among them who are more socially conscious and have a spirit of initiative, should take possession of all the means of production, of all the wealth—land, raw materials, houses, machines, food stocks, etc., and to the best of their ability, initiate new forms of social life. We would wish that the land workers who today work for masters should no longer recognise the landowners' property rights but continue and intensify production on their own account, establishing direct contacts with workers in industry and transport for the exchange of goods and services; that industrial workers, including engineers and technicians, should take possession of the factories and continue and intensify production for their own benefit and that of the whole community; immediately switching production in those factories which today turn out useless or harmful goods to supplying the articles most urgently required to satisfy the needs of the public; that the railwaymen should continue to operate the railways but in the service of the community; that committees composed of volunteers or elected by the people should take over, under the direct control of the population, all available accommodation to house, as well as is possible in the circumstances, those most in need; that other committees, always under the direct control of the people, should deal with provisioning and the distribution of consumer goods; that all the members of the bourgeoisie should of necessity have to "muck in" with those who were the proletarian masses and work like everybody else in order to enjoy the same benefits as everybody else. And all this must be done immediately, on the very day, or the morrow of the successful insurrection, without waiting for orders from central committees or from any other kind of authority.

This is what the anarchists want, and it is in fact what would naturally happen if the revolution were to be a truly social revolution and not just a political change, which after a few convulsions would lead things back to what they were formerly. For, if one did not deprive the bourgeoisie of its economic power at once, it would in a short time recapture the political power which the insurrection had torn from its grasp. And in order to take away economic power from the bourgeoisie, it is necessary to organise immediately a new economic structure based on justice and equality. Economic needs, at least the most essential ones, cannot be interrupted; they must be satisfied immediately. "Central Committees" either do nothing or act when their services are no longer required.[6]

VI
26. Anarchist Propaganda

It must be admitted that we anarchists, in outlining what we would like the future society to be—a society without bosses and without gendarmes—have, in general, made everything look a bit too easy.

While on the one hand we reproach our adversaries for being unable to think beyond present conditions and of finding communism and anarchy unattainable, because they imagine that man must remain as he is today, with all his meanness, his vices and his fears, even when their causes have been eliminated, on the other hand we skate over the difficulties and the doubts, assuming that the morally positive effects which will result from the abolition of economic privilege and the triumph of liberty have already been achieved.

So, when we are told that some people won't want to work, we immediately have a string of excellent reasons to show that work, that is the exercise of our faculties and the pleasure to produce, is at the root of man's well-being, and that it is therefore ridiculous to think that healthy people would wish to withdraw from the need to produce for the community when work would not be oppressive, exploited, and despised, as it is today.

And if they bring up the inclinations to, or the anti-social, criminal ways of, a section, however small, of the population, we reply that, except in rare and questionable cases of congenital sickness which it is the task of alienists to deal with, crimes are of social origin and would change with a change of institutions.

Perhaps this exaggerated optimism, this simplification of the problems had its *raison d'être* when anarchism was a beautiful dream, a hurried anticipation, and what was needed was to push forward to the highest ideal and inspire enthusiasm by stressing the contrast between the present hell and the desired paradise of tomorrow.

But times have changed. Statal and capitalist society is in a state of crisis, of dissolution, or reconstruction depending on whether revolutionaries are able, and know how, to influence with their concepts and their strength, and perhaps we are on the eve of the first attempts at realisation.

It is necessary therefore to leave a little on one side the idyllic descriptions and visions of future and distant perfection and face things as they are today and as they will be in what one can assume to be the foreseeable future.[1]

When anarchist ideas were a novelty which amazed and shocked, and it was only possible to make propaganda for a distant future (and even the attempts at insurrection, and the prosecutions we freely invited and accepted, only served the purpose of drawing the public's attention to our propaganda), it could be enough to criticise existing society and present an exposition of the ideal to which we aspire. Even the questions of tactics were, in fact, simply questions of deciding which were the best ways of propagating one's ideas and preparing individuals and masses for the desired social transformation.

But today the situation is more mature, circumstances have changed . . . and we must be able to show not only that we have more reason on our side than have the parties because of the nobility of our ideal of freedom, but also that our ideas and methods are the most practical for the achievement of the greatest measure of freedom and well-being that is possible in the present state of our civilisation.[2]

Our task is that of "pushing" the people to demand and to seize all the freedom they can and to make themselves responsible for providing their own needs without waiting for orders from any kind of authority. Our task is that of demonstrating the uselessness and harmfulness of government, provoking and encouraging by propaganda and action, all kinds of individual and collective initiatives.

It is in fact a question of education for freedom, of making people who are accustomed to obedience and passivity consciously aware of their real power and capabilities. One must encourage people to do things for themselves, or to think they are doing so by their own initiative and inspiration even when in fact their actions have been suggested by others, just as the good school teacher when he sets a problem his pupil cannot solve immediately, helps him in such a way that the pupil imagines that he has found the solution unaided, thus acquiring courage and confidence in his own abilities.

This is what we should do in our propaganda. If our critic has ever made propaganda among those who we, with too much disdain, call politically "unconscious," it will have occurred to him to find himself making an effort not to appear to be expounding and forcing on them a well-known and universally accepted truth; he will have tried to stimulate their thought and get them to arrive with their own reason at conclusions which he could have served up ready-made, much more easily so far as he was concerned, but with less profit for the "beginner" in politics. And if he ever found himself in a position of having to act as leader or teacher in some action or in propaganda, when the others were passive he would have tried to avoid making the situation obvious so as to stimulate them to think, to take the initiative, and gain confidence in themselves.[3]

The daily paper [*Umanità Nova*] is but one of our means of action. If instead of awakening new forces, and encouraging more ambitions and enthusiastic activity, it were to absorb all our forces and stifle all other initiatives, it would be a misfortune rather than an affirmation of vigour, and witness to our strength, vitality, and boldness.

Furthermore there are activities which cannot by definition, be carried out by the paper or by the press. Since the paper has to address itself to the public it must of necessity speak in the presence of the enemy, and there are situations in which the enemy must not be informed. The comrades must make other arrangements for these situations . . . elsewhere![4]

Must organisation be secret or public?

In general terms the answer is obviously that one must carry out in public what it is convenient that everybody should know and in secret what it is agreed should be withheld from the public at large.

It is obvious that for us who carry on our propaganda to raise the moral level of the masses and induce them to win their emancipation by their own efforts and who have no personal or sectarian ambitions to dominate, it is an advantage where possible to give our activities a maximum of publicity to thereby reach and influence with our propaganda as many people as we can.

But this does not depend only on our wishes; it is clear that if, for example, a government were to prohibit us from speaking, publishing, or meeting and we had not the strength to openly defy the ban, we should seek to do all these things clandestinely.

One must, however, always aim to act in the full light of day, and struggle to win our freedoms, bearing in mind that the best way to obtain a freedom is that of taking it, facing necessary risks; whereas very often a freedom is lost, through one's own fault, either through not exercising it or using it timidly, giving the impression that one has not the right to be doing what one is doing.

Therefore, as a general rule we prefer always to act publicly . . . also because the revolutionaries of today have qualities, some good and others bad, which reduce their conspiratorial capacities in which the revolutionaries of fifty or a hundred years ago excelled. But certainly there can be circumstances and actions which demand secrecy, and in which case one must act accordingly.

In any case, let us be wary of those "secret" affairs which everybody knows about, and first among them, the police.[5]

Isolated, sporadic propaganda which is often a way of easing a troubled conscience or is simply an outlet for someone who has a passion for argument, serves little or no purpose. In the conditions of unawareness and misery in which the masses live, and with so many forces against us, such propaganda is forgotten and lost before its effect can grow and bear fruit. The soil is too ungrateful for seeds sown haphazardly to germinate and make roots.

What is needed is continuity of effort, patience, coordination, and adaptability to different surroundings and circumstances.

Each one of us must be able to count on the cooperation of everybody else; and that wherever a seed is sown it will not lack the loving care of the cultivator, who tends it and protects it until it has become a plant capable of looking after itself, and in its turn, of sowing new, fruitful, seeds.[6]

27. An Anarchist Programme[1]

1. Aims and Objectives

We believe that most of the ills that afflict mankind stem from a bad social organisation; and that Man could destroy them if he wished and knew how.

Present society is the result of age-long struggles of man against man. Not understanding the advantages that could accrue for all by cooperation and solidarity; seeing in every other man (with the possible exception of those closest to them by blood ties) a competitor and an enemy, each one of them sought to secure for himself, the greatest number of advantages possible without giving a thought to the interests of others.

In such a struggle, obviously the strongest or more fortunate were bound to win, and in one way or another subject and oppress the losers.

So long as Man was unable to produce more than was strictly needed to keep alive, the conquerors could do no more than put to flight or massacre their victims, and seize the food they had gathered.

Then when with the discovery of grazing and agriculture a man could produce more than what he needed to live, the conquerors found it more profitable to reduce the conquered to a state of slavery, and put them to work for their advantage.

Later, the conquerors realised that it was more convenient, more profitable and certain to exploit the labour of others by other means: to retain for themselves the exclusive right to the land and working implements, and set free the disinherited who, finding themselves without the means of life, were obliged to have recourse to the landowners and work for them, on their terms.

Thus, step by step through a most complicated series of struggles of every description, of invasions, wars, rebellions, repressions, concessions won by struggle, associations of the oppressed united for defence, and of the conquerors for attack, we have arrived at the present state of society, in which some have inherited the land and all social wealth, while the mass of the people, disinherited in all respects, is exploited and oppressed by a small possessing class.

From all this stems the misery in which most workers live today, and which in turn creates the evils such as ignorance, crime, prostitution, diseases due to malnutrition, mental depression, and premature death. From all this arises a special class (government) which, provided with the necessary means of repression, exists to legalise and protect the owning class from the demands of the workers; and then it uses the powers at its disposal to create privileges for itself and to subject, if it can, the owning class itself as well. From this the creation of another privileged class (the clergy), which by a series of fables about the will of God, and about an after-life etc., seeks to persuade the oppressed to accept oppression meekly, and (just as the government does), as well as serving the interest of the owning class, serves its own. From this the creation of an official science which, in all those matters serving the interests of the ruling class, is the negation of true science. From this the patriotic spirit, race hatred, wars, and armed peace, sometimes more disastrous than wars themselves. From this the transformation of love into torment or sordid commerce. From this hatred, more or less disguised, rivalry, suspicion among all men, insecurity, and universal fear.

We want to change radically such a state of affairs. And since all these ills have their origin in the struggle between men, in the seeking after well-being through one's own efforts and for oneself and against everybody, we want to make amends, replacing hatred by love, competition by solidarity, the individual search for personal well-being by the fraternal cooperation for the well-being of all, oppression and imposition by liberty, the religious and pseudo-scientific lie by truth.

Therefore:

1. Abolition of private property in land, in raw materials, and the instruments of labour, so that no one shall have the means of living by the exploitation of the labour of others, and that everybody, being assured of the means to produce and to live, shall be truly independent and in a position to unite freely among themselves for a common objective and according to their personal sympathies.
2. Abolition of government and of every power which makes the law and imposes it on others: therefore abolition of monarchies, republics, parliaments, armies, police forces, magistratures, and any institution whatsoever endowed with coercive powers.
3. Organisation of social life by means of free association and federations of producers and consumers, created and modified according to the wishes of their members, guided by science and experience, and free from any kind of imposition which does not spring from natural needs, to which everyone, convinced by a feeling of overriding necessity, voluntarily submits.
4. The means of life, for development and well-being, will be guaranteed to children and all who are prevented from providing for themselves.
5. War on religions and all lies, even if they shelter under the cloak of science. Scientific instruction for all to advanced level.
6. War on rivalries and patriotic prejudices. Abolition of frontiers; brotherhood among all peoples.
7. Reconstruction of the family, as will emerge from the practice of love, freed from every legal tie, from every economic and physical oppression, from every religious prejudice.

This is our ideal.

2. Ways and Means

We have outlined under a number of headings our objectives and the ideal for which we struggle.

But it is not enough to desire something; if one really wants it adequate means must be used to secure it. And these means are not arbitrary, but instead cannot but be conditioned by the ends we aspire to and by the circumstances in which the struggle takes place, for if we ignore the choice of means we would achieve other ends, possibly diametrically opposed to those we aspire to, and this would be the obvious and inevitable consequence of our choice of means. Whoever sets out on the highroad and takes a wrong turning does not go where be intends to go but where the road leads him.

It is therefore necessary to state what are the means which in our opinion lead to our desired ends, and which we propose to adopt.

Our ideal is not one which depends for its success on the individual considered in isolation. The question is of changing the way of life of society as a whole; of establishing among men relationships based on love and solidarity; of achieving the full material, moral and intellectual development not for isolated individuals, or members of one class or of a particular political party, but for all mankind—and this is not something that can be imposed by force, but must emerge through the enlightened consciences of each one of us and be achieved with the free consent of all.

Our first task therefore must be to persuade people.

We must make people aware of the misfortunes they suffer and of their chances to destroy them. We must awaken sympathy in everybody for the misfortunes of others and a warm desire for the good of all people.

To those who are cold and hungry we will demonstrate how possible and easy it could be to assure to everybody their material needs. To those who are oppressed and despised we shall show how it is possible to live happily in a world of people who are free and equal; to those who are tormented by hatred and bitterness we will point to the road that leads to peace and human warmth that comes through learning to love one's fellow beings.

And when we will have succeeded in arousing the sentiment of rebellion in the minds of men against the avoidable and unjust evils from which we suffer in society today, and in getting them to understand how they are caused and how it depends on human will to rid ourselves of them; and when we will have created a lively and strong desire in men to transform society for the good of all, then those who are convinced, will by their own efforts as well as by the example of those already convinced, unite and want to as well as be able to act for their common ideals.

As we have already pointed out, it would be ridiculous and contrary to our objectives to seek to impose freedom, love among men and the radical development of human faculties, by means of force. One must therefore rely on the free will of others, and all we can do is to provoke the development and the expression of the will of the people. But it would be equally absurd and contrary to our aims to admit that those who do not share our views should prevent us from expressing our will, so long as it does not deny them the same freedom.

Freedom for all, therefore, to propagate and to experiment with their ideas, with no other limitation than that which arises naturally from the equal liberty of everybody.

But to this are opposed—and with brute force—those who benefit from existing privileges and who today dominate and control all social life.

In their hands they have all the means of production; and thus they suppress not only the possibility of free experimentation in new ways of communal living, and the right of workers to live freely by their own efforts, but also the right to life itself; and they oblige whoever is not a boss to have to allow himself to be exploited and oppressed if he does not wish to die of hunger.

They have police forces, a judiciary, and armies created for the express purpose of defending their privileges; and they persecute, imprison and massacre those who would want to abolish those privileges and who claim the means of life and liberty for everyone.

Jealous of their present and immediate interests, corrupted by the spirit of domination, fearful of the future, they, the privileged class, are, generally speaking incapable of a generous gesture; are equally incapable of a wider concept of their interests. And it would be foolish to hope that they should freely give up property and power and adapt themselves to living as equals and with those who today they keep in subjection.

Leaving aside the lessons of history (which demonstrates that never has a privileged class divested itself of all or some of its privileges, and never has a government abandoned its power unless obliged to do so by force or the fear of force), there is enough contemporary evidence to convince anyone that the bourgeoisie and governments intend to use armed force to defend themselves, not only against complete expropriation, but equally against the smallest popular demands, and are always ready to engage in the most atrocious persecutions and the bloodiest massacres.

For those people who want to emancipate themselves, only one course is open: that of opposing force with force.

It follows from what we have said that we have to work to awaken in the oppressed the conscious desire for a radical social transformation, and to persuade them that by uniting they have the strength to win; we must propagate our ideal and prepare the required material and moral forces to overcome those of the enemy, and to organise the new society, and when we will have the strength needed we must, by taking advantage of favourable circumstances as they arise, or which we can ourselves create, to make the social revolution, using force to destroy the government and to expropriate the owners of wealth, and by putting in common the means of life and production, and by preventing the setting up of new governments which would impose their will and to hamper the reorganisation of society by the people themselves.

All this is however less simple than it might appear at first sight. We have to deal with people as they are in society today, in the most miserable moral and material condition; and we would be deluding ourselves in thinking that propaganda is enough to raise them to that level of intellectual development which is needed to put our ideas into effect.

Between man and his social environment there is a reciprocal action. Men make society what it is and society makes men what they are, and the result is therefore a kind of vicious circle. To transform society men must be changed, and to transform men, society must be changed.

Poverty brutalises man, and to abolish poverty men must have a social conscience and determination. Slavery teaches men to be slaves, and to free oneself from slavery there is a need for men who aspire to liberty. Ignorance has the effect of making men unaware of the causes of their misfortunes as well as the means of overcoming them, and to do away with ignorance people must have the time and the means to educate themselves.

Governments accustom people to submit to the Law and to believe that Law is essential to society; and to abolish government men must be convinced of the uselessness and the harmfulness of government.

How does one escape from this vicious circle?

Fortunately existing society has not been created by the inspired will of a dominating class, which has succeeded in reducing all its subjects to passive and unconscious instruments of its interests. It is the result of a thousand internecine struggles, of a thousand human and natural factors acting indifferently, without directive criteria; and thus there are no clear-cut divisions either between individuals or between classes.

Innumerable are the variations in material conditions; innumerable are the degrees of moral and intellectual development; and not always—we would almost say very rarely, does the place of any individual in society correspond with his abilities and his aspirations. Very often individuals accustomed to conditions of comfort fall on hard times and others, through exceptionally favourable circumstances succeed in raising themselves above the conditions into which they were born. A large proportion of the working class has already succeeded either in emerging from a state of abject poverty, or was never in such a situation; no worker to speak of finds himself in a state of complete social unawareness, of complete acquiescence to the conditions imposed on him by the bosses. And the same institutions, such as have been produced by history, contain organic contradictions and are like the germs of death, which as they develop result in the dissolution of institutions and the need for transformation.

From this the possibility of progress—but not the possibility of bringing all men to the necessary level to want, and to achieve, anarchy, by means of propaganda, without a previous gradual transformation of the environment.

Progress must advance contemporaneously and along parallel lines between men and their environment. We must take advantage of all the means, all the possibilities and the opportunities that the present environment allows us to act on our fellow men and to develop their consciences and their demands;

we must use all advance in human consciences to induce them to claim and to impose those major social transformations which are possible and which effectively serve to open the way to further advances later.

We must not wait to achieve anarchy, in the meantime limiting ourselves to simple propaganda. Were we to do so we would soon exhaust our field of action; that is, we would have converted all those who in the existing environment are susceptible to understand and accept our ideas, and our subsequent propaganda would fall on sterile ground; or if environmental transformations brought out new popular groupings capable of receiving new ideas, this would happen without our participation, and thus would prejudice our ideas.

We must seek to get all the people, or different sections of the people, to make demands, and impose itself and take for itself all the improvements and freedoms that it desires as and when it reaches the state of wanting them, and the power to demand them; and in always propagating all aspects of our programme, and always struggling for its complete realisation, we must push the people to want always more and to increase its pressures, until it has achieved complete emancipation.

3. The Economic Struggle

The oppression which today impinges most directly on the workers and which is the main cause of the moral and material frustrations under which they labour, is economic oppression, that is the exploitation to which bosses and business men subject them, thanks to their monopoly of all the most important means of production and distribution.

To destroy radically this oppression without any danger of it reemerging, all people must be convinced of their right to the means of production, and be prepared to exercise this basic right by expropriating the land owners, the industrialists and financiers, and putting all social wealth at the disposal of the people.

But can this expropriation be put into effect today? Can we today pass directly, without intermediate steps, from the hell in which the workers now find themselves to the paradise of common property?

Facts demonstrate what the workers are capable of today.

Our task is the moral and material preparation of the people for this essential expropriation; and to attempt it again and again, every time a revolutionary upheaval offers us the chance to, until the final triumph. But in what way can we prepare the people? In what way must one prepare the conditions which make possible not only the material fact of expropriation, but the utilisation to everybody's advantage of the common wealth?

We have already said that spoken and written propaganda alone cannot win over to our ideas the mass of the people. A practical education is needed, which must be alternately cause and effect in a gradual transformation of the environment. Parallel with the workers developing a sense of rebellion against the injustices and useless sufferings of which they are the victims, and the desire to better their conditions, they must be united and mutually dependent in the struggle to achieve their demands.

And we as anarchists and workers, must incite and encourage them to struggle, and join them in their struggle.

But are these improvements possible in a capitalist regime? Are they useful from the point of view of a future complete emancipation of the workers?

Whatever may be the practical results of the struggle for immediate gains, the greatest value lies in the struggle itself. For thereby workers learn that the bosses interests are opposed to theirs and that they cannot improve their conditions, and much less emancipate themselves, except by uniting and becoming stronger than the bosses. If they succeed in getting what they demand, they will be better off: they will earn more, work fewer hours and will have more time and energy to reflect on the things that matter to them, and will immediately make greater demands and have greater needs. If they do not succeed they will be led to study the causes of their failure and recognise the need for closer unity and greater activity and they will in the end understand that to make their victory secure and definitive, it is necessary to destroy capitalism. The revolutionary cause, the cause of the moral elevation and emancipation of the workers must benefit by the fact that workers unite and struggle for their interests.

But, once again, can the workers succeed in really improving their conditions in the present state of society?

This depends on the confluence of a great number of circumstances.

In spite of what some say, there exists no natural law (law of wages) which determines what part of a worker's labour should go to him; or if one wants to formulate a law, it could not be but that: wages cannot normally be less than what is needed to maintain life, nor can they normally rise such that no profit margin is left to the boss.

It is clear that in the first case workers would die, and therefore would stop drawing any wages, and in the second the bosses would stop employing labour and so would pay no more wages. But between these two impossible extremes there is an infinite scale of degrees ranging from the miserable conditions of many land workers to the almost respectable conditions of skilled workers in the large cities.

Wages, hours, and other conditions of employment are the result of the struggle between bosses and workers. The former try to give the workers as little as possible and get them to work themselves to the bone; the latter try, or should try to work as little, and earn as much, as possible. Where workers accept any conditions, or even being discontented, do not know how to put up effective resistance to the bosses demands, they are soon reduced to bestial conditions of life. Where, instead, they have ideas as to how human beings should live and know how to join forces, and through refusal to work or the latent and open threat of rebellion, to win the bosses respect, in such cases, they are treated in a relatively decent way. One can therefore say that within certain limits, the wages he gets are what the worker (not as an individual, of course, but as a class) demands.

Through struggle, by resistance against the bosses, therefore, workers can up to a certain point, prevent a worsening of their conditions as well as obtaining real improvement. And the history of the workers' movement has already demonstrated this truth.

One must not however exaggerate the importance of this struggle between workers and bosses conducted exclusively in the economic field. Bosses can give in, and often they do in face of forcefully expressed demands so long as the demands are not too great; but if workers were to make demands (and it is imperative that they should) which would absorb all the bosses profits and be in effect an indirect form of expropriation, it is certain that the bosses would appeal to the government and would seek to use force to oblige the workers to remain in their state of wage slavery.

And even before, long before workers can expect to receive the full product of their labour, the economic struggle becomes impotent as a means of producing the improvements in living standards.

Workers produce everything and without them life would be impossible; therefore it would seem that by refusing to work they could demand whatever they wanted. But the union of all workers, even in one particular trade, and in one country is difficult to achieve, and opposing the union of workers are the bosses organisations. Workers live from day to day, and if they do not work they soon find themselves without food; whereas the bosses, because they have money, have access to all the goods in stock and can therefore sit back and wait until hunger reduces their employees to a more amenable frame of mind. The invention or the introduction of new machinery makes workers redundant and adds to the large army of unemployed, who are driven by hunger to sell their labour at any price. Immigration immediately creates problems in the countries where better working conditions exist, for the hordes of hungry workers, willy-nilly, offer the bosses an opportunity to depress wages all round. And all these facts, which necessarily derive from the capitalist system, conspire in counteracting and often destroying advances made in working class consciousness and solidarity. And in every case the overriding fact remains that production under capitalism is organised by each capitalist for his personal profit and not, as would be natural, to satisfy the needs of the workers in the best possible way. Hence the chaos, the waste of human effort, the organised scarcity of goods, useless and harmful occupations, unemployment, abandoned land, under-use of plant, and so on, all evils which cannot be avoided except by depriving the capitalists of the means of production and, it follows, the organisation of production.

Soon then, those workers who want to free themselves, or even only to effectively improve their conditions, will be faced with the need to defend themselves from the government, with the need to attack the government, which by legalising the right to property and protecting it with brute force, constitutes a barrier to human progress, which must be beaten down with force if one does not wish to remain indefinitely under present conditions or even worse.

From the economic struggle one must pass to the political struggle, that is to the struggle against government; and instead of opposing the capitalist millions with the workers' few pennies scraped together with difficulty, one must oppose the rifles and guns which defend property with the more effective means that the people will be able to find to defeat force by force.

4. The Political Struggle

By the political struggle we mean the struggle against government. Government is the *ensemble* of all those individuals who hold the reins of power, however acquired, to make the law and to impose it on the governed, that is the public.

Government is the consequence of the spirit of domination and violence with which some men have imposed themselves on other, and is at the same time the creature as well as the creator of privilege and its natural defender.

It is wrongly said that today government performs the function of defender of capitalism but that once capitalism is abolished it would become the representative and administrator of the general interest. In the first place capitalism will not be destroyed until the workers, having rid themselves of government, take possession of all social wealth and themselves organise production and consumption in the interests of everybody without waiting for the initiative to come from government which, however willing to comply, would be incapable of doing so.

But there is a further question: if capitalism were to be destroyed and a government were to be left in office, the government, through the concession of all kinds of privileges, would create capitalism anew for, being unable to please everybody it would need an economically powerful class to support it in return for the legal and material protection it would receive.

Consequently privilege cannot be abolished and freedom and equality established firmly and definitely without abolishing government—not this or that government but the very institution of government.

As in all questions of general interest, and especially this one, the consent of the people as a whole is needed, and therefore we must strain every nerve to persuade the people that government is useless as well as harmful, and that we can live better lives without government.

But, as we have repeated more than once, propaganda alone is impotent to convince everybody—and if we were to want to limit ourselves to preaching against government, and in the meantime waiting supinely for the day when the public will be convinced of the possibility and value of radically destroying every kind of government, then that day would never come.

While preaching against every kind of government, and demanding complete freedom, we must support all struggles for partial freedom, because we are convinced that one learns through struggle, and that once one begins to enjoy a little freedom one ends by wanting it all. We must always be with the people, and when we do not succeed in getting them to demand a lot we must still seek to get them to want something; and we must make every effort to get them to understand that however much or little they may demand should be obtained by their own efforts and that they should despise and detest whoever is part of, or aspires to, government.

Since government today has the power, through the legal system, to regulate daily life and to broaden or restrict the liberty of the citizen, and because we are still unable to tear this power from its grasp, we must seek to reduce its power and oblige governments to use it in the least harmful ways possible. But this we must do always remaining outside, and against, government, putting pressure on it through agitation in the streets, by threatening to take by force what we demand. Never must we accept any kind of legislative position, be it national or local, for in so doing we will neutralise the effectiveness of our activity as well as betraying the future of our cause.

The struggle against government in the last analysis, is physical, material.

Governments make the law. They must therefore dispose of the material forces (police and army) to impose the law, for otherwise only those who wanted to would obey it, and it would no longer be the law, but a simple series of suggestions which all would be free to accept or reject. Governments have this power, however, and use it through the law, to strengthen their power, as well as to serve the interests of the ruling classes, by oppressing and exploiting the workers.

The only limit to the oppression of government is the power with which the people show themselves capable of opposing it. Conflict may be open or latent; but it always exists since the government does not pay attention to discontent and popular resistance except when it is faced with the danger of insurrection.

When the people meekly submit to the law, or their protests are feeble and confined to words, the government studies its own interests and ignores the needs of the people; when the protests are lively, insistent, threatening, the government, depending on whether it is more or less understanding, gives way or resorts to repression. But one always comes back to insurrection, for if the government does not give way, the people will end by rebelling; and if the government does give way, then the people gain confidence in themselves and make ever increasing demands, until such time as the incompatibility between freedom and authority becomes clear and the violent struggle is engaged.

It is therefore necessary to be prepared, morally and materially, so that when this does happen the people will emerge victorious.

A successful insurrection is the most potent factor in the emancipation of the people, for once the yoke has been shaken off, the people are free to provide themselves with those institutions which they think best, and the time lag between passing the law and the degree of civilisation which the mass of the population has attained, is breached in one leap. The insurrection determines the revolution, that is, the speedy emergence of the latent forces built up during the "evolutionary" period.

Everything depends on what the people are capable of wanting.

In past insurrections unaware of the real reasons for their misfortunes, they have always wanted very little, and have obtained very little.

What will they want in the next insurrection?

The answer, in part, depends on our propaganda and what efforts we put into it.

We shall have to push the people to expropriate the bosses and put all goods in common and organise their daily lives themselves, through freely constituted associations, without waiting for orders from outside and refusing to nominate or recognise any government or constituted body in whatever guise (constituent, dictatorship, etc.) even in a provisional capacity, which ascribes to itself the right to lay down the law and impose with force its will on others.

And if the mass of the population will not respond to our appeal we must—in the name of the right we have to be free even if others wish to remain slaves and because of the force of example—put into effect as many of our ideas as we can, refuse to recognise the new government and keep alive resistance and seek that those localities where our ideas are received with sympathy should constitute themselves into anarchist communities, rejecting all governmental interference and establishing free agreements with other communities which want to live their own lives.

We shall have to, above all, oppose with every means the reestablishment of the police and the armed forces, and use any opportunity to incite workers in non anarchist localities to take advantage of the absence of repressive forces to implement the most far reaching demands that we can induce them to make.

And however things may go, to continue the struggle against the possessing class and the rulers without respite, having always in mind the complete economic, political and moral emancipation of all mankind.

5. Conclusion

What we want, therefore, is the complete destruction of the domination and exploitation of man by man; we want men united as brothers by a conscious and desired solidarity, all cooperating voluntarily for the well-being of all; we want society to be constituted for the purpose of supplying everybody with the means for achieving the maximum well-being, the maximum possible moral and spiritual development; we want bread, freedom, love, and science for everybody.

And in order to achieve these all-important ends, it is necessary in our opinion that the means of production should be at the disposal of everybody and that no man, or groups of men, should be in a position to oblige others to submit to their will or to exercise their influence other than through the power of reason and by example.

Therefore: expropriation of landowners and capitalists for the benefit of all; and abolition of government.

And while waiting for the day when this can be achieved: the propagation of our ideas; unceasing struggle, violent or non-violent depending on the circumstances, against government and against the boss class to conquer as much freedom and well-being as we can for the benefit of everybody.

PART TWO

We follow ideas and not men, and rebel against this habit of embodying a principle in a man.

—Malatesta speaking at the Berne Congress of the International, 1876

Some of us, and Max Nettlau and Luigi Bertoni in particular, often suggested to Malatesta that he should write his Memoirs which would have been such a great contribution to contemporary history as well as to a better understanding of the events in which he was directly involved; and he would reply: "Yes, one day . . . but there is no hurry; I will think about it when there aren't more important things to do, when I'm an old man." But as he always found more important things to do, and never admitted to being old, he never wrote his Memoirs.

—Luigi Fabbri in his biography *Malatesta* (Buenos Aires, 1945)

Notes for a Biography

1

> ... So I left for Switzerland with Cafiero. At the time I was sickly, I spat blood and was said to be consumptive, more or less.... While crossing the Gothard during the night (at that time there was no tunnel and one had to cross the snowy mountain in a diligence) I had caught cold, and arrived at the house where Bakunin was staying in Zurich, with a feverish cough.
>
> After the first greetings. Bakunin made up a camp bed, and invited me—he almost forced me—to lie on it, covered me with all the blankets he could lay hands on and urged me to stay there quietly and sleep. And all this was accompanied by attention, and motherly tenderness, which gripped my heart.
>
> While I was wrapped up in bed, and all present imagined that I was sleeping, I heard Bakunin whispering nice things about me and then adding sadly: "What a shame that he should be so sick; we shall lose him very soon; he won't last more than six months."

That touching description of his first meeting with Bakunin in 1872 was written by Malatesta in 1926[1] when he was in his 73rd year and Bakunin had been fifty years in his grave.

Others at the time referred to Malatesta's ill-health. Cafiero (in a letter 1875) spoke of "poor Malatesta is sick with consumption" and thought that no doubt the intentions of their persecutors was "to stifle a life so young and noble, within the stinking and silent walls of a prison cell."[2] Borghi points out that Malatesta's "respiratory system remained his weak point throughout his life" and adds "I will never forget the crises provoked by the bronchial attacks he suffered in the stinking cell in Milan during the cold winter of 1920–21."[3]

His companion during the last years of his life, Elena Melli, in a letter to Damiani (July 28, 1932) describes the last weeks of his life: "He had got over the bronchial-pneumonia, as well as the relapse he suffered a few weeks ago. It seemed as if he was better, and out of danger, but he was getting weaker all the time; one could see it from one day to the next. Even he did not believe that he was dying but another attack on the left side suffocated him. . . . During those last few days he could hardly breathe, he was suffocating in spite of all the oxygen he took—1,500 litres in five hours. . . . He died on Friday, the 22nd [July 1932] at 12:20 p.m.[4]

2

George Woodcock in his recent history of Anarchism writes:

> In the middle of 1871, however a new group of militants appeared, different in character from those veterans of earlier struggles who had first gathered around Bakunin. The leaders among them, Carlo Cafiero, Errico Malatesta, and Carmelo Palladino, were all young men in their early twenties, the educated sons of Southern Italian landowners; all of them came from regions where peasant poverty was endemic . . . ; they were in fact the Italian equivalent of the conscience-stricken Russian noblemen who in the same decade felt the burning urge to "go to the people."[5]

At least so far as Malatesta is concerned, the comparison does not fit the facts that are available.

(Of Palladino not a great deal is known other than that he was a young lawyer who had been very active in the Naples section of the International from 1869–1871; that he visited Bakunin in company with Cafiero towards the end of 1872 and went to Locarno in 1874 after the failure of the Italian insurrectionary movement of that year but eventually returned to Cagnamo Varamo "where he died many years later in tragic circumstances."[6]

Carlo Cafiero (born in Barletta in 1846 of a "rich and reactionary family"[7]) was a member of the London International whom Marx intended should be used to help convert Italy and Spain to Marxism. On his return to Italy it was he who was converted instead, and in part by Malatesta's efforts. Bakunin completed the "conversion" the following year. He remained active until 1882, when he championed the social democratic cause. A year later Cafiero suffered a mental breakdown from which he never recovered. He died in a mental home in 1892.

Errico Malatesta was born in Santa Maria Capua Vetere (a garrison town with a population of 10,000 in the province of Caserta) on December 14, 1853. We know very little about his family's background. The popular view that he was descended from nobility is baseless. Fabbri[8] describes Malatesta's father as "a man of moderately liberal ideas" as well as "a rich landowner." According to Nettlau[9] the family came from the "petit bourgeoisie and engaged in commerce," and this description is confirmed by Borghi[10] who recounts that Malatesta was always highly amused by his alleged descent from Sigismundo Malatesta "the famous tyrant of Rimini" who in the 15th century erected a temple to God and his mistress Isotta. No noble blood coursed through his veins. "His mother and father were retiring and modest landowners."

From Malatesta's own account of his first meeting with Bakunin in 1872[11] we learn that by then his mother and father as well as a brother and sister had died from "chest complaints," and in another article of political reminiscences, of Giuseppe Fanelli, he mentions that at the time (1871) "I was a student and lived with my brother and an old aunt who was mother to us after the death of our parents."[12]

> The International had been introduced in Italy by bourgeois who in their love for justice, had deserted their class, and in 1872 and also later in many places, the majority, at least the leadership and active elements were not workers but young people from the middle- and lower-middle-class.[13]

3

In the middle of 1871 Malatesta was not in his "early twenties" but just over 17 years old, and already active in the political struggle.

When he was fourteen he protested over a local injustice by addressing to King Victor Emmanuel II what Fabbri[14] describes as an "insolent and threatening letter" which Authority took sufficiently seriously to order his arrest (March 25, 1868). With the help of friends his father secured his release from prison and as well as from the threat of being sent to a special school "in view of the fact that his family had so neglected his education as a loyal subject of the Crown."[15]

At supper on the night of his release his father tried to reproach his son or at least warn him to be more prudent in future. But Fabbri tells us that the young Malatesta's reply was so intransigent that all his father could say, with tears in his eyes was "My poor boy, it displeases me to tell you, but at this rate you will end up on the gallows."[16]

Two years later (1870) according to Angiolini[17] he was arrested and sentenced in Naples following a demonstration and "sent down" from the University of Naples (where he was studying medicine) for a year.

Malatesta's schooling started in the *lycée* of Santa Maria but he was soon to move with his parents to Naples where he attended the Scolopian school (a religious order devoted to education) and studied the classics.[18]

> I was then (1868) a youth dedicated to the study of rhetoric, Roman History and Gioberti's philosophy. My teachers did not succeed in stifling in me the forces of nature, so that I was able to preserve in the stupid and corrupting environment of a modern school my intellectual sanity and the purity of my heart.[19]

From the Scolopians he went to the Medical School at the University of Naples. He can have at most completed three years of his medical studies before joining the International and the years following that momentous decision were so packed with political and revolutionary activity that it is unlikely that he ever completed his medical studies.[20]

4

At the age of 14 he was a budding Republican and in due course applied for membership of the "Universal Republican Alliance," but Mazzini turned down the application on the grounds that his tendencies were too socialistic and that he would soon have gone over to the International. Malatesta had not heard of the International until then. His insatiable curiosity had to be satisfied and he set about finding out more; in the course of his search he met a number of members of the Italian section of the International and came under the influence of Fanelli and Palladino. He joined the International in 1871, a few months after the "inspiring" events of the Paris Commune. His entry into the Naples section was the beginning of a new phase of activity within the section. As well as a group of workers, many of Malatesta's student friends followed him.[21] He was also indicating not only a great capacity for work but an ability to inspire those around him, a gift he retained throughout his life.

Many years later he was to describe the life of a militant in those days of "enthusiasm" when the Internationalists were "ever ready for any sacrifice for the cause and were inspired by the rosiest hopes."[22]

> Everyone gave to propaganda all they could, as well as what they could not afford; and when money was short we gladly sold household objects, facing, in a resigned way, the reprimands from our respective families. For propaganda we neglected our work and our studies. In any case the revolution was to take place at any moment and would put all matters to rights! Often one went to prison, but came out with more energy than before; persecutions only awakened our enthusiasm. It is true that the persecutions at that time were jokes compared with what took place later. At that time the regime had emerged from a series of revolutions; and the authorities, from the beginning stern so far as the workers, especially in the country, were concerned, showed a certain respect for freedom in the political struggle, a kind of embarrassment at being similar to the Bourbon and Austrian rulers, which however disappeared as the regime became consolidated and the struggle for national independence receded into the background.[23]

But he also does not hesitate to point to all the false political assumptions with which, at the time, they fed their enthusiasms.

> We believed in the general discontent, and since the poverty that afflicted the mass of the people was truly insupportable, we thought it would be enough to set an example, and with weapons in our hands, launch the slogan "down with the gentlefolk," for the working masses to set about the bourgeoisie and take possession of the land, the factories and all they had produced by their efforts and that had been taken away from them. And then of course we had a mystical faith in the virtues of the people, in its abilities, in its equalitarian and libertarian instincts.
>
> Facts demonstrated then and later (and they had before as well) how far we were from the truth. It was only too clear that hunger, when there is no awareness of individual rights and a guiding idea to action, does not result in revolutions; at most it creates sporadic risings which the *signori*, if they have any sense, can much more easily control by distributing bread and throwing a few coppers to the clamouring mob from their balconies, than by ordering the carabineers to fire on them. And if our wishes had not blinded our powers of observation, we could easily have noted the depressing, and therefore counter-revolutionary effect of hunger, and the fact that our propaganda was most effective in the least depressed regions and among those workers, mostly artisans, who were in less difficult financial straits.

Unlike many revolutionaries who never saw the wood of reality for the trees of their dreams, Malatesta was at an early stage in his political life subjecting all the hopes and theories of his contemporaries and teachers to the critical test of reality. It is important to stress however that whereas as so often happens, the starry-eyed missionary-type of revolutionary and the action-above-all-else activist who despises those who dare to stop to think, soon lose their missionary zeal, and turn their activism to more mundane pursuits, Malatesta never abandoned his revolutionary activity nor did he lose his optimism, an optimism which must be seen much more as confidence in himself and his closest friends than as blind faith in some anarchist or socialist millennium.[24]

In a rare autobiographical article written in 1884,[25] when he was thirty, and intended both as a warning and an incitement to the youth at that time, he describes his own feelings as a teenager, his dreams of "an ideal world" and his faith in the "republic"—in the cause of which he had seen the inside of a royal prison for the first time—only to be aware as be entered the world of reality what problems had to be surmounted to achieve his ideal world, and the fact that the republic was a government like any other—and sometimes even worse.

5

Early in life Malatesta understood the dangers of the cult of the personality without, nevertheless, ever under-estimating any man's worth, or failing to recognise exceptional qualities in others, or the influences they exerted on his own development. The fact that in his early youth he had to choose between a galaxy of "great men"—Garibaldi, Mazzini, Marx, and Bakunin—may have given him an early insight into the dangers that stemmed from associating ideas with personalities. Indeed at the eighth Congress of the International Working Men's Association held in Berne in October 1876 Malatesta (who was one of the Italian delegates) protested against the habit of calling themselves or of being known as Bakuninists, "since we are not, seeing that we do not share all Bakunin's theoretical and practical ideas, and because above all, we follow ideas and not men, and rebel against this habit of embodying a principle in a man."[26]

And of Mazzini he refers to the way "possibly irritated at being deprived of that kind of pontificate that he had exercised for many years over the revolutionary movement, violently attacked the Commune and the International and held back his followers from the steps that they were about to take."[27] And he writes of Garibaldi's followers and "their *duce*"[28] (Mussolini had himself referred to as "*il duce*," and since Malatesta's reference to Garibaldi was written in 1928, at the height of Mussolini's power, his use of the term for Garibaldi can hardly be considered flattering!)

Yet presumably because he combated the idea of superman, he was as generous in pointing to the qualities and achievements of those of his contemporaries and "mentors," as he was uncompromising in his criticism of their personal weaknesses and what he considered their political mistakes. This approach is well illustrated by Malatesta's article of recollections of Kropotkin which is included at the end of these Notes, and in his short but generous defence of Mazzini (1922):

> We were against Mazzini for his way of understanding the social struggle, for the providential mission that he attributed to Italy and to Rome, for his religious dogmatism.
>
> There were always, as happens in the heat of the struggle, excesses and misunderstanding on both sides; but in the spirit of objectivity we recognise that at the bottom of our hearts and in the sentiments that inspired us: we were Mazzinians just as Mazzini was an Internationalist.
>
> Fundamental differences of method existed and remain, just as there were and still are basic differences in philosophical concepts; but the animating spirit was the same. Love among men, brotherhood among peoples, social justice and solidarity, the spirit of sacrifice, of duty. And furthermore the decisive and unreconcilable hatred of the institution of monarchy.[29]

6

Of the influences in his own development Bakunin takes pride of place. Malatesta referred to him as "the great revolutionary, he who we all look upon as our spiritual father." His greatest quality was his ability to "communicate faith, the desire for action and sacrifice to all those who had the opportunity of meeting him. He would say that one needed to have *le diable au corps*; and he certainly had it in him and in his spirit.

> I was a Bakuninist, as were all my comrades of those far off days. Today—and for very many years—I would no longer describe myself as such.
>
> Ideas have developed and been modified. Today I find that Bakunin in political economy and in the interpretation of history, was too Marxist; I find that his philosophy was conducted without possible issue in the contradiction between the mechanical concept of the universe and the faith in will over the fate of mankind. But all this of no great importance. Theories are uncertain and changing concepts; and philosophy, consisting of hypotheses inhabiting the clouds, has

> little or no influence on life. And Bakunin always remains, in spite of all possible disagreements, our great master and inspiration.
>
> What is living is his radical criticism of the principle of authority and of the State that embodies it; living is always the struggle against the two lies, the two guises, in which the masses are oppressed and exploited: democratic and dictatorial; and living is his masterly denunciation of that false socialism he called soporific, and which aims, consciously or unconsciously at consolidating the dominion of the bourgeoisie lulling workers to inactivity with useless reforms. And living are, above all, the intense hatred against all that degrades and humiliates man and the unlimited love of liberty for all.[30]

7

But as he himself wrote of that period "though none of us had read Marx, we were still too Marxist."[31] Fabbri considered that the period of transition between the anarchism of the First International and the anarchism that he expounded to the end of his life occurred during the seven or eight years from the publication of the *l'Associazione* (London, 1890) to *l'Agitazione* (Ancona, 1897). Nevertheless, the same writer observes that already in *La Questione Sociale* (Florence, 1884) "certain fundamental aspects of his evolution are fairly clearly revealed." It was in *l'Agitazione* that Malatesta published six articles on "Individualism in Anarchism," "Harmony and Organisation" in which, without polemicising openly with Kropotkin, he gives an interpretation of anarchism which is in open contradiction with the Kropotkinian view expressed in the *Conquest of Bread* and his other writings of the time.[32]

He describes his "evolution" in a letter to Fabbri[33] in which he confirmed the latter's view that since 1897 he had modified his views on small details only. At the time "I had more faith, more hope in syndicalism—or rather, in the syndicates—than I have now; and communism seemed then a more simple and an easier solution than it appears now." And he goes on to point out that there was a greater difference between his ideas of 1897 and those of 1872–73–74. "Then we were 'kropotkinians' even before Kropotkin (in fact Kropotkin found those ideas which he made his own, already widely held by us before he entered the 'bakuninist' wing of the international movement)." He refers to this at greater length in an article on the Question of Revisionism (1927) and also in his Kropotkin "Recollections" appended to these Notes.

8

Malatesta was the "complete" anarchist propagandist. Early in his political life he lost any illusions he might have had about historical inevitability and realised that only if people could be shaken out of their apathy and "pushed" ("spingere" is a favourite word of his which one constantly meets in his writings) to think and act for themselves, would things change. He was therefore an indefatigable propagandist of the written and spoken word. But also because he was aware of the limits of propaganda as such he was also an activist, viewing direct action, intelligently conceived, as a vital aspect of the task of preparing the environment for revolution. The third ingredient in this "complete" anarchist propagandist was that he began as an Internationalist and remained one to the end of his days.

(Unlike our intellectual expatriates who denounce everything English and live like puckasahibs in countries which, apart from the climate and the low cost of living and cheap labour, are still a century behind perfidious Albion in their way of life and their laws, Malatesta was truly the Internationalist because he loved mankind without ceasing to love Italy:

"Is it not absurd"—he once wrote in answer to a shocked comrade—"to believe that he who loves all countries, who looks on the world as his ideal country and seeks to make it the effective country for all men, linked in brotherhood in work and for mutual well-being, should make an exception of the country in which he was born and the people with whom he has greater affinities and links? . . . *Long Live Italy*, yes, a thousand times yes: And *Long live all the countries of the world*. And, it is understood, not the political States, all of which we want to see destroyed, but the people, emancipated from all political and economic oppression."[34]

If Malatesta devoted much of his activity and thought to the Italian political scene it was because he felt more able to make an effective contribution to the struggle in a country and among people with whom he shared—among other things—a common language. But as he put it:

> For us, our country is the whole world; for us every human achievement is ours just as is every human shame. Italy is part of the world, and though for its liberation we specially devote our efforts, it is only because here our activity can be more effective because here we have relatives, friends and comrades who we specially love. . . . But all this is so obvious, so elementary, so common-place and has so often been said that one has to make an effort to repeat it.[35]

9

Because of the special attention he was accorded by government and police in Italy, Malatesta spent nearly half his life in exile. His first period of exile in 1878 began when he was twenty-five. He returned to Italy in 1883 only to leave for South America the following year; he did not return until 1897 when he edited *l'Agitazione* but by 1899 was again in exile. He returned to Italy in 1913–14 for barely a year, and did not manage to set foot in his country again until 1919 where he spent the next 13 years until his death in 1932 (except for a brief visit to Switzerland in 1922 on the occasion of the 50th anniversary of the St. Imier conference of the International which he had attended as the delegate for the Naples Section is his youth). Thus Malatesta spent thirty-five years of his life in exile—much of it filled with activity but also much of it frustrated by inactivity. What is clear however, is that even in exile he never lost touch with the Italian political situation.

At the time of writing these lines the *Sunday Telegraph* (25.10.64) illustrates a review of Mr. Joll's work on *The Anarchists*[36] with a reproduction of the photograph of Malatesta used on the cover of this volume and captioned "Dangerous Type." Professor George Woodcock in his *History* perpetuates instead the romantic picture of the "knight errant" ranging through Europe and the Levant "in search of revolutionary adventure." Others accused Malatesta in his time, of being a coward who never stopped to face the music—that is the consequences of his actions. Malatesta *was* a "dangerous type" but not in the sense clearly implied by the *Sunday Telegraph* which titles its review "Futile Gang." He was dangerous so far as governments were concerned, but admired and respected as a man of integrity and vision by people from all walks of life throughout the world. His life was full of those incidents which are "romantic" when viewed in retrospect and by those literati who in a lifetime have never said boo to a goose even in anger, but it was quite clear that after the early years when Malatesta and his friends courted arrest and imprisonment as part of their propaganda activities, he did not consider that his effectiveness as a propagandist was greater in prison than at liberty even in exile. On the other hand this did not prevent him from taking big risks, but they were what could be called calculated risks.

Malatesta, as I see him, was neither a romantic nor a martyr type. But neither did he lack a sense of humour, or underestimate his worth as a political thinker and personality; but he was never an exhibitionist, nor a poseur. He obviously sought approval and a following but always on the strength of his arguments and never by compromising them or by encouraging the cult of *his personality*. The fact is that Malatesta's ideas and activities provoked heated discussion not only among the Italian Left but within the anarchist movement itself. It is only since his death that his ideas have ceased to be the centre of heated discussion in the Italian anarchist movement. Perhaps now the discussion will be taken up in the English speaking movement!

10

That Malatesta was far from being the revolutionary in search of adventure is surely illustrated by the relatively inactive years—1900 to 1919—spent in London which were interrupted only by his participation in the Anarchist International Congress in Amsterdam (1907) and that period of less than a year (1913–14) in Italy. His contribution to the Congress is noteworthy for its practical suggestions and approach. I refer to Malatesta's contributions to it in the concluding section of this volume.

Malatesta's return to Italy (1913–14) is a model of the thoroughness and the energy with which he set about any task, or assignment he undertook (and one must bear in mind that by then he was sixty, an age when many other revolutionaries were dead, or resting on their laurels and writing their memoirs).

His decision was prompted by a number of considerations principal among them the political "hunch" that the Italian situation, following the unpopular Tripolitanian war was ripe for some "practical" initiative. At the time the Italian anarchist movement was torn by internal and personal polemics, largely the work of a handful of "comrades" who in due course transferred their activities to the bourgeois parties, as generally is the case, and it was with a view to once again bringing together the movement that Cesare Agostinelli the Ancona hatter and Malatesta's old comrade in arms approached him in London, and Fabbri who was, at the time, doing a teaching job in a village in Emilia, about his idea of starting an anarchist paper in Ancona. Both responded enthusiastically. Fabbri was detailed to draft a circular announcing the forthcoming publication which Malatesta suggested should be called *Volontà*. The first issue appeared in Ancona, June 1913, and edited by Malatesta from London, WC1. Fabbri writes that "right from the start the new periodical bore the imprint of earlier Malatestian newspapers."[37] But so far as the presentation went, Malatesta, from London was writing to his friend (June 13): "What do you think of the first issue of *Volontà?* Typographically its horrible. The quality of the paper makes me shudder. Light inking on grey paper—type too crammed etc. Still . . . we will improve." On the 16th June he writes to Agostinelli "The 2nd issue has arrived. Much better, well done! If we go on improving we shall end up by doing something really good. Tonight I will send you the editorial. It should reach you by Thursday. Try to keep space for it. I am late—and I am expecting a telling-off. But in future I hope I will make amends and not deserve your strictures . . ."[38] I quote this extract because it seems to me to shed more light on Malatesta's character, his simplicity, and human warmth and comradeship than anything a third party could write on the subject.

And in the course of his letter to Fabbri, Malatesta lets him onto a secret "which will please you: I have decided to come to Italy." And to Luigi Bertoni editor of the bilingual anarchist fortnightly *Le Réveil/Il Risveglio*, published for many years in Geneva, he wrote (July 3, 1913) "I have decided to leave for Italy towards the end of the month. Frankly I find it impossible to produce a paper from this distance to meet the needs of the present situation; and furthermore I am loath to spur others on to act while I am safely tucked away [in London]."[39]

Malatesta's activity as an organiser, a propagandist and revolutionary agitator during that period of less than a year can be given in some detail thanks to the fact that in the course of an allied bombardment of Ancona, during the last war, a police station was destroyed. Two anarchists, searching among the debris, found the police dossier on Malatesta which Borghi published as an appendix to the post-war edition of his biography of Malatesta.[40] The material printed comes from the diary of the Captain of the Carabineers of Ancona.

"Malatesta's return from London was the signal for a reawakening of the anarchist movement in Ancona," which had been reduced to a number of "disorganised and inactive groups" without resources. "Malatesta immediately set about reorganising it. He made revolutionary propaganda at meetings and gatherings; by leaflets and through articles in the weekly journal *Volontà* of which he is the editor and which is the organ of the party."

"In November 1913 after having drawn together all the anarchist elements in Ancona he successfully started a Circle of Social Studies where members and sympathisers meet for readings on social subjects, discussions, and propaganda meetings, which are frequently presided over by Malatesta himself. In a short time in Ancona anarchists and sympathisers number some 600 individuals consisting predominantly of dock porters, workers, and criminal elements of the town." A list of the most prominent anarchists in the town apart from Malatesta "who is the undisputed leader" follows. "They number 33, and to judge from their trades and professions, and their ages are clearly a representative cross section of the working community. They include shoemakers, carpenters, dockworkers, street traders, barbers, shop assistants, and one student. Their ages range from the early twenties, predominate in the thirties."

The Captain also notes in his diary that Malatesta had a season ticket which allowed him to travel anywhere on State railway networks, and "he very frequently travels keeping in contact with the more prominent leaders and in constant touch with the other anarchist groups." And one feels that the next entry is made with a mixture of fear and admiration for the man:

> His qualities as an intelligent, combative speaker who seeks to persuade with calm, and never with violent, language, are used to the full to revive the already spent forces of the party and to win converts and sympathisers, never losing sight of his principal goal which is to draw together the forces of the party and undermine the bases of the State, by hindering its workings, paralyze its services, and doing anti-militarist propaganda, until the favourable occasion arises to overturn and destroy the existing State.

Those who underestimate the perception of the police must surely make an exception here! But then Malatesta was always pointing out to those who sought to put words into his mouth which he had never uttered, in order to launch their attacks on him, that what he had to say was crystal clear and could not be misunderstood. And, one can now add, that not even a policeman could miss the points he made!

From August 1913 to May 1914 the Captain lists 37 noteworthy "anarchist demonstrations" in the province at 21 of which Malatesta took part either as the speaker or one of a panel of speakers.

How many private meetings he attended during those months, even the Captain cannot tell for as he notes: "The organisational work of Malatesta is difficult to penetrate, by reason of the prudence with which he acts, and the discretion of his trusted friends, and the circumspection with which he acts."

And his comrade in arms and biographer, Fabbri,[41] recounts that during his short return to Italy Malatesta also lectured and spoke at meetings in the principal cities of Italy: Rome, Milan, Florence, Turin, Leghorn etc., and in his capacity as journalist attended the conferences of the various parties and workers' organisations of the Left which interested him above all in order to assess what part they might be expected to play in the revolutionary upheaval he pinned his hopes on.

11

It was at the end of Malatesta's brief return to Italy that the "Red Week" (June 1914) exploded. *Freedom* published the following report of "The General Strike and the Insurrection in Italy" by Malatesta himself, who was back in London having only just managed to escape arrest.[42]

> The events which have taken place recently are of the greatest importance, not so much in themselves, but as an indication of the disposition of the Italian people and of what we can anticipate in the near future.
>
> The immediate cause of the outbreak was a massacre of unarmed demonstrators by the gendarmes of the town of Ancona.
>
> For a year the revolutionary and labour organisations of all political shades had been carrying on an agitation in favour of several victims

of military despotism and for the abolition of *disciplinary battalions*, to which are sent all young soldiers known to hold anti-monarchical and anti-bourgeois opinions. The treatment is barbarous, and the unhappy young men are submitted to all kinds of moral and physical tortures.

As the meetings and demonstrations were held all over Italy, but on different dates, they seemed to make but little impression on the Government; and the Trades Council of Ancona proposed, therefore to organise manifestations in the whole country on the same day, that day to be the date of the official celebration of the establishment of Italian unity and Monarchy. As on these occasions great military reviews are always held, the comrades thought that the Government would be obliged to postpone the review in order to hold the troops to preserve "order" and the attention of the whole public would be drawn to the object of the demonstration.

The idea put forward by the Ancona comrades was everywhere received with enthusiasm by all the opposition parties. The Minister ordered the police to prevent any public demonstrations. Of course, that did not deter us. In fact, we had counted on the police prohibition to give more publicity to the demonstration and to instigate the masses to resistance.

To stop the people who were leaving a meeting-hall from going to the central square to demonstrate, the gendarmes fired on the unarmed crowd, killing three workers, and wounding twenty more. After this massacre, the gendarmes, frightened, rushed to the barracks for shelter, and the people were left masters of the town. Without anybody mentioning the word, a general strike was soon complete, and workers collected at the Trades Council to hold a meeting.

The Government tried to prevent the events of Ancona from being telegraphed to other parts of the country; but nevertheless by-and-by the news became known, and strikes broke out in all the towns of Italy. The two Federal labour organisations of Italy, the General Confederation of labour, which is reformist, and the *Unione Sindacale*, with revolutionary tendencies, proclaimed a general strike, and the same was done by the Railwaymen's Union.

These strikes and demonstrations in several towns provoked new conflicts with police, and new massacres. At once, without any common understanding, one place ignorant of what the other was doing, as communications were broken off, the movement assumed everywhere an insurrectional character, and in many places the Republic, which meant for the people the autonomous Commune, was proclaimed.

All was going splendidly; the movement was developing, and the railway strike, spreading on all lines, paralyzed the Government; the workers were beginning to take measures of practical Communism in view of reorganising social life on a new basis; when suddenly the Confederation of labour, by an act which has been qualified as treachery, ordered the strike off, thereby throwing the workers into confusion and discouraging them.

The Government was not slow to profit by this condition, and began to restore "order."

If it had not been for the betrayal of the Confederation, though we could not yet have the revolution for the lack of necessary preparation and understanding, the movement would certainly have assumed larger proportions and a much greater importance.

In every way these events have proved that the mass of the people hate the present order; that the workers are disposed to make use of all opportunities to overthrow the. Government; and that when the fight is directed against the common enemy—that is to say, the Government and the bourgeoisie—all are brothers, though the names of Socialist, Anarchist, Syndicalist, or Republican may seem to divide them.

Now it is up to revolutionaries to profit by these good dispositions.

12

Shortly after his return to London war broke out (August 1914) and not only was any anarchist activity made more difficult by the physical restrictions it imposed, but the fact that the anarchist movement itself was divided in its attitude to the conflagration meant that much of its activity would be neutralised by internal polemics. In *Freedom*, November 1914 we find articles by Kropotkin, Jean Grave, Tcherkessoff, and a letter by the Belgian anarchist

Verbelen all putting forward arguments why anarchists should support the Allied cause. And to rebut their rationalisations was Malatesta's contribution: "Anarchists have forgotten their Principles" (see Appendix I). The title was unfortunate since, as Malatesta notes in the first paragraph it applied to a minority of anarchists, even if among them were "comrades whom we love and respect most," yet the author of the recent study of *The Anarchists* has used the title, to imply that Malatesta was a lone voice in a pro-war anarchist wilderness:

> He [Malatesta] quarrelled with Kropotkin over Kropotkin's support for the war; and he remained a voice of the anarchist conscience constantly declaring that—to quote the title of one of his English articles of 1914—"The Anarchists have forgotten their principles."[43]

As Mr. Joll notes later: "[in 1919] Malatesta returned to Italy in triumph" (p.179) and that Kropotkin's "position" when he returned to Russia in the summer of 1917 "was a curious one, for his support of the war had alienated him from nearly all the revolutionaries on the left" (p.180).

Indeed, but for the fact that the then editor of *Freedom*, Thomas Keell, who was as opposed to the war as Malatesta and the overwhelming majority of the anarchist movement, was concerned as editor of an anarchist journal to give the "pro-war anarchists" more than a fair hearing, Kropotkin and his supporters would have found themselves in the political wilderness sooner than they did.

When Italy joined the allies Malatesta reiterated his opposition to war in an article headed *Italy Also!* (*Freedom*, June 1915). In it he laments that in spite of "the fact that the great majority of Socialists and Syndicalists, and all the Anarchists (except a very few) were solid against war" which "gave us the hope that Italy would escape the massacre and keep all her forces for the works of peace and civilisation," Italy "has been dragged into the slaughter." And he adds:

> We do not know, for want of reliable information, the present situation in Italy, and what are the true factors that have determined so quick a change in her attitude. But one redeeming feature is revealed by the news received in London.

> The Italian government has felt that it was not safe to make war without suppressing every liberty, and putting in prison a great number of Anarchists.
>
> This means that the Anarchists remain loyal to their flag to the last, and what is more important, that the Government fears their influence on the masses.
>
> This gives us the assurance that as soon as the war fever has calmed down we will be able to begin again our own war—the war for human liberty, equality, and brotherhood—and in better conditions than before, because the people will have had another experience, and what a terrible one! . . .

And in 1916 Malatesta replies to the pro-war Manifesto signed by Kropotkin, Jean Grave, Malato, and thirteen other "old comrades" in the editorial columns of *Freedom*[44] in which he recognises the "good faith and good intentions" of the signatories as being "beyond all question," but must dissociate himself from "comrades who consider themselves able to reconcile anarchist ideas and cooperation with the Governments and capitalist classes of certain countries in their strife against the capitalists and Governments of certain other countries."

But this he had already done in a letter to *Freedom*[45] in the first months of the war in answer to Kropotkin's article in which he argued that "an anti-militarist propagandist ought never to join the anti-militarist agitation without taking in his inner self a solemn vow that in case a war breaks out, notwithstanding all efforts to prevent it, he will give the full support of his action to the country that will be invaded by a neighbour, whosoever the neighbour may be. Because, if the anti-militarists remain mere onlookers on the war, they support by their inaction the invaders; they help them to make slaves of the conquered populations; they aid them to become still stronger, and thus to be a still stronger obstacle to the Social Revolution in the future."

Malatesta's reply was couched in conciliatory terms though it must have been obviously clear to him that there was no possibility of Kropotkin "seeing his error" in view of the known fact that he had been for ten years "preaching against the 'German danger.'"

Dear Comrade—Allow me to say a few words on Kropotkin's article on Anti-militarism published in your last issue. In my opinion, anti-militarism is the doctrine which affirms that military service is an abominable and murderous trade, and that a man ought never to consent to take up arms at the command of the masters, and never fight except for the Social Revolution.

Is this to misunderstand anti-militarism?

Kropotkin seems to have forgotten the antagonism of the classes, the necessity of economic emancipation, and all the Anarchist teachings; and says that an anti-militarist ought always to be ready, in case a war breaks out, to take arms in support of the "country that will be invaded"; which considering the impossibility, at least for the ordinary workman, of verifying in time who is the real aggressor, practically means that Kropotkin's "anti-militarist" ought always to obey the orders of his government. What remains after that of anti-militarism, and, indeed, of Anarchism too?

As a matter of fact, Kropotkin renounces anti-militarism because he thinks that the national questions must be solved before the social question. For us, national rivalries and hatreds are among the best means the masters have for perpetuating the slavery of the workers, and we must oppose them with all our strength. And so to the right of the small nationalities to preserve, if you like, their language and their customs, that is simply a question of liberty, and will have a real and final solution only when, the States being destroyed, every human group, nay, every individual, will have the right to associate with, and separate from, every other group.

It is very painful for me to oppose a beloved friend like Kropotkin, who has done so much for the cause of Anarchism. But for the very reason that Kropotkin is so much esteemed and loved by us all, it is necessary to make known that we do not follow him in his utterances on the war.

I know that this attitude of Kropotkin is not quite new, and that for more than ten years he has been preaching against the "German danger"; and I confess that we were in the wrong in not giving importance to his Franco-Russian patriotism, and in not foreseeing where his anti-

> German prejudices would land him. It was because we understood that he meant to invite the French workers to answer a possible German invasion by making a Social Revolution—that is, by taking possession of the French soil, and trying to induce the German workers to fraternise with them in the struggle against French and German oppressors. Certainly we should never have dreamt that Kropotkin could invite the workers to make common cause with governments and masters.
>
> I hope he will see his error, and be again on the side of the workers against all the Governments and all the bourgeois: German, English, French, Russian, Belgian, etc.
>
> Yours fraternally,
> E. Malatesta

13

Malatesta spent many, years of his exile in London. When he arrived in 1900 he was forty-seven and at the height of his intellectual powers, and apart from the period 1913–14 spent so actively in Italy, remained in London until the end of 1919. Why did the old Internationalist apparently remain relatively inactive for so many years? It is significant that even Nettlau in his detailed biography of Malatesta has nothing to say about those years other than references to his anti-war stand and the criminal libel case against Malatesta (in 1913) which earned him a three month's prison sentence and a recommendation for deportation, which was not however proceeded with by the Home Secretary thanks to widespread demonstrations and protests which had made clear in what high esteem Malatesta was held by a wide public in this country.

One knows that Keell, for most of those years closely connected with *Freedom*, as printer and later as editor too had a high regard for him, and in the *Freedom Bulletin* of December 1932 which was a Malatesta Memorial number, Keell recounts that "if he were asked to write an article he would at first refuse, saying we should get English comrades to write for an English paper; but in the end he usually agreed." Judging by the number of his articles one finds in the files of *Freedom* for those years one can only conclude that he was not often asked! To what extent was Malatesta inhibited from working with the English movement and contributing to *Freedom* because of his differences with Kropotkin (with whom he was always careful to avoid engaging in public polemic—though this did not prevent him from pursuing his own line of thought in all his Italian writings)? Nettlau in an important series of articles on Malatesta after his death explains that his reluctance to join issue with Kropotkin was not for "reasons of friendship, but because he thought that the position Kropotkin had established for himself in the public mind in the large countries, by his personality, his intelligence and prestige, was an asset of great importance to the anarchist movement" and that only when Kropotkin sought to use it in favour of the Allies in the First World War did Malatesta feel obliged to challenge his old friend and comrade.[46]

14

As well as contributing to a large number of journals during his lifetime, (and of course many of his articles were translated and published in journals throughout the world) Malatesta was the editor of a number, never however for a long time, mainly because of police attention or government suppression. The list includes *Questione Sociale* (Florence, 1883–84; Buenos Aires 1885; Paterson, NJ, 1899–1900), *l'Associazione* (Ancona, 1889–90), *l'Agitazione* (Ancona, 1897–98), *Volontà* (Ancona, 1913–14), *Umanità Nova* (1920–22), *Pensiero e Volontà* (1924–26).[47] Malatesta never wrote a full scale work on his ideas, and the means by which he thought they could be achieved, even though one finds him hinting in a letter to Fabbri that he might do something to please Fabbri in this respect, just as he never wrote his memoirs in spite of all kinds of attractive offers by publishers to do so.[48] His pamphlets mostly written at the end of the last century include *Anarchy* (1891) and those famous dialogues *Fra Contadini* (1884), *Al Caffè* (1902), *In Tempo di Elezioni* (1890) which had an immense success at the time though we are all too sophisticated today to have our propaganda in this form (it's now done "live" on Television!).

15

After the years of frustration in London during the 1914–18 War, Malatesta after much difficulty managed to return to Italy at the end of 1919 and the next three years (apart from a period of ten months in prison) were probably among the most active and rewarding in his long lifetime even though once again the hoped-for insurrection did not materialise, and the defeat of the working-class movement in Italy was to be marked by Mussolini's "march" to power. As well as editing the daily anarchist paper *Umanità Nova*, Malatesta addressed meetings all over Italy, and was engaged in seeking to bring together all the revolutionary elements in the Socialist and republican parties, and in the Trade Union movement. A detailed study of this period would be a rewarding task for it would not only give a clear picture of Malatesta at work and his method of working, but also show to what extent a movement without large resources, and including in its ranks all shades of anarchism, including anti-organisers and believers in organisation, could work together for a common cause.

One would, of course, see the shortcomings, and the weaknesses, but one would also find, in my opinion, even greater shortcomings in the other anti-fascist, and revolutionary movements in spite of (or perhaps because of?) their authoritarian structure. The anarchists failed to stop Mussolini, but so too did the Socialist and Communist parties as well as the Trades Union organisations.

Umanità Nova managed to survive for over two years, against all kinds of physical difficulties, from paper rationing to the destruction of the printing works and offices by gangs of young fascist thugs, and at its peak had a daily circulation of 50,000 copies. At the height of the agitation among the industrial workers, Malatesta, Borghi (who was then secretary of the Unione Sindacale Italiana, the revolutionary syndicalist Union which had sprung into life after the war and had a membership of more than 500,000), and some 80 other anarchists were arrested (October 1920) and were held in prison awaiting trial until the following July. At their trial which lasted four days, and which Malatesta used to great effect to plead his political cause, they were acquitted by the jury and set free.[49] He moved to Rome where *Umanità Nova* had been transferred in May 1921, and resumed his activity on the paper "giving it an orientation more in keeping with the situation" (Fabbri) and at the same time "seeking to draw together all the revolutionary and libertarian forces of resistance." His task was made more difficult because he now not only had to combat the opposition and sabotage of the reformist union leadership but also the hostility of the newly created Communist Party, which was trying to destroy and discredit all the working class forces which were not its creatures.

There was too, Fabbri points out, the beginnings of an internal crisis within the anarchist movement itself, (which, in certain parts of Italy because of fascist gangsterism was being reduced to impotence) and Malatesta used all his tact and experience to keep the movement together. During this period, as well as participating in the internal activities of the movement, he played a large part in the creation of the "Workers' Alliance" which sought to bring together the anti-fascist forces and which included all the workers organisations. Faced with the growing provocation of the fascists, the Alliance played its last card: the general strike. At the end of July the general strike took place and—according to Fabbri—"was successful throughout the country, at least where circumstances still permitted; but the desperate attempt nevertheless did not achieve its objective and was drowned in blood by the fascist hordes and the official police."

So far as propaganda activities were concerned the situation rapidly worsened. By now it was virtually impossible to distribute *Umanità Nova* outside Rome and district, for parcels were either seized, by the postal authorities or at news agents kiosks and burnt, a fate suffered not only by the anarchist press but by all anti-fascist journals. In the circumstances *Umanità Nova* ceased its daily publications in August 1922 and appeared as a weekly until the end of the year when Malatesta and a number of anarchists connected with the paper were arrested and charged. But it was obviously only a pretext to destroy the paper, for they were shortly afterwards released without trial. (Mussolini's "March" on Rome took place in October 1922.)

16

Seeing no immediate possibility of continuing his activities as a propagandist, Malatesta put his pen to one side and took up his tool bag and, at the age of seventy started work again as an electrician-mechanic. He occasionally wrote however in two other anarchist journals which continued intermittently for a little while longer: *Il Libero Accordo* an old anarchist journal edited by Temistocle Monticelli, and *Fede!* a weekly started by Gigi Damiani.[50]

Malatesta's 70th birthday (December 1923) was the occasion for public meetings in Paris, Buenos Aires, and elsewhere, and even in Rome and other parts of Italy it was celebrated but only at private meetings in view of the political repression. But equally important was the decision of many of his friends to give him the opportunity to continue to contribute to anarchist ideas, free from the day-to-day need to earn his living at his trade. And in fact at the beginning of 1924 he issued the first number of the bi-monthly magazine *Pensiero e Volontà*.[51] In the first year of publication Press censorship was introduced after the murder (June 1924) of Matteotti, the socialist deputy (whose death caused such widespread revulsion as to threaten the fascist regime) and the magazine appeared regularly (24 issues) but its existence became more and more difficult. Only 16 issues appeared in 1925, and the feature "news of the fortnight" was forbidden by the authorities. In due course even theoretical articles were banned by the Censor and in 1926 16 issues appeared as well as five others heavily censored. The last issue was dated October 10, 1926. Before the next issue was due to appear, the anarchist, Anteo Zamboni, had made his unsuccessful attempt on Mussolini's life, and this was a pretext for the fascist government to suppress the whole anti-fascist, as well as the simply independent, press in Italy. Nettlau[52] considers that Malatesta published in *Pensiero e Volontà* "many of his most mature writings" (and readers of this volume have an opportunity to judge for themselves since I have drawn heavily on them) and Fabbri adds that through it Malatesta had been able "to remain in contact with comrades in all parts of Italy and abroad, and continue to participate, within the limits of what was possible, in the active movement."

With the suppression of *Pensiero e Volontà* Malatesta's voice in Italy was silenced "forever," though he contributed a number of important articles to the international anarchist press, and which Nettlau, rightly I think, considers as "invaluable and the most notable production of modern Anarchist literature, something based upon an experience and keen reflection . . ."[53] The quality of these writings can be judged by his Recollections on Kropotkin which was probably the last of these occasional writings penned during the last five years of his life.[54] Notable too is his long introductory piece to Nettlau's thoroughgoing study of the International in Italy 1928[55] and his serene, uncompromising polemic with the Revisionists (Makhno and others) in 1927.[56]

It was not new for Malatesta to have his steps dogged by policemen, and his movements noted by the police of the world. From the end of 1926 until he died in 1932 he lived in Rome under house arrest. A permanent police post was established in the porch of the house where he lived with his companion and her daughter, as well as a police guard day and night outside his flat. Whoever came to see him was arrested; and when he went out anybody approaching him was arrested. His mail was opened and not always delivered to him. Fabbri and other comrades in Paris and Switzerland tried to persuade him to leave Italy but he insisted that if he were capable of doing anything it would be by remaining in Italy and not in exile. By 1930 when he seems to have lost hope of any early change of regime and was prepared to leave, it was then too late.

17

Malatesta must have met a great many of the most active as well as the "eminent" anarchists in the international movement, for there were periods in his lifetime when he travelled extensively, often taking part in the struggles in the countries he visited, and one feels that the absence of dogmatism from his approach to anarchism and the struggle was impressed on him by his experiences of the different problems and revolutionary possibilities that distinguished one country from another. Nettlau has briefly summarised Malatesta's activities outside Italy.[57]

His travels and temporary residence provided him with new local experience, and he helped on his side the local comrades.

In Switzerland he knew Locarno and Lugano at various times; Bakunin's Russian friends in 1872, 1873, up to 1875; James Guillaume and the Jurassians, Zürich and Berne, Geneva when the *Révolté* was founded (February, 1879), and on other occasions, for the last time in 1914 on his flight from Italy.

He was in Paris for many months, 1879, 1880, and beginning of 1881; very active in the first Anarchist groups there, soon expelled, returning again, arrested, imprisoned for returning. He nevertheless started in 1889 *L'Associazione* in Nice, but had soon to leave; he was in Paris to observe the May Day movement of 1890, and no doubt on other occasions, but never resident, passing through there in 1914 on his hurried return to London.

In the autumn of 1875 he travelled to Spain; visited Madrid, Cadiz, and Barcelona, and saw the militants of the then proscribed, 1891 and secretly continued, International. He made an open journey, a great lecturing tour, from November, 1891, to January, 1892; but the intimate purpose was the preparation of Revolutionary Days in May, 1892. The tragic Jerez (Andalusia) revolt intervened, and he had to break his journey and leave quickly, reaching London via Lisbon this time.

In Egypt, 1878 and 1882, and in Rumania, 1879, he lived in the Italian *milieu*, though he came to Egypt in 1882 for a revolutionary purpose connected with the natives' revolt in the days of Arabi Pasha. He intended, for romantic reasons (rivalry in combativeness of the young Internationalists with the young Garibaldians), to join the Serbians in their war against Turkey, 1876, but was twice stopped in Austria-Hungary and sent back to Italy.

He passed some time in Belgium in 1880 and a few days in 1881. He visited the country in 1893 during the political general strike, also 1907 during the violent Antwerp dock strike. Holland he knew at the time of the Amsterdam Anarchist Congress, 1907.

In London he saw the early days of the Socialist movement and knew Joseph Lane and Frank Kitz very well. Returning in October 1889, one of his first visits was to the Socialist League, where he saw William Morris. My acquaintance with him dates from that same evening and lasted until a letter of his to me of May 31, 1932, was the last one I got from him.

He lectured in New York and most of the Eastern industrial towns in the United States where Italian workers live (1899–1900). To Cuba, 1900, for Spanish lectures.

In the Argentine Republic, his activities from 1885 to the first half of 1889, mark the beginning of a more intense and coordinated movement there.

After the Russian revolution of 1917—I do not know at what stage of the ensuing events—he wished to go to Russia, to see things with his own eyes, but the British Government refused to let him depart.

This covers about all his known movement, though I do not pretend that I can retrace all his steps.

His last journey abroad was made in September, 1922, when a Jessinese comrade led him across the high mountains on smuggler paths in Switzerland, where he met the Italian Anarchists residing there in Biel, and the local and international comrades in St. Imier, at a private conference in commemoration of the St. Imier Congress of 1872, of which he was the sole survivor. When the meeting was over, the Swiss police with their order of expulsion of 1879 wanted to get hold of him, but he had just that moment been spirited away and returned to Italy.

18

One other aspect of Malatesta's political life which deserves to be studied in some detail but to which I must be content with only a brief reference, is his attitude to police officials and to imprisonment.

In his time the ordinary policeman in Italy was more often than not some "poor devil"—as he would say—from the hungry South, less interested in protecting the State or of satisfying his personal lust for power, than in ensuring that he and his family could afford a square meal once a day. So Malatesta never missed an opportunity to "seduce" his captors by pointing out to them the relationship between the anarchist struggle and their struggle to live, and there are dozens of delightful anecdotes which illustrate Malatesta's successful technique with policemen and jailers.[58] I would say that the times have changed, that the proportion of "poor devils" engaged in these jobs has considerably decreased in the past forty years, and that Malatesta who was a pragmatist, would today probably adopt quite another tactic. (Even the cover picture to this volume would indicate that the "rapport" with the British "bobby" in 1912 was not flowing with brotherly love even in one so experienced in handling policemen!)

In his youth, as he has already told us earlier in these Notes, being arrested and going to prison were part of the young revolutionaries' apprenticeship: "persecution only awakened our enthusiasm." But he also pointed out that in those days police persecution was a "joke compared with what took place later." It seems clear that during the 16 months he spent in prison awaiting trial for his part in the abortive attempt at insurrection in Benevento in 1877 (which resulted in the acquittal of all concerned)[59] Malatesta had decided that he could better serve his ideas outside than behind prison bars and whenever, therefore, he knew that his activities were about to be curtailed by the authorities, he generally chose the road of exile rather than long months in prison awaiting trial.

Some of the most vulgar and vocal of his political enemies accused him of cowardice, of running away when he should be facing the music;[60] on one occasion in the early twenties, they accused him of cowardice because he took shelter in a doorway during an exchange of shots between police and demonstrators.[61] Malatesta in spite of his rhetorical sortie to the jury at his trial in 1922 "though I am a man with a cause (*un uomo di fede*) I am not a hero." The spirit is willing, the flesh is weak' say the mystics. I love life, I love many people who love me . . ."[62] was playing his cards for one end only, acquittal in order to resume the struggle for revolution as the only answer to the threat of fascism. Had Malatesta and Borghi been free to continue their propaganda during those 10 vital months awaiting trial who knows how the political situation might have developed. It might well have ended in the way it did. But can anyone say that their imprisonment *furthered the revolutionary cause?*

Malatesta was neither a coward nor a hero; he was a courageous and determined man who used these qualities with intelligence. As it was this did not prevent him from spending more time in prison than he would have liked! To the jury at his trial in 1922 he said: "Though I have only served seven months of the sentences imposed on me—all the other sentences were either quashed or annulled by amnesties—yet Authority has managed to make me spend, in bits and pieces, more than ten years of my life in prison."[63] That is, *awaiting* trial, which more often than not ended in acquittal. Those of us accustomed to British penal procedure will find it difficult to understand how, for instance Malatesta, should have been kept in prison in Italy in 1883 from May to November, awaiting trial and then when found guilty and sentenced to three years imprisonment, released pending appeal, during which time he edited an anarchist paper in Florence (and also tended the sick in the cholera epidemic in Naples). And then managing to escape in the nick of time when he learned that his appeal had failed! Instead of three years in an Italian prison Malatesta spent them in Argentina (1885–89) where he did much to help build up the anarchist and syndicalist movement in that country (the only one, apart from Italy, Spain, and Russia in very exceptional circumstances, which in later years managed to publish a daily anarchist paper for a number of years).[64]

Malatesta, the mature revolutionary, took "calculated" risks, that is, he was prepared to face imprisonment if he felt the revolutionary possibilities justified the risk and he had a chance of fulfilling his assignment before being arrested. Thus in 1897 after the fall of the Crispi government there were possibilities of doing anarchist propaganda openly in Italy, and though his three year sentence of 1883 could be executed until November of that year when it would then automatically lapse, Malatesta thought it worth taking the risk and returned secretly to Ancona in March where he lived in a room from which he edited the weekly anarchist journal *l'Agitazione*. To avoid capture by the Italian police who had been alerted of his disappearance from London he had to refrain from any public activities or appearance at propaganda meetings; the fact that the police suspected that he might be in Ancona also meant that all his contacts with the local comrades, many of them known to, or watched by, the police, had to be conducted with the utmost circumspection. Because he could not by force of circumstances be distracted from his editorial functions by meetings and demonstrations, Fabbri[65] considers *l'Agitazione* "historically and theoretically," the most important publication edited by Malatesta. (I have unfortunately been unable to see a single copy of this journal though many of Malatesta's articles have been included in the two volumes of selections published in Naples in the post-War years.[66])

Malatesta would have continued to live clandestinely even after his earlier sentence had automatically expired because he feared that the police would arrest him on any pretext just to keep him from his propaganda which was producing results, and was obviously not to the liking of the then Italian government. Through no indiscretion on his part the police came to know of his hideout and he was arrested but set free the same day. That was in November. Between then and January Malatesta now free to take part in public activities intensified his work, but, as he had expected, the authorities did not leave him alone for long. On the 18th January 1898, during a public demonstration he and eight other comrades including the manager of the weekly were arrested in the street and charged with "criminal association."

One of the interesting aspects of this trial was that whereas in past trials most anarchists denied the charge on the grounds that they were opposed to organisation, Malatesta and his friends not only declared that they were organised, but also demanded the right of anarchists to join a formal organisation. This gave rise to agitation throughout Italy for "the freedom to organise," promoted by the Anarchist Socialist Federation of Romagna, and supported energetically from the columns of *l'Agitazione*, which continued publication in spite of further arrests of those who had taken Malatesta's place on the paper (among them Fabbri, a young man of 20). By the time the trial took place, four months later, over 3,000 anarchists, in the name of many groups and clubs had signed a public manifesto in which they declared their political beliefs, and affirmed that they were members of a "party," and in complete agreement with the accused. More support came from all parts of the world.

Thus the trial, writes Fabbri, was converted into a battle for public rights, as well as being, as many others were, an excellent medium for anarchist propaganda. It lasted a whole week, at the end of which Malatesta was given a seven month sentence, seven other comrades received six months and one was acquitted. Nevertheless this was a victory in that from then on the right of anarchists to organise themselves was recognised, and though this did not prevent them from being arrested and charged with "subversive" activities, the penalties were less severe and the powers of arrest were less arbitrary. Or were they?

A month after Malatesta's trial widespread popular riots in Milan took place which were violently put down with many dead and wounded among the demonstrators. *l'Agitazione* was banned and most of the members of the publishing group, who were still free, were arrested. Parliament approved emergency laws, and *domicilio coatto* (banishment to the penal islands) was reintroduced under worse conditions than before. So when Malatesta's sentence expired in August (and his seven comrades, a month earlier) instead of being released they were held in prison and sentenced to five years *domicilio coatto.*

19

Malatesta was sent to Ustica and he soon decided that he would not willingly spend five years on this inhospitable island, and began laying his plans for escape. The Government having also guessed his intentions, had Malatesta transferred to the island of Lampedusa, a more difficult island from which to escape! What the government had overlooked was the sympathetic "governor" on Lampedusa who was so impressed by Malatesta and the other "politicals" that he gave them a free hand, "and closed his eyes to what was going on."[67] Malatesta made his plans for escape carefully and unhurriedly. Not only did he find a way of establishing contact with those on the mainland, but Fabbri recounts that even the socialist Oddino Morgari, who visited the island, in his capacity of Parliamentary deputy, was privy to his plans. On the night of May 9, 1899, Malatesta, Vivoli, a comrade from Florence, and a civil detainee swam to a fishing boat anchored some way out (with a Sicilian socialist Lovetere aboard) boarded her and set sail for Malta. Their escape was discovered the next day because of the unexpected visit to the island of a government inspector sent to investigate rumours circulating in Rome about Malatesta's escape plans! But they were too late. Malatesta reached Malta where he remained a week awaiting a ship to take him to England. A few days later he was back with the Defendi family in Islington. But within a matter of a few weeks he was on his way to Paterson, New Jersey, at the invitation of the Italian comrades there who wanted him to take over the editorship of their periodical *La Questione Sociale.* However, he remained in the United States only a few months, during which time as well as editing the paper he addressed many public meetings, in Italian and Spanish, throughout the continent. Before returning to London he spent ten days in Cuba where he had been invited to address a number of meetings. In spite of difficulties by the police who at first prohibited his meetings and then agreed to their being held so long as he didn't use the word anarchy, Malatesta managed to address four meetings but then decided that it was not worth going on with the tour and returned to New York in March. In April he was back in London.

Fabbri writes that "personal reasons determined his decision to return to London" but gives no indication whether these were political or domestic. There was obviously no political reason for returning to London, but there might well have been for leaving the United States. Nettlau writes that Malatesta's support for organisation always met with strong opposition from the individualist anarchists.[68] His invitation to edit the anarchist journal in Paterson coincided with the announcement that the former editor Giuseppe Ciancabilla was starting another paper, *Aurora,* with the support of "all" the comrades. Though I, and readers of these notes, may see no point now in establishing the facts of Malatesta's activities during those months, in detail, I referred to it in the first place in ordering to illustrate Malatesta's practical attitude to the propaganda value of imprisonment. His arrest, trial and imprisonment in 1898, was in his opinion good propaganda, the culmination of long months of clandestine activity as editor of *l'Agitazione.* The prospect of five years in the penal islands was not. Hence his determination to escape at all costs. Perhaps those five years, with the exception of the months in the Americas, were not as rewarding as he might have wished, but I suggest that they were better spent both so far as he was concerned and the anarchist movement, than if he had served his five years in *domicilio coatto.*

The other reason for referring to the months in the States is to state the facts concerning an incident in which Malatesta was the central figure. At a meeting he was addressing in West Hoboken (now Union City, New Jersey) heated discussion followed in which one member of the audience challenged the speaker, and when Malatesta "put him in his place" he was obviously so incensed that he drew out a revolver and fired at him hitting him in the leg. He was disarmed by a man "one of the most tolerant you could find, and a member of Malatesta's group"[69] the man, who months later was to return to Italy to assassinate King Humbert: Gaetano Bresci.

The false rumour was circulated that Malatesta's assailant was another anarchist, and one can understand with what relish this tit-bit of political scandal was repeated by the anarchists' detractors on every possible occasion. Some thirty years after the shooting it was revived with the publication of Max Nomad's *Rebels and Renegades* and the anarchists in the United States through their journals had to repeat the true facts, but they could never delete the falsehoods committed to print in Nomad's book. Indeed thirty years after Nomad, George Woodcock (who should have known better than to rely on Nomad for source material) in his history of anarchism (American edition) repeats the lie, naming Ciancabilla as Malatesta's would-be assassin.

In itself the shooting incident is a minor incident in a long and full life and it is as such that it is treated in these Notes. But from the point of view of anarchist propaganda the Nomad-Woodcock version could do great harm even now, and for this reason the facts of the shooting incident are presented as an Appendix,[70] because I hope that English historians who may want to include Malatesta in their magnus opus, and are barred from consulting the original sources by language problems, will at least consult this work rather than Nomad's concoction of half-truths and pure invention!

20

At the beginning of these notes I quoted a passage from Woodcock's History in which he describes Malatesta and other young Internationalists as "the Italian equivalent of the conscience-stricken Russian noblemen" who in the same decade felt the burning urge to go to the people, and produced evidence to try to show that the analogy was not a correct one. I return to it now because

Malatesta's character was so unlike this generalisation, and his approach to the social problems so different, that only by fully appreciating this can one put his sixty years militancy in proper perspective.

All the evidence points to the fact that Malatesta did not have a sheltered youth, even though it is clear that his family had the means to allow him to pursue his studies without having to worry about his next meal. His entry into politics was typical of a normal, impulsive "teenager" and just as so many young people in this country were drawn into some kind of political commitment by the enthusiasm that surrounded the first Aldermaston March, so many in Malatesta's time must have felt the same way as a result of the daring exploits of Garibaldi and his "liberators." (And according to Nettlau it is possible that Malatesta as a young boy actually witnessed the liberators in action when Santa Maria and Capua were the centres of fierce struggles.) But what is surely significant in Malatesta's case is that in a matter of three or four years he had "seen through," as well as sympathised with, the Garibaldians and the Mazzinians, and also "discovered" Bakunin and the International. And his mental development took place in the course of political activities of all kinds which gave him an early taste of Authority and government. By contrast both Bakunin and Kropotkin entered the struggle following a relatively long intellectual preparation. Kropotkin was in his 30th year when he made his "first journey abroad" and began reading all the "socialistic literature" he could lay hands on. In his Memoirs he writes:

> I spent days and nights in reading, and received a deep impression which nothing will efface. . . . The more I read the more I saw that there was before me a new world, unknown to me, and totally unknown to the learned makers of sociological theories—a world that I could know only by living in the Workingmen's Association and by meeting the workers in their everyday life. I decided accordingly to spend a couple of months in such a life. . . .[71]

For Bakunin it was in Dresden in 1842—when he was 28—that, to quote Carr, he "was ready to proclaim to the world his conversion to the cause of revolution."

> The winter of 1841–42 which he spent alone in Berlin seems to have been the decisive period of Bakunin's conversion. He devoured greedily the mass of pamphlets and dissertations with which the young Hegelians under the very nose of the censors, were flooding Germany. . . . By the time he settled again in Dresden in the summer of 1842, Bakunin was a full-blown young Hegelian. Ruge discovered that he had "outstripped all the old donkeys in Berlin."[72]

For Malatesta, "going to the people" involved total identification with the working people *as one of them*. And this he did early in life. As soon as he came into his inheritance he handed the properties to his working tenants and what money came to him was used for propaganda. In his early twenties he learned the trade of mechanic in the workshop of a friend and Internationalist, one Agenore Natta of Florence.[73] Throughout his long life Malatesta earned his living as a mechanic-electrician, except when the political situation demanded, and the anarchist movement could afford to keep him, while he devoted his activities full time to the political struggle. Just as he was always opposed to permanent Union officials and organisers, so was he opposed to revolutionaries, being "kept" by the movement. It was not only a matter of principle, that is a rule based on experience, of the harmful effects that inevitably accrued from full-time officials, but also an expression of his own independent spirit, which could not be free unless he were also financially independent of the anarchist movement.

This is why it is wrong to portray Malatesta as the professional agitator and revolutionary, in fact, as well as in the interest of the anarchist movement. For if his life is as important to the anarchist movement as are his ideas, it is just because he was neither the professional revolutionary nor "the saint," neither the "prophet" nor the "man of destiny." Malatesta was always a comrade among comrades, ever seeking to forward his point of view but never seeking to dominate an argument with the weight of his personality. In this connection it is significant that as a speaker he never used oratorical tricks, just as in his writings he was always concerned with convincing readers by the clarity, the logic, and sheer commonsense of his arguments. And because of this approach, rather than in spite of it, all his writings, and I am sure his speeches too, are full of real human warmth for they are based on understanding of the problems (as well as the difficulties in overcoming them) that face all those who are willing and anxious to do something to radically change society.

Malatesta was fully aware of the dangers, as well as the advantages, that the "eminence" or "notoriety" he and a few others enjoyed in the international anarchist movement and in the world of Left politics. It is probably true to say that he went out of his way to underestimate his worth so far as the anarchist movement was concerned, but to exploit his standing in the working class movement whenever he thought it imperative to bring together all the movements and parties of the so-called revolutionary Left to accept an *Entente* on specific issues. Malatesta was always very "politically conscious," without ever becoming, however, a politician. He explored every political opening—as some of his political enemies were to remind him years later, without however adding the important point, that Malatesta the anarchist emerged unscathed from his excursions along "the paths of political evil"! His anarchism was not in his head but in his heart, or to quote his words "This feeling is the love of mankind, and the fact of sharing the sufferings of others. . . ." But in order to achieve his ends he was always guided by his "head"—that is by his observation and understanding of the human and material problems to be overcome.

21

In a much publicised recent work on *The Anarchists*, the author,[74] from his cloistered university outpost pronounces sentence on "a disappointed life" when he declares that at the end of Malatesta's life (1932) "The Italian State was . . . a stronger and more formidable adversary than it had ever been." But surely, Malatesta's life was full, and rich, and satisfying; his ideas still stimulating, and informed by the kind of common sense and humanity millions of our fellow beings have yet to discover.

And is there no lesson to be learned about what *matters* in our lives, as individuals, and as a civilisation, when, more than thirty years after his death, Malatesta the man and his ideas, are being presented to the English speaking public more or less for the first time, while at the same time the world is desperately trying to forget that Mussolini and the other sordid actors in that "age of disgrace" ever existed? A thought surely, which those historians who are now so busily writing the obituary notices of anarchism might do well to ponder over!

V.R.

Appendix I

Anarchists Have Forgotten Their Principles
by E. MALATESTA (*Freedom*, November 1914)

At the risk of passing as a simpleton, I confess that I would never have believed it possible that Socialists—even Social Democrats—would applaud and voluntarily take part, either on the side of the Germans or on that of the Allies, in a war like the one that is at present devastating Europe. But what is there to say when the same is done by Anarchists—not numerous, it is true, but having among them comrades whom we love and respect most?

It is said that the present situation shows the bankruptcy of "our formulas"—i.e., of our principles—and that it will be necessary to revise them.

Generally speaking, every formula must be revised whenever it shows itself insufficient when coming into contact with fact; but it is not the case today, when the bankruptcy is not derived from the shortcoming of our formulas, but from the fact that these have been forgotten and betrayed.

Let us return to our principles.

I am not a "pacifist." I fight, as we all do, for the triumph of peace and of fraternity among all human beings; but I know that a desire not to fight can only be fulfilled when neither side wants to, and that so long as men will be found who want to violate the liberties of others, it is incumbent on these others to defend themselves if they do not wish to be eternally beaten; and

I also know that to attack is often the best, or the only, effective means of defending oneself. Besides, I think that the oppressed are always in a state of legitimate self-defence, and have always the right to attack the oppressors. I admit, therefore, that there are wars that are necessary, holy wars: and these are wars of liberation, such as are generally "civil wars"—i.e., revolutions.

But what has the present war in common with human emancipation, which is our cause?

Today we hear Socialists speak, just like any bourgeois, of "France," or "Germany," and of other political and national agglomerations—results of historical struggles—as of homogeneous ethnographic units, each having its proper interests, aspirations, and mission, in opposition to the interests, aspirations, and mission of rival units. This may be true relatively, so long as the oppressed, and chiefly the workers, have no self-consciousness, fail to recognise the injustice of their inferior position, and make themselves the docile tools of the oppressors. There is, then, the dominating class only that counts; and this class, owing to its desire to conserve and to enlarge its power, even its prejudices and its own ideas, may find it convenient to excite racial ambitions and hatred, and send its nation, its flock, against "foreign" countries, with a view to releasing them from their present oppressors, and submitting them to its own political and economical domination.

But the mission of those who, like us, wish the end of all oppression and of all exploitation of man by man, is to awaken a consciousness of the antagonism of interests between dominators and dominated, between exploiters and workers, and to develop the class struggle inside each country, and the solidarity among all workers across the frontiers, as against any prejudice and any passion of either race or nationality.

And this we have always done. We have always preached that the workers of all countries are brothers, and that the enemy—the "foreigner"—is the exploiter, whether born near us or in a far-off country, whether speaking the same language or any other. We have always chosen our friends, our companions-in-arms, as well as our enemies, because of the ideas they profess and of the position they occupy in the social struggle, and never for reasons of race or nationality. We have always fought against patriotism, which is a survival of the past, and serves well the interests of the oppressors; and we were proud of being internationalists, not only in words, but by the deep feelings of our souls.

And now that the most atrocious consequences of capitalist and State domination should indicate, even to the blind, that we were in the right, most of the Socialists and many Anarchists in the belligerent countries associate themselves with the Governments and the bourgeoisie of their respective countries, forgetting Socialism, the class struggle, international fraternity, and the rest.

What a downfall!

It is possible that present events may have shown that national feelings are more alive, while feelings of international brotherhood are less rooted, than we thought; but this should be one more reason for intensifying, not abandoning, our anti-patriotic propaganda. These events also show that in France, for example, religious sentiment is stronger, and the priests have a greater influence than we imagined. Is this a reason for our conversion to Roman Catholicism?

I understand that circumstances may arise owing to which the help of all is necessary for the general well-being: such as an epidemic, an earthquake, an invasion of barbarians, who kill and destroy all that comes under their hands. In such a case the class struggle, the differences of social standing must be forgotten, and common cause must be made against the common danger; but on the condition that these differences are forgotten on both sides. If any one is in prison during an earthquake, and there is a danger of his being crushed to death, it is our duty to save everybody, even the gaolers—on condition that the gaolers begin by opening the prison doors. But if the gaolers take all precautions for the safe custody of the prisoners during and after the catastrophe, it is then the duty of the prisoners towards themselves as well as towards their comrades in captivity to leave the gaolers to their troubles, and profit by the occasion to save themselves.

If, when foreign soldiers invade the *sacred soil of the Fatherland*, the privileged class were to renounce their privileges, and would act so that the "Fatherland" really became the common property of all the inhabitants, it would then be right that all should fight against the invaders. But if kings wish to remain kings, and the landlords wish to take care of *their* lands and of *their* houses, and the merchants wish to take care of *their* goods, and even sell them at a higher price, then the workers, the Socialists and Anarchists, should leave them to their own devices, while being themselves on the look-out for an opportunity to get rid of the oppressors inside the country, as well as of those coming from outside.

In all circumstances, it is the duty of the Socialists, and especially of the Anarchists, to do everything that can weaken the State and the capitalist class, and to take as the only guide to their conduct the interests of Socialism; or, if they are materially powerless to act efficaciously for their own cause, at least to refuse any voluntary help to the cause of the enemy, and stand aside to save at least their principles—which means to save the future.

All I have just said is theory, and perhaps it is accepted, in theory, by most of those who, in practice, do just the reverse. How, then, could it be applied to the present situation? What should we do, what should we wish, in the interests of our cause?

It is said, on this side of the Rhine, that the victory of the Allies would be the end of militarism, the triumph of civilisation, international justice, etc. The same is said on the other side of the frontier about a German victory.

Personally, judging at their true value the "mad dog" of Berlin and the "old hangman" of Vienna, I have no greater confidence in the bloody Tsar, nor in the English diplomatists who oppress India, who betrayed Persia, who crushed the Boer Republics; nor in the French bourgeoisie, who massacred the natives of Morocco; nor in those of Belgium, who have allowed the Congo atrocities and have largely profited by them—and I only recall some of their misdeeds, taken at random, not to mention what all Governments and all capitalist classes do against the workers and the rebels in their own countries.

In my opinion, the victory of Germany would certainly mean the triumph of militarism and of reaction; but the triumph of the Allies would mean a Russo-English (i.e., a knouto-capitalist) domination in Europe and in Asia, conscription and the development of the militarist spirit in England, and a Clerical and perhaps Monarchist reaction in France.

Besides, in my opinion, it is most probable that there will be no definite victory on either side. After a long war, an enormous loss of life and wealth, both sides being exhausted, some kind of peace will be patched up, leaving all questions open, thus preparing for a new war more murderous than the present.

The only hope is revolution; and as I think that it is from vanquished Germany that in all probability, owing to the present state of things, the revolution would break out, it is for this reason—and for this reason only—that I wish the defeat of Germany.

I may, of course, be mistaken in appreciating the true position. But what seems to me elementary and fundamental for all Socialists (Anarchists, or others) is that it is necessary to keep outside every kind of compromise with the Governments and the governing classes, so as to be able to profit by any opportunity that may present itself, and, in any case, to be able to restart and continue our revolutionary preparations and propaganda.

A young Errico Malatesta

Appendix II

Pro-Government Anarchists
by E. MALATESTA (*Freedom*, April 1916)

A manifesto has just appeared, signed by Kropotkin, Grave, Malato, and a dozen other old comrades, in which, echoing the supporters of the Entente Governments who are demanding a fight to a finish and the crushing of Germany, they take their stand against any idea of "premature peace."

The capitalist Press publishes, with natural satisfaction, extracts from the manifesto, and announces it as the work of "leaders of the International Anarchist Movement."

Anarchists, almost all of whom have remained faithful to their convictions, owe it to themselves to protest against this attempt to implicate Anarchism in the continuance of a ferocious slaughter that has never held promise of any benefit to the cause of Justice and Liberty, and which now shows itself to be absolutely barren and resultless even from the standpoint of the rulers on either side.

The good faith and good intentions of those who have signed the manifesto are beyond all question. But, however painful it may be to disagree with old friends who have rendered so many services to that which in the past was our common cause, one cannot—having regard to sincerity, and in the interest of our movement for emancipation—fail to dissociate oneself from comrades who consider themselves able to reconcile Anarchist ideas and cooperation with the Governments and capitalist classes of certain countries in their strife against the capitalists and Governments of certain other countries.

During the present war we have seen Republicans placing themselves at the service of kings, Socialists making common cause with the ruling class, labourists serving the interests of capitalists; but in reality all these people are, in varying degrees, Conservatives—believers in the mission of the State, and their hesitation can be understood when the only remedy lay in the destruction of every Governmental chain and the unloosing of the Social Revolution. But such hesitation is incomprehensible in the case of Anarchists.

We hold that the State is incapable of good. In the field of international as well as of individual relations it can only combat aggression by making itself the aggressor; it can only hinder crime by organising and committing still greater crime.

Even on the supposition—which is far from being the truth—that Germany alone was responsible for the present war, it is proved that, as long as governmental methods are adhered to, Germany can only be resisted by suppressing all liberty and reviving the power of all the forces of reaction. Except the popular Revolution, there is no other way of resisting the menace of a disciplined Army but to try and have a stronger and more disciplined Army; so that the sternest anti-militarists, if they are not Anarchists, and if they are afraid of the destruction of the State, are inevitably led to become ardent militarists.

In fact, in the problematical hope of crushing Prussian Militarism, they have renounced all the spirit and all the traditions of Liberty; they have Prussianised England and France; they have submitted themselves to Tsarism; they have restored the prestige of the tottering throne of Italy.

Can Anarchists accept this state of things for a single moment without renouncing all right to call themselves Anarchists? To me, even foreign domination suffered by force and leading to revolt, is preferable to domestic oppression meekly, almost gratefully, accepted, in the belief that by this means we are preserved from a greater evil.

It is useless to say that this is a question of an exceptional time, and that after having contributed to the victory of the Entente in "this war," we shall return, each into his own camp, to the struggle for his own ideal.

If it is necessary today to work in harmony with the Government and the capitalist to defend ourselves against "the German menace," it will be necessary afterwards, as well as during the war.

However great may be the defeat of the German Army—if it is true that it will be defeated—it will never be possible to prevent the German patriots thinking of, and preparing for, revenge; and the patriots of the other countries, very reasonably from their own point of view, will want to hold themselves in readiness so that they may not again be taken unawares. This means that Prussian Militarism will become a permanent and regular institution in all countries.

What will then be said by the self-styled Anarchists who today desire the victory of one of the warring affiances? Will they go on calling themselves anti-militarists and preaching disarmament, refusal to do military service, and sabotage against National Defence, only to become, at the first threat of war, recruiting-sergeants for the Governments that they have attempted to disarm and paralyze?

It will be said that these things will come to an end when the German people have rid themselves of their tyrants and ceased to be a menace to Europe by destroying militarism in their own country. But, if that is the case, the Germans who think, and rightly so, that English and French domination (to say nothing of Tsarist Russia) would be no more delightful to the Germans than German domination to the French and English, will desire first to wait for the Russians and the others to destroy their own militarism, and will meanwhile continue to increase their own country's Army.

And then, how long will the Revolution be delayed? How long Anarchy? Must we always wait for the others to begin?

The line of conduct for Anarchists is clearly marked out by the very logic of their aspirations.

The war ought to have been prevented by bringing about the Revolution, or at least by making the Government afraid of the Revolution. Either the strength or the skill necessary for this has been lacking.

Peace ought to be imposed by bringing about the Revolution, or at least by threatening to do so. To the present time, the strength or the skill is wanting.

Well! there is only one remedy: to do better in future. More than ever we must avoid compromise; deepen the chasm between capitalists and wage-slaves, between rulers and ruled; preach expropriation of private property and the destruction of States as the only means of guaranteeing fraternity between the peoples and Justice and Liberty for all; and we must prepare to accomplish these things.

Meanwhile it seems to me that it is criminal to do anything that tends to prolong the war, that slaughters men destroys wealth, and hinders all resumption of the struggle for emancipation. It appears to me that preaching "war to the end" is really playing the game of the German rulers, who are deceiving their subjects and inflaming their ardour for fighting by persuading them that their opponents desire to crush and enslave the German people.

Today, as ever, let this be our slogan: Down with Capitalists and Governments, all Capitalists and all Governments!

Long live the peoples, all the peoples!

Appendix III

Fact and Fiction on the Shooting Incident at a Meeting Addressed by Malatesta in West Hoboken in 1899

This minor incident in a very full life would have been put in its proper perspective but for the exaggerated importance attributed to it, as well as the falsification of the facts, by writers more concerned with satisfying their publishers' interest and with entertaining the reading public, than with establishing the facts as well as getting them in their proper perspective.

"Max Nomad"—described in the publisher's blurb of the original American edition of his book *Rebels and Renegades*[1] as "the pen-name of a political emigrant from prewar [1914–18] Europe who has been either a sympathetic observer of, or an active participant in the extreme left-wing revolutionary movements" in some European countries as well as in the United States since—devotes the first of his "sketches of persons still living, who have been prominently identified with revolutionary or labour movements," to Malatesta. The sketch, nearly fifty pages long is a combination of the kind of concoction of half truths one would expect from a newspaper hack and the anti-libertarian hysteria of one who at the time [1932], at least, was a revolutionary of the authoritarian school, an admirer of Lenin and Trotsky as well as Stalin and William Z. Foster. Suffice it to say, that in the mid-twentieth century Max Nomad's name crops up in the columns of the

American *Socialist Call* and in the *New Leader* peddling anti-Communism and still as anti-anarchist as ever!

In *Rebels and Renegades,* Nomad writes of Malatesta's stay in America:

> The inevitable discussions as to the merits or demerits of organisation now began again, and this time almost cost him his life. During one of these disputes G. Ciancabilla, the leader of the "anti-organizzatori" seeing that the majority were siding with the old champion, emphasised his own argument by emptying his revolver into the body of his opponent. The hero escaped, and Malatesta, unable to leave the place on account of his wound, was arrested. He refused to name his assailant, although the police left him for a time without any treatment in the hope of forcing him to give the desired information. Ciancabilla remained a prophet among the guardians of the Holy Grail of unrestrained individual liberty, and died a few years later in California where he edited a paper with the fitting title *La Protesta Umana.*

It was an easy matter to demolish Nomad's fantasy: Ciancabilla was not at the meeting at which Malatesta was shot at; and his assailant was one Domenico Pazzaglia, a barber, "unknown to most of the comrades and ignored by the few who knew him."[2] The anarchist monthly *man!* (March 1933)[3] further points out that Ciancabilla disapproved of Pazzaglia's act. The July number of that journal published a letter from Nomad in which he apologised for confusing Ciancabilla with Pazzaglia, but asserts that the latter was a follower of Ciancabilla that is, presumably an "anti-organizzatore." Was Ciancabilla such?

In 1897 he was editor of the socialist paper *Avanti!* (Forward) and published a most interesting interview with Malatesta which took place in "a small railway station, in between trains, and we talked for about an hour, arm in arm, walking up and down the platform under the very noses of two carbineers and a plain clothes detective, detailed to keep a watch on stations."[4]

Apart from the relationship between the two men, which was to become more intimate when Ciancabilla became an anarchist, what is interesting about the preamble to this interview is that this was the period when Malatesta was living incognito in Ancona and the object of a nation-wide police hunt! Was Ciancabilla's preamble one of the many attempts to put the police off the scent, or did he really meet Malatesta in "a small railway station"? I must confess that I am curious to know the answer! Anyway, it was during this period that Ciancabilla as well as a number of other socialists, among them Mamolo Zamboni (father of the Zamboni who years later—in 1926—made the unsuccessful attempt on Mussolini's life) joined the anarchists under the influence of Malatesta. I find it surprising therefore that in so short a time Ciancabilla should have become the spokesman of the individualist section of the Italo-American anarchist movement. Not only was he the Italian translator of Kropotkin's *Conquest of Bread* (we know, Mussolini also translated Kropotkin!) but even in September 1899 he was expressing the view in *Questione Sociale* that he could not conceive individual or collective well-being without order, social services, and "a harmonious society based on associations and collectivities functioning organically."[5]

Thirty years after his libel on Ciancabilla and on Malatesta (for Nomad's potted historical sketch can be faulted factually on every page—irrespective of his sneers and guffaws) George Woodcock's history of anarchism was published in the United States as a paperback,[6] and because Professor Woodcock was content to rely on Nomad rather than Nettlau, Fabbri, Borghi, or even his erstwhile comrades in the English speaking world, for his references to Malatesta, he repeated the Nomad libel, presumably unaware of Nomad's subsequent rectification. Not only must one charge Woodcock with not having checked his sources, especially when they are Marx Nomad; but when he was politely informed of his error by anarchists in the United States, he felt it sufficient to change two words in the passage complained of when his *History* appeared in an English edition[7] to put the record right. I must reproduce the whole paragraph from the American edition in order also to illustrate the slapdash way these professionals of the written word happily churn out the words by the thousand:

> As a result of the tense atmosphere which followed the 1898 rising, Malatesta was not released at the end of his prison term, but instead, with a number of other leaders of the movement, was sent to exile for

> five years on the island of Lampedusa. He did not stay there long. One stormy day he and three of his comrades seized a boat and put out to sea in defiance of the high waves. They were lucky enough to be picked up by a ship on its way to Malta, whence Malatesta sailed to the United States. There his life once again took a sensational turn, which this time almost brought it to an end. He became involved in a dispute with the individualist anarchists of Paterson, who insisted that anarchism implied no organisation at all, and that every man must act solely on his impulses. At last, in one noisy debate, the individual impulse of a certain Ciancabilla directed him to shoot Malatesta who was badly wounded but who obstinately refused to name his assailant. Ciancabilla fled to California, and Malatesta eventually recovered; in 1900 he set sail for London which by now had become his favourite place of exile.

In the Pelican edition, Professor Woodcock deletes the two references to Ciancabilla by name and in place of the first substitutes "a Comrade" and for the second "the would-be assailant." Thus is serious history written: a named comrade becomes "a Comrade" (with a capital C) and "Ciancabilla" becomes the "would-be-assailant" and in Professor Woodcock's two editions both "fled to California." Not in the interests of history but in order to debunk the Woodcocks and the army of self-appointed historians who have neither the love of their *métier* nor a sense of responsibility towards their readers, I have quoted the paragraph from Woodcock's history in full. I do not propose to analyze the paragraph for factual errors,[8] the reader can do this for himself by comparing it with my brief account of this period. I cannot resist however, underlining what I think is the prize sentence from Professor Woodcock's paragraph: "One stormy day he and three of his comrades seized a boat and put out to sea in defiance of the high waves!"

Appendix IV

Pietro Kropotkin—Ricordi E Critiche Di Un Vecchio Amico (Peter Kropotkin—Recollections and Criticisms of an Old Friend) by E. Malatesta (*Studi Sociali*, April 15, 1931)

Peter Kropotkin is without doubt one of those who have contributed perhaps most—perhaps more even than Bakunin and Elisée Reclus—to the elaboration and propagation of anarchist ideas. And he has therefore well deserved the recognition and the admiration that all anarchists feel for him.

But in homage to the truth and in the greater interest of the cause, one must recognise that his activity has not all been wholly beneficial. It was not his fault; on the contrary, it was the very eminence of his qualities which gave rise to the ills I am proposing to discuss.

Naturally, Kropotkin being a mortal among mortals could not always avoid error and embrace the whole truth. One should have therefore profited by his invaluable contribution and continued the search which would lead to further advances. But his literary talents, the importance and volume of his output, his indefatigable activity, the prestige that came to him from his reputation as a great scientist, the fact that he had given up a highly privileged position to defend, at the cost of suffering and danger, the popular cause, and furthermore the fascination of his personality which held the attention of those who had the good fortune to meet him, all made him acquire a notoriety and an influence such that he appeared, and to a great extent he really was, the recognised master for most anarchists.

As a result of which, criticism was discouraged and the development of the anarchist idea was arrested. For many years, in spite of the iconoclastic and progressive spirit of anarchists, most of them so far as theory and propaganda were concerned, did no more than study and quote Kropotkin. To express oneself other than the way he did was considered by many comrades almost as heresy.

It would therefore be opportune to subject Kropotkin's teachings to close and critical analysis in order to separate that which is ever real and alive from that which more recent thought and experience will have shown to be mistaken. A matter which would concern not only Kropotkin, for the errors that one can blame him for having committed were already being professed by anarchists before Kropotkin acquired his eminent place in the movement: he confirmed them and made them last by adding the weight of his talent and his prestige; but all us old militants, or almost all of us, have our share of responsibility.

In writing now about Kropotkin I do not intend to examine his teachings. I only wish to record a few impressions and recollections, which may I believe, serve to make better known his moral and intellectual stature as well as understanding more clearly his qualities and his faults.

But first of all I will say a few words which come from the heart because I cannot think of Kropotkin without being moved by the recollection of his immense goodness. I remember what he did in Geneva in the winter of 1879 to help a group of Italian refugees in dire straits, among them myself; I remember the small attentions, I would call maternal, which he bestowed on me when one night in London having been the victim of an accident I went and knocked on his door; I recall the innumerable kind actions towards all sorts of people; I remember the cordial atmosphere with which he was surrounded. Because he was a really good person, of that goodness which is almost unconscious and needs to relieve all suffering and be surrounded by smiles and happiness. One would have in fact said that he was good without knowing it; in any case he didn't like one saying so, and he was offended when I wrote in an article on the occasion of his 70th birthday that his goodness was the first of his qualities. He would rather boast of his energy and courage—perhaps because these latter qualities had been developed in, and for, the struggle, whereas goodness was the spontaneous expression of his intimate nature.

I had the honour and good fortune of being for many years linked to Kropotkin by the warmest friendship.

We loved each other because we were inspired by the same passion, by the same hopes . . . and also by the same illusions.

Both of us were optimistic by temperament (I believe nevertheless that Kropotkin's optimism surpassed mine by a long chalk and possibly sprung from a different source) and we saw things with rose tinted spectacles—alas! everything was too rosy—we then hoped, and it is more than fifty years ago, in a revolution to be made in the immediate future which was to have ushered in our ideal society. During these long years there were certainly periods of doubt and discouragement. I remember Kropotkin once telling me: "My dear Errico, I fear we are alone, you and I, in believing a revolution to be near at hand." But they were passing moods; very soon confidence returned; we explained away the existing difficulties and the scepticism of the comrades and went on working and hoping.

Nevertheless it must not be imagined that on all questions we shared the same views. On the contrary, on many fundamentals we were far from being in agreement, and almost every time we met we would have noisy and heated discussions; but as Kropotkin always felt sure that right was on his side, and could not calmly suffer to be contradicted, and on the other hand, had great respect for his erudition and deep concern for his uncertain health, these discussions always ended by changing the subject to avoid undue excitement.

But this did not in any way harm the intimacy of our relationship, because we loved each other and because we collaborated for sentimental rather than intellectual reasons. Whatever may have been our differences of interpretation of the facts, or the arguments by which we justified our actions, in practice we wanted the same things and were motivated by the same intense feeling for freedom, justice and the well-being of all mankind. We could therefore get on together.

And in fact there was never serious disagreement between us until that day in 1914 when we were faced with a question of practical conduct of capital importance to both of us: that of the attitude to be adopted by anarchists to the [First World] War. On that occasion Kropotkin's old preferences for all that which is Russian and French were reawakened and exacerbated in him, and he declared himself an enthusiastic supporter of the *Entente*. He seemed to forget that he was an Internationalist, a socialist, and an anarchist; he forgot what he himself had written only a short time before about the war that the Capitalists were preparing, and began expressing admiration for the worst Allied statesmen and Generals, and at the same time treated as cowards the anarchists who refused to join the *Union Sacré*, regretting that his age and his poor health prevented him from taking up a rifle and marching against the Germans. It was impossible therefore to see eye to eye: for me he was a truly pathological case. All the same it was one of the saddest, most painful moments of my life (and, I dare to suggest, for him too) when, after a more than acrimonious discussion, we parted like adversaries, almost as enemies.

Great was my sorrow at the loss of the friend and for the harm done to the cause as a result of the confusion that would be created among the comrades by his defection. But in spite of everything the love and esteem which I felt for the man were unimpaired, just as the hope that once the moment of euphoria had passed and the foreseeable consequences of the war were viewed in their proper perspective, he would admit his mistake and return to the movement, the Kropotkin of old.

Kropotkin was at the same time a scientist and a social reformer. He was inspired by two passions: the desire for knowledge and the desire to act for the good of humanity, two noble passions which can be mutually useful and which one would like to see in all men, without being, for all this, one and the same thing. But Kropotkin was an eminently systematic personality and he wanted to explain everything with one principle, and reduce everything to unity and often, did so, in my opinion, at the expense of logic.

Thus he used science to support his social aspirations, because in his opinion, they were simply rigorous scientific deductions.

I have no special competence to judge Kropotkin as a scientist. I know that he had in his early youth rendered notable services to geography and geology, and I appreciate the great importance of his book on Mutual Aid, and I am convinced that with his vast culture and noble intelligence, could have made a greater contribution to the advancement of the sciences had his thoughts and activity not been absorbed in the social struggle. Nevertheless it seems to me that he lacked that something which goes to make a true man of science; the capacity to forget one's aspirations and preconceptions and observe facts with cold objectivity. He seemed to me to be what I would gladly call, a poet of science. By an original intuition, he might have succeeded in foreseeing new truths, but these truths would have needed to be verified by others with less, or no imagination, but who were better equipped with what is called the scientific spirit. Kropotkin was too passionate to be an accurate observer.

His normal procedure was to start with a hypothesis and then look for the facts that would confirm it—which may be a good method for discovering new things; but what happened, and quite unintentionally, was that he did not see the ones which invalidated his hypothesis.

He could not bring himself to admit a fact, and often not even to consider it, if he had not first managed to explain it, that is to fit it into his system.

As an example I will recount an episode in which I played a part.

When I was in the Argentinian Pampas (in the years 1885 to 1889), I happened to read something about the experiments in hypnosis by the School of Nancy, which was new to me. I was very interested in the subject but had no opportunity at the time to find out more. When I was back again in Europe, I saw Kropotkin in London, and asked him if he could give me some information on hypnosis. Kropotkin flatly denied that there was any truth in it; that it was either all a fake or a question of hallucinations. Some time later I saw him again, and the conversation turned once more onto the subject. To my great surprise I found that his opinion had completely changed; hypnotic phenomena had become a subject of interest deserving to be studied. What had happened then? Had he learned new facts or had he had convincing proofs of those he had previously denied? Not at all. He had, quite simply, read in a book, by I don't know which German physiologist, a theory on the relationship between the two hemispheres of the brain which could serve to explain, well or badly, the phenomena of hypnosis.

In view of this mental predisposition which allowed him to accommodate things to suit himself in questions of pure science, in which there are no reasons why passion should obfuscate the intellect, one could foresee what would happen over those questions which intimately concerned his deepest wishes and his most cherished hopes.

Kropotkin adhered to the materialist philosophy that prevailed among scientists in the second half of the 19th century, the philosophy of Moleschott, Buchner, Vogt, and others; and consequently his concept of the Universe was rigorously mechanistic.

According to his system, Will (a creative power whose source and nature we cannot comprehend, just as, likewise, we do not understand the nature and source of "matter" or of any of the other "first principles")—I was saying, Will which contributes much or little in determining the conduct of individuals—and of society, does not exist and is a mere illusion. All that has been, that is and will be, from the path of the stars to the birth and decline of a civilisation, from the perfume of a rose to the smile on a mother's lips, from an earthquake to the thoughts of a Newton, from a tyrant's cruelty to a saint's goodness, everything had to, must, and will occur as a result of an inevitable sequence of causes and effects of mechanical origin, which leaves no possibility of variety. The illusion of Will is itself a mechanical fact.

Naturally if Will has no power, if everything is necessary and cannot be otherwise, then ideas of freedom, justice and responsibility have no meaning, and have no bearing on reality.

Thus logically all we can do is to contemplate what is happening in the world, with indifference, pleasure or pain, depending on one's personal feelings, without hope and without the possibility of changing anything.

So Kropotkin, who was very critical of the fatalism of the Marxists, was, himself the victim of mechanistic fatalism which is far more inhibiting.

But philosophy could not kill the powerful Will that was in Kropotkin. He was too strongly convinced of the truth of his system to abandon it or stand by passively while others cast doubt on it; he was too passionate, and too desirous of liberty and justice to be halted by the difficulty of a logical contradiction, and give up the struggle. He got round the dilemma by introducing anarchism into his system and making it into a scientific truth.

He would seek confirmation for his view by maintaining that all recent discoveries in all the sciences, from astronomy right through to biology and sociology coincided in demonstrating always more clearly that anarchy is the form of social organisation which is imposed by natural laws.

One could have pointed out that whatever are the conclusions that can be drawn from contemporary science, it was a fact that if new discoveries were to destroy present scientific beliefs, he would have remained an anarchist in spite of science, just as he was an anarchist in spite of logic. But Kropotkin would not have been able to admit the possibility of a conflict between science and his social aspirations and would have always thought up a means, no matter whether it was logical or not, to reconcile his mechanistic philosophy with his anarchism.

Thus, after having said that "anarchy is a concept of the Universe based on the mechanical interpretation of phenomena which embrace the whole of nature including the life of societies" (*I confess I have never succeeded in understanding what this might mean*) Kropotkin would forget his mechanistic concept as a matter of no importance, and throw himself into the struggle with the fire, enthusiasm, and confidence of one who believes in the efficacy of his Will and who hopes by his activity to obtain or contribute to the achievement of the things he wants.

In point of fact Kropotkin's anarchism and communism were much more the consequence of his sensibility than of reason. In him the heart spoke first and then reason followed to justify and reinforce the impulses of the heart.

What constituted the true essence of his character was his love of mankind, the sympathy he had for the poor and the oppressed. He truly suffered for others, and found injustice intolerable even if it operated in his favour.

At the time when I frequented him in London, he earned his living by collaborating to scientific magazines and other publications, and lived in relatively comfortable circumstances; but he felt a kind of remorse at being better off than most manual workers and always seemed to want to excuse himself for the small comforts he could afford. He often said, when speaking of himself and of those in similar circumstances: "If we have been able to educate ourselves and develop our faculties; if we have access to intellectual satisfactions and live in not too bad material circumstances, it is because we have benefited, through an accident of birth, by the exploitation to which the workers are subjected; and therefore the struggle for the emancipation of the workers is a duty, a debt which we must repay."

It was for his love of justice, and as if by way of expiating the privileges that he had enjoyed, that he had given up his position, neglected the studies he so enjoyed, to devote himself to the education of the workers of St. Petersburg and the struggle against the despotism of the Tsars. Urged on by these same feelings he had subsequently joined the International and accepted anarchist ideas. Finally, among the different interpretations of anarchism he chose and made his own the communist-anarchist programme which, being based on solidarity and on love, goes beyond justice itself.

But as was obviously foreseeable, his philosophy was not without influence on the way he conceived the future and on the form the struggle for its achievement should take.

Since, according to his philosophy that which occurs must necessarily occur, so also the communist-anarchism he desired, must inevitably triumph as if by a law of Nature.

And this freed him from any doubt and removed all difficulties from his path. The bourgeois world was destined to crumble; it was already breaking up and revolutionary action only served to hasten the process.

His immense influence as a propagandist as well as stemming from his great talents, rested on the fact that he showed things to be so simple, so easy, so inevitable, that those who heard him speak or read his articles were immediately fired with enthusiasm.

Moral problems vanished because he attributed to the "people," the working masses, great abilities and all the virtues. With reason he praised the moral influence of work, but did not sufficiently clearly see the depressing and corrupting effects of misery and subjection. And he thought that it would be sufficient to abolish the capitalists' privileges and the rulers' power for all men immediately to start loving each other as brothers and to care for the interests of others as they would for their own.

In the same way he did not see the material difficulties, or he easily dismissed them. He had accepted the idea, widely held among the anarchists at the time, that the accumulated stocks of food and manufactured goods, were so abundant that for a long time to come it would not be necessary to worry about production; and he always declared that the immediate problem was one of consumption, that for the triumph of the revolution it was necessary to satisfy the needs of everyone immediately as well as abundantly, and that production would follow the rhythm of consumption. From this idea came that of "taking from the storehouses" ("presa nel mucchio"), which he popularised and which is certainly the simplest way of conceiving communism and the most likely to please the masses, but which is also the most primitive, as well as truly utopian, way. And when he was made to observe that this accumulation of products could not possibly exist, because the bosses normally only allow for the production of what they can sell at a profit, and that possibly at the beginning of a revolution it would be necessary to organise a system of rationing, and press for an intensification of production rather than call upon [the people] to help themselves from a storehouse which in the event would be nonexistent, Kropotkin set about studying the problem at first hand and arrived at the conclusion that in fact such abundance did not exist and that some countries were continually threatened by shortages. But he recovered [his optimism] by thinking of the great potentialities of agriculture aided by science. He took as examples the results obtained by a few cultivators and gifted agronomists over limited areas and drew the most encouraging conclusions, without thinking of the difficulties that would be put in the way by the ignorance and aversion of peasants to what is change, and in any case to the time that would be needed to achieve general acceptance of the new forms of cultivation and of distribution.

As always, Kropotkin saw things as he would have wished them to be and as we all hope they will be one day; he considered as existing or immediately realizable that which must be won through long and bitter struggle.

At bottom Kropotkin conceived nature as a kind of Providence, thanks to which there had to be harmony in all things, including human societies.

And this has led many anarchists to repeat that "*Anarchy is Natural Order*," a phrase with an exquisite Kropotkinian flavour.

If it is true that the law of Nature is Harmony, I suggest one would be entitled to ask why Nature has waited for anarchists to be born, and goes on waiting for them to triumph, in order to destroy the terrible and destructive conflicts from which mankind has always suffered.

Would one not be closer to the truth in saying that anarchy is the struggle, in human society, against the disharmonies of Nature?

I have stressed the two errors which, in my opinion, Kropotkin committed—his theory of fatalism and his excessive optimism, because I believe I have observed the harmful results they have produced on our movement.

There were comrades who took the fatalist theory—which they euphemistically referred to as determinism—seriously and as a result lost all revolutionary spirit. The revolution, they said, is not made; it will come when the time is ripe for it, and it is useless, unscientific and even ridiculous to try to provoke it. And armed with such sound reasons, they withdrew from the movement and went about their own business. But it would be wrong to believe that this was a convenient excuse to withdraw from the struggle. I have known many comrades of great courage and worth, who have exposed themselves to great dangers and who have sacrificed their freedom and even their lives in the name of anarchy while being convinced of the uselessness of their actions. They have acted out of disgust for present society, in a spirit of revenge, out of desperation, or the love of the grand gesture, but without thinking thereby of serving the cause of revolution, and consequently without selecting the target and the opportune moment, or without bothering to coordinate their action with that of others.

On the other hand, those who without troubling themselves with philosophy have wanted to work towards, and for, the revolution, have imagined the problems as much simpler than they are in reality, did not foresee the difficulties, and prepare for them . . . and because of this we have found ourselves impotent even when there was perhaps a chance of effective action.

May the errors of the past serve to teach us to do better in the future.

I have said what I had to say.

I do not think my strictures on him can diminish Kropotkin, the person, who remains, in spite of everything one of the shining lights of our movement.

If they are just, they will serve to show that no man is free from error, not even when he is gifted with the great intelligence and the generous heart of a Kropotkin.

In any case anarchists will always find in his writings a treasury of fertile ideas and in his life an example and an incentive in the struggle for all that is good.

Police photographs of Malatesta, 1898.

PART THREE

No, I would not like to return to the old times . . . simply to follow the same road and find ourselves back to where we are now. To want to, one should also be able to take with one the results of fifty years activity and all the experience acquired in that time. And in that case it would be the "good old days."

—From Malatesta's preface to Nettlau's *Bakunin e l'Internazionale in Italia dal 1864 al 1872* (1928)

We do not boast that we possess absolute truth; on the contrary, we believe that social truth is not a fixed quantity, good for all times, universally applicable or determinable in advance. . . . Our solutions always leave the door open to different and, one hopes, better solutions.

—*Umanità Nova*, 1921

June 9/12

MALATESTA RELEASE COMMITTEE.

A MARCH

will take place from

Mile End Waste

TO GREAT

PROTEST MEETING

AT

TRAFALGAR SQUARE.

SPEAKERS:

BEN TILLETT, CUNNINGHAN-GRAHAM, GUY BOWMAN, MRS. TOM MANN & others.

A Band will be in attendance.

Trade Unions invited to bring banners.

All workers should attend here (Mile End Waste) at 1.45 p.m. on Sunday Next.

Watch "Daily Herald" for further particulars.

"Workers Friend" Printers, 163, Jubilee Street, Mile End, E.

MALATESTA:

A MASS MEETING to demand the immediate RELEASE OF MALATESTA

Will Be Held In **TRAFALGAR SQUARE** TO-MORROW AT 4 P.M.

CENTRE PLINTH:

BEN TILLETT, R. B. CUNNINGHAME-GRAHAM, GEORGE LANSBURY, M.P., J. C. WEDGWOOD, M.P., GUY BOWMAN, MRS. TOM MANN, MRS. AGNES HENRY. Chairman: JAMES MACDONALD.

WEST PLINTH:

F. J. PASSMORE, A. COOK, W. E. PARKER, NINA BOYLE, LESLIE BOYNE, CARL QUINN, A. RAY. Chairman: GUY A. ALDRED.

EAST PLINTH:

J. GRIFFITHS, C. R. LEE, M. KAVANAGH; MRS. BAKER, P. E. TANNER, M. SHUGAR, A. B. MACE, J. TOCHATTI. Chairman: W. PONDER.

PROCESSIONS START:

Hammersmith: The Grove, 2.30 P.M. Islington: Highbury Corner, 2.15 P.M.
Harlesden: Manor Park Road, 2.15 P.M. Mile End: The Waste, 2 P.M.

BANDS AND BANNERS WILL ACCOMPANY EACH PROCESSION.

D. Herald
June 8/12

Malatesta's Relevance for Anarchists Today

An Assessment

I

Malatesta's critical essay of recollections of Kropotkin was one of the last things he wrote, and that was thirty-four years ago; and some of his writings selected for this volume go back to the '90s. There have been tremendous social upheavals and economic developments in these thirty years which Malatesta, were he writing these concluding lines for me, would be the first to recognise and take into account in formulating anarchist tactics in the '60s of the twentieth century. But we should be wary of confusing technological and scientific discoveries and advancement with political progress and social awareness. Obviously in the past thirty years in the fields of technology and science mankind has made strides which only fifty years ago might have been considered impossible. On the other hand the growth of radical political thought and awareness during the latter half of the 19th century is a phenomenon not experienced since. Indeed the characteristic of our age is that though we have developed the new sciences to the point where we know more about ourselves, about our motivations, our behaviour patterns, our unconscious thoughts; where we know more about the workings of the ruling groups; and of the economic and financial system; where as a result of mass communications secret diplomacy and political scandals, cannot remain uncovered, as easily as in the past, revolutionary avant-garde movements are at their lowest ebb, and Western Man seems unable to project, let alone realise a way of life that combines the full satisfaction of material needs with individual fulfilment and happiness.

It is significant that in the affluent nations of the world, where at last the material conditions for the realisation of socialism have been achieved, there is no longer a socialist movement worthy of the name. And that in the hungry half of the world the movements of "liberation" are nationalistic and intensely hierarchical and political, and rarely influenced by radical revolutionary ideas of social and economic justice.

The temptation is to conclude that the age of classical revolution is passed. As one sociologist put it

> Modern revolutionary theory was conceived at an early stage of Capitalism, in a world of scarcity and ruthless exploitation, when one could think only of a life and death struggle between rich and poor in which the poor had nothing to lose but his chains. Since then a situation has developed in advanced industrialist countries where there are too many people who could lose only by revolution. They would therefore prefer to see a peaceful transformation toward a more enlightened social organisation.[1]

It is undoubtedly true that the power structure at the top has undergone very considerable change in the past thirty years, and that a growing proportion of the population, by reason of its economic and/or social status, now has a stake in capitalist society and will resist any attempt at radical change. But because the revolutionary theory, as quoted by Mannheim, has been shown to be fallacious anyway, (the poor being more concerned with their next meal than with their chains, are thus prepared to *follow* any demagogue who promises them a square meal every day in return for their political servitude) and revolutionary movements, at all times, a small section of the community, the chances of a revolutionary upheaval in this respect have not been made all that much more difficult by the "managerial revolution" on the other side.

To assume that these elements in themselves represent a formidable physical obstacle, which daily grows larger, is to ignore the lessons of Algeria and

Kenya for instance and to exaggerate white militancy in Southern Rhodesia and South Africa. In the former, the withdrawal of the military might of the respective Metropolitan powers revealed the bankruptcy of the militant boasting of the "colons." We have yet to see how militant they will be in S. Rhodesia and South Africa if and when they are resisted by armed Africans, and not by moral arguments and the Luthuli tactics of non-violence, which it could be argued, have been shown to be inadequate in dealing with these two situations of injustice.

Mannheim, in his observations on dictatorship, points out that "given modern social techniques, a minority will never hand over power to an unarmed majority." He follows this eminently Malatestian and anarchist remark with "Revolution against any totalitarian power, once entrenched, is nearly hopeless. No established totalitarian regime, whatever its political creed, can be broken from within; it takes an external war to unseat it." From which, in his opinion, "it follows that the utopian hopes of the Communists that their dictatorship would gradually fade away are even more visionary than many of their other over-optimistic expectations."

While agreeing with Mannheim that the "withering away" of the State theory of the Marxists is "visionary," assuming that it was ever expressed by them in good faith, one cannot allow Mannheim's equally utopian faith in the positive role of "external war to unseat" totalitarian power to pass unchallenged. His simplifications hardly stand up to examination. The last war (1) unseated the Hitler and Mussolini gangs (2) aided Franco's regime—at a time when according to Mannheim's arguments it could have destroyed it (3) consolidated the power of the Stalin regime in Russia (4) and as a result of its possession of the Atomic Bomb and the financial advantages resulting from its late entry in the War, the United States emerged as the dominating world Power, politically and economically.

Thus if it can be shown that "external war" has unseated dictatorship it has also consolidated others, as well as creating new ones in the process! So that on balance, considering the price mankind pays in death and destruction, any advantages that can be enjoyed by the survivors are not political but if anything economic ones. The characteristic of modern war is the technological progress that it stimulates and subsidises at all costs.

Most of us welcome the labour-saving gadgets that are now within the reach of our purses, but without considering the terrible price at which this technological breakthrough has been bought nor the price our children and future generations will have to pay to liquidate our debt of folly. Some of us do, and that minority in the affluent society is the guarantee that human values will survive in an environment of milk and gadgets just as they emerged in one of abject poverty lorded over by an aristocracy of undisguised wealth and privilege.

Malatesta's analysis of Capitalism is still valid; mass production needs, and even creates, mass markets. Yet the *raison d'être* of capitalist economics is still *profits*, and therefore the "artificial scarcity of goods" which Malatesta referred to in the 1920s as "a characteristic" of that system, still obtains, and in that case it is reasonable to suppose that the "affluence" we enjoy in the West is not the result of a change of heart among capitalists, but the chance effect of a cause serving at the same time other interests.

Have the capitalists then, in serving their interests at the same time silenced popular opposition by dangling the carrot of full employment and "affluence" in front of the working people? They haven't, and not only are they unable to guarantee full employment (assuming that they considered it to be good business) but neither can they control their employees' demands, for as Malatesta pointed out, the more successful they are in pressing their demands the more will they demand.

In other words, general prosperity, which also means more education as well as more material things, does not result in a passive or contented acceptance of a class structure and a privileged society. Just as the intentions of mass communications (apart from being profitable business) which are to condition the mass-reading public, also produce the opposite effect on large numbers of people, so prosperity (more education) produces growing feelings of resentment among wage earners at having to be ordered about by another, simply because he disposes of the means of production. There is a growing cynicism about the alleged superior qualities of those who control our political life, as well as less acceptance than in the past of the ostentatious ways of life of the wealthy parasites in our midst. State funerals for politicians are obvious attempts to rehabilitate the former, and football pools, with the occasional huge prize winnings, an open sesame to the millionaires' club for the man in the street. But the dilemma of capitalism cannot be solved by these obvious tricks, whatever they may do in the short term to distract attention from the major issues.

Even assuming that the problems of world hunger and poverty can and will be satisfactorily solved in the next twenty years, and I make the assumption only in order to argue for the validity of anarchy in a world in which the basic material needs of life *have* been satisfied, the fact is, if the capitalist, or state-socialist, systems succeed in solving the problems of production and distribution in a way that ensures the basic necessities to maintain health for every individual in the world, they will still not have touched the problem of Authority.

Having filled the empty bellies they are, willy-nilly feeding minds, until then exclusively obsessed by food, with ideas, with ambitions, dreams, power, love. Thus having solved the problem of hunger the ruling elite would surround itself with doting followers, but also in a short time have to contend with the pressures from those hungry for the fruits of power as well as from those simply desirous of running their own lives without being bossed around from above.

Malatesta, speaking for the latter, did not make the mistake of confusing them with those he described as "strong, intelligent, passionate individuals, with strong material or intellectual needs, who finding themselves by chance, among the oppressed, seek, at all costs to emancipate themselves, and do not resent becoming oppressors. . . . "They are rebels but not anarchists," he concluded, because they had both the feelings and mentality of "unsuccessful bourgeois" and when they do succeed they not only become bourgeois "in fact" but are "not the least unpleasant among them." The anarchist movement has to this day been unable to protect itself from the Colin Wilsons and other "rebels" of this world who were never anarchists. Since we cannot prevent anyone from calling himself by whatever name he likes, all we can do, declared Malatesta, is to "try to prevent any confusion, or at least seek to reduce it to a minimum," even if there may be circumstances in which we "find them alongside us." This, it seems to me is a positive reaction; the alternatives lead to sectarianism, isolation, and in anarchist terms, to an extreme form of individualism.

Malatesta also avoided the mistake, not uncommon in anarchist movements, of seeking to counteract the ill-effects, or the failure, of one extreme by opting for another. The answer to the excesses of "propaganda by the deed" was not Tolstoyan "passive anarchy" any more than organisation with party discipline was the answer to uncoordinated actions, or faith in the inevitability of anarchy. Similarly the failure of insurrectionary attempts in the early days of the movement led to the excessive faith, of some, in the powers of the "general strike," while others concerned by the insufficient influence exerted by anarchists in the workers' organisations and revolutionary parties, either sought to contract out of society (by starting isolated communities) or became so involved in Trades Union and party activities, that many ended up by being *their* spokesmen.

In steering a middle course, Malatesta was undoubtedly guided by a long experience and observation of the fate of these extreme attitudes and groupings, no less than by his clear image of the role of anarchists in the social struggle. Far from this middle course implying compromise and reformism, Malatesta sought to ensure that the anarchist movement should always retain its fundamental characteristics but without thereby being condemned to sterility and the role of passive observers of the world political scene.

Apart from the early years, when he too was carried away by the bakuninist ideas of successful local insurrections setting the world on fire, Malatesta was only too aware of the improbability of achieving the anarchist revolution in a foreseeable future, and one can therefore understand why he should have steered clear of both kinds of anarchist extremists: those who were convinced of the impossibility of ever achieving anarchism (such as the individualists) no less than those who thought it could be ushered in overnight by toppling a few heads of State, by a successful General Strike, or by a mass syndicalist organisation.

For these reasons he avoided dogmatic postures and refused to win applause by oratorical flourishes. He could not, for instance, conceive of a world or even a community in which *absolute* freedom reigned. "Mutual Aid" is not "a Law of Nature"—"natural Man is in a state of continuous conflict with his fellows. . . ." He was an anarchist because it corresponded "better than any other way of social life" to the kind of life *he* wished to live, which for him included, "the good of all" a consideration, in Malatesta's case, free from sentimental or oratorical overtones in view of his realistic appraisal of human problems.

In 1920 when he was editor of the anarchist daily, *Umanità Nova* and inciting, as well as, hoping for far-reaching popular action, he was never tempted to write-down or simplify the problems of social revolution: "The needs, tastes, aspirations, and interests of mankind"—he wrote—"are neither similar nor naturally harmonious; often they are diametrically opposed and antagonistic. On the other hand, the life of each individual is so conditioned by the life of others that it would be impossible, even assuming it were convenient to do so, to isolate oneself, and live one's own life. Social solidarity is a fact from which no one can escape."

Having presented what is, in his opinion a realistic picture of the human situation Malatesta suggests that

> [Social Solidarity] can be freely and consciously accepted and in consequence benefit all concerned, or it can be accepted willy-nilly, consciously or otherwise, in which case it manifests itself by the subjection of one to another, by the exploitation of some by others.

Organisation is surely one of the basic manifestations of human solidarity and one is not surprised to find Malatesta in 1897 defining anarchy as "society *organised* without authority'. To say, as Joll condescendingly does, that he "had always accepted some degree of organisation," in order to conclude that in the polemic between Malatesta and the then anarcho-syndicalist, Monatte, it was the latter "who was right," is to distort the questions at issue between the two militants at the Amsterdam Congress of 1907. Indeed Malatesta went so far as to point out in that same piece of 1897 that

> were we to believe that organisation was not possible without authority we would be authoritarians because we would still *prefer* authority, which fetters and impoverishes life, to *disorganisation* which makes life impossible (my italics)

and everything he wrote subsequently emphasised the need for, without making a cult out of, organisation. Organisation is "a necessary aspect of social life" from which nobody can escape

> and even the most extreme anti-organisers not only are subject to the general organisation of the society they live in, but in the voluntary actions in their lives, and in their rebellion against organisation, they unite among themselves, they share out their tasks, they *organise* with whom they are in agreement, and use the means that society puts at their disposal.

As to organisation of the anarchist movement, not only did he consider it "useful and necessary." In his view activity in isolation, when possibilities existed to coordinate, or join it, with the activities of a strong group condemned one to impotence, and to wasting one's efforts in small ineffectual action.

Here again, Malatesta's approach was anything but dogmatic. For his experience on the daily anarchist paper made him question, in retrospect, the wisdom (and I assume this to mean the effectiveness, from the point of view of propaganda) of seeking to reconcile all the anarchist currents of thought in one paper, in a period of political ferment such as Italy was passing through in the immediate post-war years. If one juxtaposes these with the following observations

> Isolated, sporadic propaganda . . . serves little or no purpose. In the conditions of awareness and misery in which the masses live, and with so many forces against us, such propaganda is forgotten and lost before its efforts can grow and bear fruit. The soil is too ungrateful for seeds sown haphazardly to germinate and make roots

one is probably justified in concluding that Malatesta felt that when propaganda was at a low ebb it was time for anarchists of all shades to sink their tactical differences, and seek to combine in propagating the ideas, the ends, they held in common, but that when the movement was strong, and the political environment promising from a revolutionary point of view, they should unite where possible but not hesitate to have their respective organs of expression.

A critical study of the international anarchist press—not just simply a bibliography—would not only be revealing, but important in an attempt to further anarchist ideas. In the past fifty years the whole economics of printing and publishing have radically changed—and unfavourably from the point of view of the minority press. Equally the voice of mass communications has centupled in that time, and relatively therefore the difficulties of getting a hearing for anarchist ideas ever greater. Yet throughout the world the anarchist groups and movements each go on struggling to produce their papers and their journals without any attempt at coordinating their efforts or even establishing the most elementary kind of information service which would help to provide factual background material on political and other events of topical interest, while leaving each journal free to contribute its own interpretation.

Far from suggesting that the anarchist press should be centralised (such an attempt was made in Spain by the CNT-FAI Committees in 1938 with disastrous consequences). I am suggesting that internationally its resources could be used more effectively if they were coordinated. I am also suggesting that such coordination would not only improve the topical content of the various journals, but would also result in the discussion of anarchist ideas and tactics by anarchists internationally. In Malatesta's time there was a ferment of ideas singularly lacking today in the anarchist movement.

Do we really know all the answers? Have we restated anarchism in current terms with all the wealth of sociological research at our disposal? Have we re-examined anarchist tactics in the light of the momentous events technological and political that have taken place in the past thirty years? Have we understood the developments in the capitalist system, and in government in these post-war years and have we made an analysis of their significance in anarchist terms? I think not, and I say this as an assiduous reader of anarchist literature of all kinds in four languages, as well as in all humility, in view of my close association with the publishing activities of Freedom Press over many years.

In the course of compiling this volume I have been made only too aware of the inadequacies of anarchist propaganda in dealing with the means which we believe will lead a universally authoritarian society in, at least, a *libertarian* direction. And as I was pointing out earlier our choice of panaceas is determined by circumstances, with the tendency to veer from one extreme to another. My political education included, for instance, unquestioning "faith" in the efficacy of the "General Strike" as the answer to every anarchist's prayer, and in the course of the years, like many of my comrades, I have called on the "general strike" to put things right, just as socialists have appealed to "revolutionary government" to solve all the problems stemming from "bad" governments!

It was only because I intended to include in the Selections a section on the "general strike" that I discovered that Malatesta had written very little on the subject and that when he did it was generally to warn against placing too high hopes in the general strike as a weapon of social change. This led me to reread some of the literature on the subject including Berkman's valuable *ABC of Anarchism* (recently reissued by Freedom Press) I append the results of my own somewhat cursory reading, more as an illustration of the extremism (one way or the other) of anarchist positions and the unquestioning acceptance of *our* panaceas, than as confirmation of Malatesta's thesis or his way of summing up the problems, and of evaluating which, in the circumstances are the best tactics, though I feel that we have something to learn in these directions too.

II

In the early '20s Malatesta was writing of the general strike that it was a powerful weapon of struggle in the hands of the workers and "is, or could be, a way and the occasion to determine a radical social revolution." The situation was analogous to that in Spain fourteen years later, a weak government unable to impose its authority; the workers on the verge of revolution; the Right using the socialist renegade Mussolini to reestablish the rule of "Law and Order." The obvious and vital difference was that whereas in Spain the revolutionary elements captured the imagination of the reformists and indifferents, and swept them forward, in Italy the dead hand of the socialist politicians and Trade Union leaders killed the revolutionary potentialities of the situation. Obviously in such a situation the General Strike as Malatesta put it, "if understood and used differently from the way the old advocates of this weapon used it" could have been a "really effective means for social transformation." Nevertheless in general terms he asked himself whether "the idea of the general strike has not done more harm than good to the revolutionary cause."

It was some years earlier, at the Anarchist Congress in Amsterdam in 1907, that Malatesta expressed his reasons which were that: Firstly, many syndicalists were advocating the general strike as a substitute for the insurrection, and secondly that they overlooked the limitations of the general strike as a weapon in the struggle against the capitalist regime.

Without having any illusions about their past achievements, Malatesta saw that at least steady progress had been made in the right direction by the insurrectionary socialist movement, before it was halted by the emergence of Marxism, "with its dogmas and fatalism" and "unfortunately, with its scientific pretences (we were in a period of full, *scientifist* euphoria), Marxism gave false hopes and also attracted or diverted most of the anarchists." They began by saying that "the revolution comes but is not made" that socialism would "inevitably come about" in the order of things, and that the political factor (which Malatesta points out is "after all simply violence in the service of economic interests") is of no importance because the economic question determines every aspect of social life. "And so insurrectionary preparation was neglected and practically abandoned. Far from despising the political struggle, the anti-insurrectional Marxists later decided that politics was the principal and almost the only means to bring about the triumph of socialism that is, once they saw the possibility of entering Parliament and of giving to the political struggle the restricted meaning of electoral struggle, and with this means they sought to extinguish in the masses all enthusiasm for insurrectional action."

It was in this atmosphere, writes Malatesta, that the idea of the general strike was launched, and "welcomed enthusiastically by those who had no faith in parliamentary action, and saw in it a new and promising road leading to popular action." The trouble was however, that most of them viewed the general strike "not as a means of drawing the masses towards insurrection, that is, of the violent destruction of the political power, and to the seizure of the land, the means of production and of all social wealth, but as a substitute for the insurrection, a way of 'starving the bourgeoisie' and obliging it to capitulate without a blow being struck." Far from starving the bourgeoisie, "we should starve ourselves first," was his cryptic comment.

That Malatesta was not exaggerating when he referred to the General Strike as a panacea and as a substitute for the insurrection is to be found in a whole number of pamphlets published at the time. In this country, for instance, the anarchist press issued Arnold Roller's well-known essay on "The Social General Strike" (Freedom Press, London, 1912) in which one reads that, "The heroic times of the battle on the barricades have gone by." The "winding lanes" in which a barricade could easily be erected and defended have been replaced in large cities by "broad long streets, in which the columns of an army can easily operate and take the barricades," and even the paving stones have been replaced by wooden blocks and asphalt "and such material is not fit for building barricades." Therefore, Roller concludes "it would be foolish for the people to begin a revolution, relying upon such insufficient means of defence." An excellent argument against barricades in Bond Street but not necessarily against insurrection!

Roller also deals with the problem of feeding the population during a general strike:

> As soon as the bakers and butchers quit working, the General Strike will be felt much more intensely, and it will be probably the first time that the ruling classes will understand and feel what it means to be hungry.... The proletarians can stop production, but they cannot stop consumption. In this way they would during the transition do the same thing as the ruling classes have done uninterruptedly for thousands of years—that is, "consume without producing." This action of the ruling classes the working class calls "exploitation"; and if the proletarians do it, the possessing classes call it "plundering," and Socialists call it "expropriation."

In 1907 Malatesta was telling his fellow delegates in Amsterdam: "Some of the enthusiasts of the general strike go so far as to admit that the General Strike involves expropriation. But then the soldiers come. Are we to let ourselves be shot down? Of course not. We should stand up to them, and that would mean Revolution. So why not say Revolution at once, instead of General Strike?

This was not simply a question of words for in Malatesta's view it went deeper than that:

> The advocates of the General Strike make people think they can do things without fighting, and thus actually spoil the revolutionary spirit of the people. It was propaganda of this kind that brought about such illogical positions as that taken up by the strikers recently at Barcelona, where they did fight the soldiers, but at the same time treated with the State. This was because they were under the delusion that it was only an economic question.

Again the idea expressed by such writers as Roller that "when the bakers and butchers quit working" the ruling classes will "probably for the first time understand what it means to be hungry" is not only doubtful, but even if it were true, the fact is that they would be no more worse off than the rest of the population and that short of everybody starving to death something must give, and it is inevitable that it will be the workers, for they and not the employers are the producers of the necessities of life. Malatesta argued thus because he was far from convinced that under capitalism there was ever over-production or that the granaries and the warehouses were stuffed with surplus food. Unlike Roller who believed that

> the crisis of over-production is the best guarantee for the success of the Social General Strike, because the products on hand permit the satisfaction of all needs before the complete reorganisation; namely, by a general "Help yourself" on the part of the workers.

Malatesta always pointed out that the characteristic of capitalism is under- rather than over-production (see Section 12 "Production & Distribution") and that it was a mistake to believe that the stocks of food and essential goods in the large cities was sufficient to feed the people for more than a few days. When pressed by Malatesta to investigate the true position, Kropotkin who, in all his writings on the subject, had been a partisan of the *prise au tas* (taking from the storehouses) view, discovered that if the imports of food into England were stopped for four weeks everybody in the country would die of starvation; and that in spite of all the warehouses in London, the capital city was never provisioned for much more than three days. Is the situation much different today in London and in all the large cities of the world?

Malatesta offered the Congress of 1907 what he called "a more or less novel conception" of the General Strike: namely "that in dealing with this question we must *begin* by considering the necessity of food." And in which case

> A peasant strike, for instance, appeared to him as the greatest absurdity. Their only tactics were immediate expropriation, and wherever we find them setting to work on those lines it is our business to go and help them against the soldiers. And then he had read somewhere that we ought to go and smash the railway bridges! He wondered whether the advocates of such foolishness ever realised that corn has to come the same way the cannons come. To adopt the policy of neither cannons nor corn is to make all revolutionists the enemies of the people. We must face the cannons if we want the corn.

"We must face the cannons if we want the corn" symbolises the commonsense which informed all Malatesta's, counsels and his own actions in the long years of his political maturity. It is his approach which even in this new scientific age in which we live, should commend itself to us today. It is not only about "cannons and corn" that his arguments have that ring of realism. I suggest that throughout the Selections this approach is applied to every major problem. For sixty years Malatesta was an anarchist because it "would correspond better than any other way of social life, to my desire for the good of all, to my aspirations towards a society which reconciles the liberty of everyone with cooperation and love among men, and not because anarchism is a scientific truth and a natural law." And for most of those sixty years without ever abandoning these feelings his feet remained firmly planted on the ground. Insurrection, General strikes, Revolution, Anarchy—yes, but the ever-recurring warning in all his theoretical and agitational writings is that the community has to go on eating every day whatever the political upheavals.

He may well have been stating the obvious but so long as it is overlooked it needs to be repeated again and again.

Monatte's taunt, after hearing Malatesta's view at the 1907 Congress was

> In listening tonight to Malatesta bitterly criticising the new revolutionary concepts, I felt that I was listening to the arguments of a distant past. To these new concepts, the brutal reality of which frightens him, Malatesta has simply offered the old Blanquist ideas which fondly imagined that it was possible to reinvigorate the world by means of a triumphant armed insurrection.
>
> Furthermore, the revolutionary syndicalists present tonight, have been reproached for having deliberately sacrificed anarchism and the revolution to syndicalism and the general strike. Well, I wish to declare, that our anarchism is as good as yours and we have no more intention than you have *de mettre notre drapeau dans notre poche* (of hiding our true colours). As everybody here, anarchy is our final object. But because times have changed, we have also modified our concept of the movement and of the revolution. The latter cannot be achieved in the meld of 1848. As to syndicalism, if in some countries in practice it has given rise to some errors and deviations, the experience is there which will prevent us from repeating them. If instead of criticising from above the past, present or even future shortcomings of syndicalism, anarchists were to become more closely involved in its activity, the hidden dangers that might be contained in syndicalism would once for all be exorcised!

Monatte exaggerated the differences between syndicalists and anarchists because he did not or for tactical reasons was not willing to take into account the opening sentences in Malatesta's exposé which made it quite clear that he would only deal with those aspects of his ideas in which "he was *in disagreement* with earlier speakers and in particular with Monatte" for to do otherwise would simply mean burdening delegates with the kind of repetitions which are permissible at meetings when one is addressing a hostile or indifferent audience. But here—he went on to add—"we are among comrades and none of you hearing me criticise what can be criticised in syndicalism will surely be tempted to take me for an enemy of workers' organisation and action; anyone who does obviously doesn't know me very well!"

Without wishing to be unkind to Monatte, who remained devoted to the cause of revolutionary syndicalism to the end of a long life, but in the interests of truth, it must be mentioned that whereas Monatte succumbed to the temptations of the Bolshevik Revolution a few years later (though he soon left them), Malatesta not only exposed the dangers from the beginning but received the announcement of Lenin's death with what was, for the revolutionary Left, no less than for some anarchists, the shocking remark "Lenin is dead. Long Live the Revolution!"

I have only apparently diverged from the subject of the pros and cons of the General Strike as a revolutionary weapon, because it seems to me that from the foregoing one can the better judge whether Malatesta's criticisms were the "arguments of the distant past" or those of a man who refused to be deflected from the realities of the present and, in the circumstances, of the foreseeable future.

It is interesting to note that French syndicalists, such as Pierre Besnard, in the '30s were defining the general strike as "la grève generale insurrectionelle et expropriatrice."[2] The general strike he explained as "a specifically syndicalist weapon" which can deal "in a *decisive* manner with all revolutionary situations whatever the initial factors of the movements set in motion. It is directly opposed to *insurrection*, the only weapon of the political parties." And he adds that it is

> by far more complete than [insurrection]. In fact whereas the latter only makes it possible to take power, the general strike not only provides the possibility of destroying that power, of getting rid of those who enjoy it, of preventing any party from capturing it, it deprives capitalism and

> the State of all means of defence, while at the same time *abolishing* individual property, replacing it by collective property.
>
> In a word, the general strike has a power of *immediate* transformation, and this power is exercised for the sole benefit of the proletariat, to whom the possession of the apparatus of production and exchange offers the means of *radically* transforming the social order.
>
> The expropriatory general strike, with violence which the proletariat will invariably be obliged to use, will be, moreover, clearly *insurrectional.*
>
> Its effect will be felt at the same time politically and economically, whereas insurrection permits a party to act only in the political field.

Surely Malatesta would be justified in rising from his grave in anger and demanding that we call a spade a spade! And he would need do no more than point to the fact that the syndicalists were now embellishing the term "general strike" with "insurrectionelle et expropriatrice" and that Besnard, syndicalist, in his interesting "programme" shares the same preoccupations as Malatesta, anarchist, when he writes

> Let us, now, examine what are the characteristics of the general strike. I have said that it signified in the first place and above all, the cessation of production, and work, under capitalism.
>
> This means that workers, then the peasants, must simultaneously stop work. Does this mean they must quit their place of work and abandon the means of production to the bosses? No. Unlike what happens during a strike, workers will have to at the same time *stop* work, *occupy* the place of production, *get rid* of the boss, *expropriate* him, and *get ready* to get production moving again, but in the interests of the revolution.
>
> The cessation of work and production will mark the end of a regime, the expropriation of the possessors of the means of production and exchange and at the same time the overthrow of State power.

"On the duration of this stoppage will depend the future of the revolutionary movement," writes Besnard. Malatesta in 1907 seeing clearly this danger declared that "rather than calling on workers to stop working we must get them to work on their own account. Failing which the general strike will become a general famine even if we had been able from the outset to seize all the goods stored in the warehouses." And again in 1920 we find him advocating the taking-over of factories as the answer to general strikes of protest (see Section 18).

To this day for syndicalists and many anarchists the general strike remains the battle cry, the short cut to the free society "if only the workers would make up their minds." As far as I know no objective study on the subject of the general strike has been made by anarchists or syndicalists since Malatesta expressed his doubts at the Anarchist Congress in 1907 and again in 1920. It is significant that the major work on the subject should be by an American professor, Wilfrid Crook, and is packed with valuable material though marred by the author's obsession with the Communist bogey.[3] A work which is more objective and valuable, though it only deals briefly with the problem, is Lady Chorley's *Armies and the Art of Revolution*,[4] a war-time publication which was presumably justified by the publishers as a work of "national interest" in so far as it would assist those engaged in "political warfare" in dealing with revolutionary situations among the defeated nations. Be that as it may, Lady Chorley has done the kind of research anarchists should have long ago engaged in. Her conclusions are of considerable interest and bear out the arguments advanced by Malatesta from his own experience. The author is "summing up"

> the rather heterogeneous evidence [of the preceding pages and trying] to arrive at some conclusions as to the value of the general strike as a revolutionary weapon. In particular, an attempt must be made to answer the question whether a general strike can in any circumstances provide conditions which will indirectly weaken the fighting power of the forces of the *status quo* government, so that an insurrection may succeed even against their opposition.
>
> It seems clear that the general strike has certain inherent weaknesses that cannot be overcome. Its object is to hold a government to ransom by the dislocation of all economic life. If the middle classes

are against the strike, this dislocation cannot be completely effected since they are competent to run skeleton necessary services. When the dislocation is complete, after a few days the strains put upon the strike organisation will probably be beyond its resources on a vast and probably quite impossible scale. Moreover, the structure of modern community life cannot survive such a dislocation for more than a few days. And if the whole structure crumbles, the resulting chaos will be a crushing liability rather than an asset. History shows that successful revolutions have invariably taken off from a springboard of properly organised community life. Whether, the community life is organised in the interests of this or that class is of no moment. The point is that it is organised. *It is a fallacy to suppose that revolutions are ever the offspring of chaos and foul night.* Relative economic chaos may ensue for a time after a successful revolution. This may be inevitable. But no leader can afford to make the production of general chaos an instrument of revolutionary policy. During a revolution, the more smoothly the machinery runs for the neutral population, the better....

A general strike, then, must succeed in its objective within the first few days. If this does not happen, it will probably collapse under the weight of the dislocation it has itself brought about before that dislocation actually brings down the whole social structure. There is a third alternative: that it should transform itself into armed revolt. Granted the opposition of the armed forces of the government, such a revolt can only be successful if the conditions created by the strike prevent the troops from exerting their full strength.... Taking it by and large, the general strike is not a good revolutionary weapon. Its main revolutionary value is as an expression of working-class solidarity. It can sometimes be used to create artificially a revolutionary situation, *but unless such a situation can be used as the taking-off point for an already planned insurrection, whose chances have been calculated, it is a useless expenditure of enormous energy. As an actual instrument of policy it is more wasteful of energy than a straight insurrection, and its failure is more likely to set back a working-class movement than the failure of an insurrection.*

The passages I have italicised in Lady Chorley's conclusions seem to me to be the particularly relevant ones in a piece full of important observations for anarchists and syndicalists, and not least for those who see in the general strike the weapon *par excellence* of the non-violent revolution.

The point surely is that where the general strike is neither purely economic or political but revolutionary in its objectives, its purpose being to replace government and all the institutions of State by other forms of social and political organisation, it is in effect the insurrection as visualised by Malatesta, and the only difference between his approach and that of any other, what I would call, practical anarchists, such as Alexander Berkman is one of emphasis, but it is crucial to the whole future development of anarchist thinking and propaganda no less than in its possibilities of developing as a movement of radical change. On the subject of "Organisation of labour for the Social Revolution" Berkman writes in the *ABC of Anarchism*

> We know that revolution begins with street disturbances, and outbreaks; it is the initial phase which involves force and violence.... This phase of the revolution is of short duration. It is usually followed by the more conscious, yet still spontaneous, destruction of the citadels of authority, the visible symbols of organised violence and brutality; jails, police stations and other government buildings are attacked, the prisoners liberated, legal documents destroyed.... But this stage passes quickly; the people's ire is soon spent. Simultaneously the revolution begins its constructive work.

But then to his imaginary interlocutor who asks whether he really thinks the reconstruction will start so soon, he rightly replies that "it must begin immediately" (the people must eat today and tomorrow warned Malatesta; and this is what the revolutionary workers in Barcelona in 1936 realised when within 48 hours of crushing the military rebellion—and without government authority they reestablished the essential services needed by the community).

But when Berkman's questioner asks "Are you not too hopeful" he replies: "No, I don't think so. I am convinced that the social revolution will not 'just happen.' It will have to be prepared, organised. Yes, indeed, organised—just as a strike is organised. In truth it will be a strike, the strike of the united workers of an entire country—*a general strike.*"

And he then goes on to argue that it is obvious unarmed masses and their barricades couldn't in these days of "armoured tanks, poison gas, and military planes" withstand "high power artillery and bombs thrown upon them from flying machines." The whole proposition is "ridiculous" and it is therefore "time to have done with this obsolete idea of revolution"

> The strength of labour is not in the field of battle. It is in the shop, in the mine and factory. There lies its power that no army in the world can defeat, no human agency conquer.
>
> In other words the social revolution can take place only by means of the *General Strike.* The General Strike, rightly understood and thoroughly carried out, is the social revolution.
>
> It is most important that we realise that the General Strike is the only possibility of social revolution. In the past the General Strike has been propagated in various countries without sufficient emphasis that its real meaning is revolution, that it is the only practical way to it. It is time for us to learn this, and when we do so the social revolution will cease to be a vague, unknown quantity. It will become an actuality, a definite method and aim, a programme whose first steps is the taking over of the instruments by organised labour.

Berkman's imaginary interlocutor expresses himself satisfied—but about another topic: "that the social revolution means construction rather than destruction"! But in all frankness, Berkman's argument just does not hold water as it stands. "You can shoot people to death but you can't shoot them to work" he declares. But, equally can it be said that without shooting them to death you can starve them back to work.

It is when Berkman implies that a revolutionary social strike will prevent any intervention by the armed forces that he seems to join company with the syndicalists, the "nonviolent" anarchists, and others whom Malatesta roundly criticised, save that Berkman does recognise there must be a "clash" between Authority and the revolutionary workers, which "involves force and violence" but which "will be of short duration." What is this but Malatesta's insurrectionary period? And why assume that the forces opposed to the struggle will not be the full force of the State's armed power?

It seems to me that for those anarchists or revolutionary socialists who cannot honestly see how violence can be avoided in any decisive confrontation between the forces of the under-privileged and those of the State which, after all, they are openly declaring daily, exist to protect privilege by violence (even law can only be enforced by the use or threat of force), it is bad propaganda in the long term to seek to suggest that the struggle to overthrow authoritarian rule as the first step in building a libertarian society will not involve violence, or a series of violent encounters with the entrenched forces of the *status quo*. Not only does one disillusion those who were led to believe that the revolution would all be plain sailing, but one appears as utopians to those practical people whose logic and commonsense are insulted by such "simplicist" arguments.

Arnold Roller in 1912 was not to know that in 1936 the people of Barcelona would defeat a carefully laid plan by the military to seize the city in less than 24 hours, and in spite of the fact that the new part of Barcelona where they met their defeat consisted of wide and straight avenues and "not winding lanes"! Or that in 1944 the Danes would ignore the problems of wood blocks and asphalt and instead "turned over trolley cars for barricades" (see Crook p.302), any more than Berkman was to know in 1929 that the Algerian resistance could successfully wage its war of independence against the cream of French military might—500,000 strong, armed with the latest weapons of horror, both military and psychological, from flame throwers, helicopters, the latest in automatic weapons and heavy armoured transport and offensive weapons, and the ruthless "paras" as well as a militant million white "colons" who certainly did not give up their privileged status without a fight, to torture, refined and crude, terrorism, bombings of civilian populations, starvation ... in a word, the French pulled every dirty trick from the militarist-imperialist bag to no avail. Ben Bella in the end was received in the Elysée as spokesmen for the Algerian people, just as in 1936 the anarchists in Catalonia were received in the Generalitat as "masters" of the city, and of the province.

It is surely significant that Malatesta who equally was not to know about these, and other, events that could be enumerated, puts forward arguments which are confirmed—not refuted—by the experience of the past thirty years. What, it seems to me, makes *his* approach so worthy of serious consideration as contemporary is that it was not only patently honest but was also illumined by an imagination which was *political* as well as human. Can one, by the same token, concede that he was probably right when he declared that the simplification of the revolutionary problems only served to "spoil the revolutionary spirit of the people"?

III

I have only touched on the subject of the General Strike. Professor Crook's angled work on the subject has probably uncovered all the sources available. What we need is an anarchist eye and imagination to interpret the 400 pages of text and probe the 70 invaluable pages of source notes, and in due course supply us with the findings!

But even a cursory glance at the general strike as a weapon of social revolution leads us to the question of "violence" and "non-violence" one of the three tactical issues over which anarchists have wasted more hours and reams of paper arguing at cross purposes. It will come as something of a shock to some anarchists reading Malatesta to learn that "non-violent revolutionary direct action" was in fact "rediscovered" not *discovered* by the "Committee of 100" in its meteoric, short-lived, but historically and socially, significant existence. When he referred to "passive anarchy" as "an error the opposite of the one which the terrorists make" he was writing in 1896. Thus it can be said that the Tolstoyan-Gandhist and Bakuninist-Malatestian trends have co-existed in the anarchist movement these past 70 years, and therefore, to present the former as a new departure in anarchist tactics—as anarchism's New Look—is as unconvincing as it is historically false!

If the barricades in Barcelona led to Franco and his vaunted "25 años de paz" ("25 years of peace"—or should it be "repression," or "apathy"?) what did Gandhism lead to in India, and where has it got the blacks in South Africa? Again, to say as the Tolstoyans do, that even assuming the barricades and insurrection had a chance of succeeding in the distant past, the power of the State backed by formidable armed forces, and the entrenched power of industrialists and financiers, today has relegated such tactics to the history books, is an argument which must be examined and appraised in the light of all the evidence from Spain, Cuba, Algeria, Egypt, and Black Africa.

But to say all this without recognising that these same "problems" equally militate against "non-violent" tactics, clearly indicates that for some non-violence is accepted as an article of faith. It probably explains the sterility of the discussions in the columns of *Freedom* in recent years. What I propose to do now is not to reopen the discussion, but simply to point out that Malatesta and those of a like mind have never suggested that the anarchist society could be brought about through violence.

What they do say is that the possibility of radical change in society depends on first destroying the entrenched power of the ruling, the privileged, minority or class in present society, seeing that all the evidence on which we can draw indicates that no ruling class abdicates its power except when opposed by a superior force, and anarchists are not alone in drawing such conclusions. But as Malatesta points out again and again, what emerges from such upheavals is not necessarily anarchy but "the resultant" of all the active forces in society. So far as the role of anarchists in such situations is concerned, they must beware of trying, or hoping, to *impose* anarchy by force, just as they must be prepared to *defend* their right to live as anarchists, with force if necessary, it being clearly understood however that in living their way of life they do not interfere with the equal freedom of others to live theirs.

Malatesta therefore remained to the end of his life a believer in the need for violent, insurrectionary, action, not for the romantic and sentimental reasons attributed to him by popular historians, but because it was the only way out of the "vicious circle" which he so succinctly defines in these terms:

> Between man and his social environment there is a reciprocal action. Men make society what it is and society makes men what they are, and the result is therefore a kind of vicious circle. To transform society men must be changed, and to transform men society must be changed.

Propaganda by the spoken and written word is not the answer. By propaganda we must encourage as many people as possible to make demands on the bosses and State by direct action; this in turn will, open the way to further penetration by anarchist propaganda among larger sections of the community and so on. Malatesta sought to create on the one hand an ever-growing mass-movement of political and social awareness as well as militancy which on the other hand would weaken the power as well as the *raison d'être* of the State, a situation which ideally would culminate in a violent "confrontation" provoked by the State in a last desperate attempt to stave off the inevitable.

In reality of course, the "confrontation" generally takes place at a much earlier stage, that is when government still feels confident of having the necessary forces to intimidate and curb those of the people who dare to challenge its authority. Russia in 1917, Spain 1936, Italy 1920 were the culminating chapters in long histories of struggle, of challenge and repression, highlights of revolutionary "breakthroughs" followed by "biennia negros," military dictatorships, and the suppression of "elementary rights." That neither in Russia, Italy, or Spain did these struggles lead to anything resembling the libertarian society—indeed they in fact ended in the victory of dictatorships—must obviously make us question the means.

If we dismiss these "failures," as the propagandists of "non-violence" invariably do, with the slogan that "violence begets violence" we shall learn nothing. The very fact that *they* are proposing to combat the violence of the State and of the privileged class, with non-violence, which they offer as a viable tactic, would indicate that *they* are not convinced that violence "begets violence." And indeed one has only to look around one to see that State violence more often than not "begets" obedience and servility, as well as bottled-up feelings of revenge which in times of upheaval often manifest themselves in horrible, anti-social acts of violence. And it is these explosions by the politically unconscious victims of the authoritarian society, and not the positive, generous practical actions of the conscious revolutionaries at such moments of history, which are seized upon by reactionary newspapermen in the heat of the struggle and perpetuated by equally reactionary, and cloistered and unimaginative historians.

Malatesta sought to base anarchist tactics on historic realities without nevertheless assuming that the pattern that emerged should or must perforce be slavishly followed. If history teaches us nothing else it is surely that we should seek to avoid repeating the mistakes of our predecessors. Thus there are certain well trodden political paths which from an anarchist point of view invariably lead to disaster. But if anarchists are to count in those social struggles which, albeit, are not anarchist, they must offer practical solutions as well as valuable criticism. It should be emphasised that our practical solutions may well be unattainable in the circumstances and yet still be practical.

Anarchists, as Malatesta was always pointing out, cannot stand on the sidelines waiting for a sign that might indicate society was ripe for anarchy. For, if they do, they will wait forever; in fact they would do better to give up because they would be left behind by events. The anarchist revolution is the culmination of a series of forward and alternating steps by man and his environment, and for them to lead eventually to anarchist ends, demands the participation of anarchists at every stage, *as anarchists.*

So long as the life of society is regulated by a privileged minority asserting and protecting itself with the complex machinery of Law and violence, and thus creating a class with a vested interest in the maintenance of the status quo, every serious challenge to its authority be it violent or non-violent will be met with the full force of the Law and legalised violence, the only language with which a privileged minority can address itself to the arguments and pressures of a majority without privileges, in any society. I do not propose to develop the insurrectionary argument here; it has already been clearly put by Malatesta. All I would add is that subsequent events have confirmed his arguments as well as his warnings. From the anarchist point of view obviously the Spanish Revolution of 1936–39 is the most significant social upheaval in our time. Though the anarchists have not yet subjected these events to the exhaustive analysis they deserve, the broad outline contained in the literature available could so easily be used to illustrate these pages of Malatesta's writings, just as his writings, because they foresaw the very problems that faced the anarchists and other revolutionaries in the Spanish struggle, could have served them as a tactical manual, the acceptance and application of which would have in all probability pushed the revolutionary possibilities to their fullest limits resulting either in the complete defeat of Franco's coup d'état in the first weeks of the struggle or in his military victory in the first six months, but without the possibility of lording over the country.

In other words, if the anarchists and syndicalist "leaders" after their spectacular victories of the first days of the military uprising had sought to exploit their richly deserved prestige in the eyes of the workers by directing all their energies and propaganda to the workers, inciting them to enlarge and consolidate the revolutionary gains of the 19th July, rather than seeking to use that prestige to cement a unity at top level with the other organisations and parties (which is what they did with scant success) they would have liberated *all* the latent and potential revolutionary forces in the country and beyond their frontiers. This may have ended in defeat within a few weeks. But it would have been defeat when the revolutionary feelings and expectations were still high—and therefore when it was possible to continue the struggle by other means. Whereas, in prolonging the struggle by sacrificing the revolution to the war of fronts, not only did the politicians, with the support of the revolutionary organisations, ensure military defeat, but also ensured that a people subjected for more than two years to great material privations as well as growing political dissensions between the parties and workers' organisations, when it did finally concede victory to Franco and his backers, was exhausted, decimated, disillusioned, bitter, and helpless. The great exodus of half a million Spaniards, who preferred exile or French concentration camps, to Spain under Franco, was no guarantee of continuity in the struggle, for they, no less than those left behind, and who escaped the repression were also exhausted, disillusioned, and . . . *divided.* Franco's proclaimed "25 years of peace" obviously does not accurately describe his years of repressive and corrupt rule. But neither would "25 years of resistance" accurately describe the opposition to his regime. And I say all this not in a critical vein (for if we must be critical, it is of my generation which supported the Spanish people's great struggle only with fine words and medical aid) but in seeking to provoke a dispassionate evaluation of anarchist tactics and principles in the light of anarchist experience in that life-and-death struggle. Spain was not only the military training ground for Hitler's troops and the testing ground for his weapons of destruction, it was also a political crucible for all the parties and movements of the Left. They all failed, not just the anarchists and the revolutionary syndicalists of the CNT, but the Socialists, the Communists, the Catalan Separatists no less than the Basque Nationalists, (and I assume that just as by anarchists I mean all shades from extreme individualists to "reluctant" Ministers, so the reader also takes socialists and communists to include all the shades and factions from Right to Left: from POUM to PSUC)!

We know that fighting a war of fronts resulted in military defeat; we know that the entry of anarchists and the two workers' organisations (UGT-CNT) into the government neither safeguarded their particular interests nor helped the armed struggle against Franco; we know that conscription did not produce military victories any more than did Russian military aid. The question Spanish anarchists have not to this day sought to answer is: *from the anarchist point of view* was the defeat in Spain a defeat of anarchist theory and tactics as distinct from the failure of anarchists to seek to apply their theory and tactics? And from what I have previously said, by "defeat" I am not referring to Franco's military victory but to the defeat of the Revolution with which a section of the Spanish people opposed, and in two thirds of Spain defeated, the military uprising in July 1936. Anarchist tactics might well have led to defeat: this has already been admitted. What we must ask ourselves is whether the alternative course, of playing the government game, produced beneficial results, irrespective of military defeat. The point I am trying to make is that there are "successful" failures; that is, where the seeds of positive future struggles have been sown. This was not only the basis of Malatesta's teachings, but also the conclusions reached by Lady Chorley:

> The object of an insurrection is to affect a seizure of power; and this has been shown in the opening chapter that straight insurrections have never been won and probably never can be won against the full strength of a professional army. But insurrections have frequently broken out spontaneously in conditions where any chance of permanent success was impossible and even occasionally have been launched deliberately in the accepted knowledge that they could achieve no positive and direct success. Regarding revolutionary strategy by and large it does not necessarily follow that such insurrections are always unjustifiable. Indirectly, they can sometimes alter the whole political situation so deeply that from a revolutionary standpoint they may be a valuable factor in long-term strategy, even though foredoomed to military failure.

And it is interesting that among the historic examples she quotes to support her conclusions is that of the Asturian Rising in 1934, which was followed by the "biennio negro" (the two black years).

> The Asturian Rising was a desperate protest against the failure of the 1931 Revolution to hold its gains and effect any deep alteration in the social system of Spain. . . . In the Asturias where the UGT was supreme, the working class rose in a revolt as determined and heroic as any in all European working class history. They held out for a fortnight, and were finally subdued by Moorish troops, foreign legionaries, and air bombing. The liquidation of the revolt was particularly cruel—some 30,000 prisoners were kept in gaol for eighteen months apart from bloodier and more spectacular acts of vengeance. . . . The working classes now had a tradition and a heroic myth. Asturias combined for them "the pride of an army in its previous feats of military glory and the pride of a Church in its religious martyrs." It was a welding iron to fuse the differences of the Left parties into a common aim. . . . It is not, therefore going too far to say that a direct result of the splendid failure in Asturias was the triumph of the Left in the elections of February 1963, the decisive turning point in the path of the revolution.[5]

For 25 years anarchists the world over have been commemorating the Spanish Revolution. If reading Malatesta convinces us that it is time we started studying the valuable lessons it can teach us, I am convinced that we would learn to waste less of our time and our other slender material resources in sloganising and gesturing; I think some of us would drop out; and I am also convinced that those who do not believe in the Kropotkinian theory of inevitability or in some kind of social spontaneous combustion, will welcome with relief the Malatestian cold-douche of commonsense, pragmatic anarchism, and far from being pessimistic as a result, we too may also discover the argument that for sixty years "captured" such an intelligence who was also, by common consent, the most active and realistic of all anarchists!

IV

The writers of all the recently published histories of anarchism are unanimous in declaring that the anarchist movement is dead. All that remains is the idea and a few anarchists dotted about the globe. Their conclusions may well be right; what I question are the arguments which lead them to their conclusion, for I find myself wondering whether the Movement they are talking about is the one I have in mind. For as I see it, it is a movement of continuous renewal rather than "an historically determined movement" as the Marxist historian Santarelli views it, and as I suspect Woodcock and Joll also do.

Not only do the historians consider that the anarchist "movement" in the 1880s was numerically stronger than it has even been since, but that it was more active, and as a movement with a popular basis, had greater opportunities of achieving its aims. Furthermore that governmental power and the means of repression were weak by contrast with what they were soon to become. To sustain such a thesis one should also be prepared to accommodate such notable exceptions as the revival of anarchist fortunes in Italy in 1913–14 and in 1919–22, as well as of anarchism as a growing influence in Spanish politics at various periods in the present century, culminating in the revolutionary events of 1936. One has also to bear in mind that the 20th is a century of revolutionary upheavals, whether we approve of them or not, by comparison to which those of the 19th century are almost small fry!

I criticise the modern historians of anarchism because it seems to me that they have either started work with an *idée fixe* and selected their facts to prove their thesis, or have started with no preconceived ideas but neither with any burning desire to get to the root of the anarchist dilemma, if such it is. They have instead contented themselves with rehashing the considerable material already available on the 19th century revolutionary movements, and seem to have fallen into the trap of assuming that writers and diarists and assiduous correspondents are necessarily the most active revolutionaries and "trend-setters." And because, as I have pointed out in the introduction to this volume, Malatesta was a reluctant writer, and too good a revolutionary and conspirator to keep a diary or file away his letters for posterity, our historians have not even bothered to read what he did write and have as a result failed to realise that not only was he a "dedicated" revolutionary but also a thinker whose ideas were forged in the social struggle and had nothing in common with the rhetorical, the "millenarian," predictions of a world of love and plenty which most of his 19th century contemporaries indulged in. Far from Malatesta being Kropotkin's "collaborator and most famous disciple" as one writer[6]—who declares that he has been "interested in the international anarchist movement since the turn of the century"—recently put it, it is abundantly clear that the personal esteem each had for the other never bridged the fundamental tactical differences which divided them for most of their lives. The fact is that both men went their own ways, neither seeking to join issue with the other (until Kropotkin declared his support for the Allies in the 1914–18 war, and Malatesta publicly disassociated himself from his friend's attitude).

From the point of view of the development of the anarchist movement the Marx-Bakunin struggle could be seen to be less significant than the Kropotkin-Malatesta confrontation that-might-have-been—and from this distance in time, not to have provoked it, seems to this writer to have been a serious tactical mistake on Malatesta's part.

Both men were undoubtedly the major "trend-setters" in the anarchist movements that saw the light in the 20th century. Woodcock succinctly summed up their different approaches in his Biography of Kropotkin[7] when he wrote:

> That this quality [Kropotkin's constitutional optimism], with its tendency to expect rapid and painless solutions to vast problems, amounted at times to a fault, was evident not only to hostile critics, but also to some who shared his fundamental ideals, for even his old friend and comrade, Malatesta, *the most realistic of all anarchists*, said after his death that he had leaned too much towards excessive optimism and theoretical fatalism (p.439)

and again in a footnote he points out that even though the two men were "close personal friends up to the time of the break over the first world war,

> they did not always agree on tactics or general ideas. Malatesta was a practical revolutionist, with a tendency towards conspiratorial ac-

> tion. *The most realist of the great anarchists,* he did not always share Kropotkin's optimism and while he accepted anarchist communism, regarded it in the light of a hypothesis to be revised and reconsidered according to changing circumstances (p.382)

I have italicised Woodcock's two references to Malatesta in order to underline my surprise that in his History, published ten years after the Biography, Malatesta becomes the "knight errant in search of revolutionary adventure" and the subject for the usual anecdotes, but has no place in the first half of his history dealing with the Idea, in which he devotes 30 pages to Godwin, 12 to Stirner, and 39 to Proudhon. That these writers are full of thought-provoking ideas no one who has bothered (or tried) to read them will deny. But what have they, except for Proudhon, to do with the second part of his History—"The Movement"?

Until recent years the names, let alone the writings, of Godwin and Stirner were unknown in the anarchist movement. As Woodcock points out of Godwin's "Political Justice," in spite of the *succès d'estime* it enjoyed at the time of publication in 1793, a century was to elapse before it was reprinted. And Godwin himself "died in obscurity. His ideas were familiar only to a restricted group of people with literary interests, and his social writings became the gospel of no political group," and he adds "The general neglect of Godwin has persisted. Never, in the nineteenth century, was he among the revered political writers."

Malatesta was for more than fifty years both at the centre of the ferment of ideas, and for most of that time an active militant in various countries. He did not enjoy the same kind of reverent esteem accorded to Kropotkin in the anarchist movement if for no other reason that his writings for the most part published in journals of which he was editor, and which were agitational papers existing to take advantage of a particular political situation (e.g., *l'Agitazione, Volontà, Umanità Nova*—I can only think of *Pensiero e Volontà* published after Mussolini's victory, as the exception to this rule) and one of Malatesta's roles in such papers was to seek to create a coordinated movement out of all the anarchist goodwill dispersed and unorganised. As a result he found himself frequently engaged in polemics generally with the extremist elements, between the out and out individualists on the one hand and those who in their concern to do something would almost veer to authoritarianism. As a result Malatesta was always a controversial figure, and not without his detractors within the anarchist circles as well as, of course, in the Left wing authoritarian parties. And one can imagine that he felt that he would do his cause more harm than good by challenging the Kropotkinian "optimism and theoretical fatalism." That it was in his opinion a stumbling block to the full development of the anarchist movement as a revolutionary and political force, emerges only too clearly from his recollections on Kropotkin, which was the last article he wrote, only a year before his death. I cannot understand how an historian of Woodcock's experience and knowledge of the anarchist trends could deliberately disregard this document of fundamental importance to an objective understanding of why the anarchist movement has failed.

I too, think the anarchist movement has failed but not because, to quote Woodcock's conclusions, "in almost a century of effort it has not even approached the fulfilment of its great aim to destroy the state and build Jerusalem in its ruins"—few anarchists would share the view that this has been the aim of the anarchist movement as such—but because most anarchists have seemed unable or have been unwilling, to distinguish between their problems as conscious individuals and the problems of society as a whole. And because they generally manage to find solutions to their basic material needs which permit them to live full lives they assume that what they have done others can also do, and either they conclude that propaganda is unnecessary, in which case they spend the rest of their lives living out their one-man-revolutions; or if they feel an urge to communicate their "discoveries" to their fellow-men tend to express and project their personal experience and solutions as applicable and possible for the community at large. Such propaganda can be shown to have produced valuable results in helping other individuals "discover" a new way of life for themselves, and even make them, in turn, into propagandists. In theory such propaganda will snowball, and in a short time an important minority of the population will be anarchists. In practice the results from such propaganda have been limited because its impact is personal and not social.

By way of illustration I recall the case of a Glasgow factory worker during the last world war who became an anarchist and developed into a brilliant public speaker. At a certain stage he realised that the factory was no place for him, and set out in a caravan to live the free life, earning a living making clothes pegs. He had applied theory to practice, was the conclusion drawn by his anarchist comrades. He has not been heard of since in the anarchist movement—which means nearly twenty years silence. Those who say that he—assuming he is still making and selling clothes pegs from his horse-drawn caravan—is still the best anarchist among us, are right in one sense: he has obviously reduced his personal material needs to a minimum and this he can acquire by making pegs and is left with a great deal of leisure to enjoy life. They are also wrong, because they overlook the equally important fact that our clothes-peg-anarchist depends on other people wanting his pegs and growing the food he and his horse need; and, most important, that very few other people have chosen to share his way of life. For if everybody decided to take to the road and earn a living making pegs, all of us, horses and anarchists would all die of hunger; and the monument to their naiveté—mountains of unwanted clothes pegs!

Woodcock makes a valid point when he writes that while it is true that anarchists are, in theory, revolutionaries

> in practice however, organised anarchism in the nineteenth and twentieth centuries was really a movement of rebellion rather than a movement of revolution. It was a protest, a dedicated resistance to the worldwide trend since the middle of the eighteenth century toward political and economic centralisation.

But one cannot share his conclusions that anarchism is a lost—albeit good—cause but that "once lost they are never won again" and that the "heritage that anarchism has left to the modern world" is

> in the incitement to return to a moral and natural view of society which we find in the writings of Godwin and Tolstoy, of Proudhon and Kropotkin, and in the stimulation such writers give to that very taste for free choice and free judgment which modern society has so insidiously induced the majority of men to barter for material goods and the illusion of security. The great anarchists call on us to stand on

> our own moral feet like a generation of princes, to become aware of justice as an inner fire and to learn that the still, small voices of our own hearts speak more truly than the choruses of propaganda that daily assault our outer ears.

For if anarchism is a lost cause then there can be no anarchist "heritage" unless one is satisfied to say that anarchists are an élite, the "princes" in a world of slaves.

Woodcock also fails to see that for a large number of anarchists "the historic anarchist movement" has no meaning. Few people come to accept an idea simply by reading an "authority." Somewhere Malatesta writes that it is action that sets people thinking—and while this is certainly true in his case for he only discovered the existence of the International and Bakunin after he had become an active Mazzinian in his early student days—and while he was not dogmatic on this and would recognise that for some, thought precedes, action, I think it is generally true that people formulate even vague social ideas as a result of their direct experience or observation of the world around them. Writers can help to clarify or develop these vague ideas, if they succeed in relating their writings to realities.

It is in this respect that Malatesta was one of the ablest and most honest of anarchist propagandists, and because the basic problems, which set in motion the vague ideas I refer to, have not in fact changed all that much in the past fifty years there is still a great deal that Malatesta can teach us, not as a prophet, but as somebody who belongs to our time and who worked and lived among the people, and always aware that he would be the last to suggest that anarchists today should blindly accept his ideas, or adopt his "anarchist programme" piecemeal or seek to relive his life as an agitator.

Malatesta has much to teach us, bearing in mind the present situation in the anarchist movements of the world, in his *approach to anarchism*, both as an idea and a way of life, and in his *political sense and realism*. To ignore *these* lessons is to condemn the anarchist movement to the political graveyard, mourned by the few dedicated custodians of the "Idea," and to periodic disinterment by historians in search of a subject.

V.R.

Notes

Introduction: Anarchy and Anarchism

1. *Pensiero e Volontà*, May 16, 1925
2. *Pensiero e Volontà*, September 1, 1925.
3. *l'Agitazione*, June 4, 1897
4. *Umanità Nova*, August 25, 1920
5. *Umanità Nova*, September 2, 1922
6. *Umanità Nova*, April 27, 1922
7. *Umanità Nova*, September 16, 1921
8. *Pensiero e Volontà*, May 15, 1924
9. *Pensiero e Volontà*, January 1, 1924
10. *Volontà*, June 15, 1913
11. *Pensiero e Volontà*, May 16, 1925
12. *Umanità Nova*, September 16, 1922
13. *Volontà*, June 15, 1913
14. *Umanità Nova*, April 27, 1922
15. *Il Risveglio*, December 20, 1922
16. *Umanità Nova*, July 25, 1920
17. *Il Programma Anarchico*, Bologna, 1920, in this volume, pp.173–88
18. *Il Programma Anarchico*, Bologna, 1920, in this volume, pp.173–88

1. Anarchist Schools of Thought

1. *Pensiero e Volontà*, July 1, 1925
2. *Umanità Nova*, February 27, 1920
3. *Pensiero e Volontà*, April 1, 1926
4. *Pensiero e Volontà*, August 8, 1924
5. *Pensiero e Volontà*, July 1, 1924
6. *Pensiero e Volontà*, July 1, 1924
7. *Pensiero e Volontà*, April 1, 1926

2. Anarchist—Communism

1. *Pensiero e Volontà*, August 25, 1926
2. *Pensiero e Volontà*, June 1, 1926
3. *Umanità Nova*, August 31, 1921
4. *Pensiero e Volontà*, April 1, 1926
5. *Il Risveglio*, November 30, 1929

3. Anarchism and Science

1. *Volontà*, December 27, 1913
2. *Umanità Nova*, April 27, 1922
3. *Pensiero e Volontà*, September 15, 1924
4. *Pensiero e Volontà*, November 1, 1924
5. *Pensiero e Volontà*, July 1, 1925
6. *Pensiero e Volontà*, November 16, 1925
7. *Pensiero e Volontà*, February 1, 1926

4. Anarchism and Freedom

1. *Umanità Nova*, September 30, 1922
2. *Umanità Nova*, September 24, 1920
3. *Umanità Nova*, November 24, 1921
4. *Umanità Nova*, September 11, 1920
5. *La Questione Sociale*, November 25, 1899
6. *La Questione Sociale*, November 25, 1899

5. Anarchism and Violence

1. *Umanità Nova*, August 25, 1921
2. *Pensiero e Volontà*, September 1, 1924
3. *Il Programma Anarchico*, Bologna, 1920, in this volume, pp.173–88
4. *Umanità Nova*, August 12, 1920
5. *Umanità Nova*, September 9, 1921
6. *Umanità Nova*, April 27, 1920
7. *Umanità Nova*, May 9, 1920
8. *Pensiero e Volontà*, April 16, 1925
9. *Fede!*, October 28, 1923
10. *Umanità Nova*, October 21, 1922
11. *Il Risveglio*, December 20, 1922
12. *Fede!*, November 25, 1923
13. *Umanità*, Nova July 18, 1920
14. *l'Anarchia* (Numero Unico), August 1896

6. Attentats

1. *Pensiero e Volontà*, September 1, 1924
2. *Pensiero e Volontà*, September 1, 1924
3. *l'Agitazione*, September 22, 1901
4. "Causa ed Effetti," September 22, 1900
5. *Umanità Nova*, December 18, 1921
6. *Umanità Nova*, December 24, 1921

7. Ends and Means

1. *l'En Dehors*, August 17, 1892
2. *Umanità Nova*, June 25, 1922

3. *l'Anarchia*, August 1896

8. Majorities and Minorities

1. *Umanità Nova*, August 11, 1922
2. *Umanità Nova*, October 6, 1921
3. *Pensiero e Volontà*, June 15, 1924

9. Mutual Aid

1. *Umanità Nova*, September 16, 1922
2. *Umanità Nova*, July 25, 1920
3. *Umanità Nova*, September 2, 1922
4. *Umanità Nova*, October 21, 1922
5. *Il Pensiero*, June 1, 1909

10. Reformism

1. *Umanità Nova*, May 10, 1922
2. *Pensiero e Volontà*, May 15, 1924
3. *Umanità Nova*, September 10, 1920
4. *Pensiero e Volontà*, March 1, 1924

11. Organisation

1. *Il Risveglio*, October 15, 1927
2. *l'Agitazione*, June 4, 1897
3. *l'Agitazione*, June 11, 1897
4. *Il Risveglio*, October 15, 1927
5. *l'Agitazione*, June 11, 1897
6. *l'Agitazione*, June 18, 1897

12. Production and Distribution

1. *Umanità Nova*, March 7, 1920
2. *Il Pensiero*, May 16, 1905
3. *Il Risveglio*, May 16, 1931
4. *Il Risveglio*, December 30, 1922
5. *Umanità Nova*, March 7, 1920
6. *Pensiero e Volontà*, May 1, 1924
7. *Umanità Nova*, October 4, 1922
8. *Umanità Nova*, May 9, 1920
9. *Il Risveglio*, December 30, 1922
10. *Pensiero e Volontà*, August 25, 1926

13. The Land

1. *Umanità Nova*, May 15, 1920

14. Money and Banks

1. *Umanità Nova*, April 18, 1922
2. *Umanità Nova*, October 7, 1922

15. Property

1. *Il Risveglio*, November 30, 1929
2. *Umanità Nova*, May 10, 1922
3. *Umanità Nova*, April 18, 1922
4. *Il Risveglio*, November 31, 1929

16. Crime and Punishment

1. *Umanità Nova*, August 27, 1920
2. *Pensiero e Volontà*, August 15, 1924
3. *Umanità Nova*, September 30, 1922
4. *Umanità Nova*, August 19, 1922
5. *Umanità Nova*, September 30, 1922
6. *Umanità Nova*, September 2, 1920
7. *Umanità Nova*, September 2, 1920
8. *Umanità Nova*, September 2, 1920
9. *Umanità Nova*, August 10, 1922
10. *Il Risveglio*, February 11, 1933

17. Anarchists and the Working Class Movements

1. *Il Risveglio*, October 1–15, 1927
2. *Umanità Nova*, March 14, 1922
3. *Umanità Nova*, April 13, 1922
4. *Umanità Nova*, April 6, 1922
5. *Umanità Nova*, April 13, 1922
6. *Umanità Nova*, April 6, 1922
7. *Pensiero e Volontà*, April 16, 1925
8. *Umanità Nova*, April 6, 1922
9. *Fede!*, September 30, 1922
10. *Pensiero e Volontà*, February 16, 1925

18. The Occupation of the Factories

1. *Umanità Nova*, March 17, 1920
2. Confederazione Generale del Lavoro (the reformist Trade Union organization).
3. *Umanità Nova*, June 28, 1922
4. *Pensiero e Volontà*, April 1, 1924

19. Workers and Intellectuals

1. *Umanità Nova*, August 10, 1922
2. *Umanità Nova*, October 20, 1921
3. *Pensiero e Volontà*, May 16, 1925
4. *Umanità Nova*, October 20, 1921

20. Anarchism, Socialism, and Communism

1. *Umanità Nova*, September 3, 1921
2. *l'Agitazione*, September 23, 1897
3. *l'Anarchia*, August 1896
4. *l'Agitazione*, May 15, 1897
5. *Umanità Nova*, August 31, 1921
6. *l'Agitazione*, May 15, 1897
7. *Fede!*, October 28, 1923
8. *l'Anarchia*, August 1896

21. Anarchists and the Limits of Political Co-Existence

1. *Umanità Nova*, May 1, 1920
2. *Umanità Nova*, May 4, 1922
3. *Umanità Nova*, June 25, 1922
4. *Umanità Nova*, August 26, 1922
5. *Pensiero e Volontà*, June 1, 1924
6. *Pensiero e Volontà*, August 1, 1926
7. *Umanità Nova*, November 25, 1922
8. *Pensiero e Volontà*, May 1, 1924

22. The Anarchist Revolution

1. *Pensiero e Volontà*, June 15, 1924
2. *Umanità Nova*, October 28, 1921
3. *Umanità Nova*, September 30, 1920
4. *Umanità Nova*, April 22, 1920
5. *Umanità Nova*, August 30, 1921
6. *Il Risveglio*, December 30, 1922
7. *Umanità Nova*, November 25, 1922
8. *Pensiero e Volontà*, June 15, 1924
9. *Pensiero e Volontà*, June 1, 1926
10. *Pensiero e Volontà*, July 1, 1926
11. *Pensiero e Volontà*, June 16, 1926
12. *Pensiero e Volontà*, August 1, 1926
13. *Il Risveglio*, December 14, 1929
14. *Il Risveglio*, November 30, 1929
15. *Vogliamo*, June 1930
16. *Vogliamo*, June 1930

23. The Insurrection

1. *Umanità Nova*, August 12, 1920
2. *Umanità Nova*, August 7, 1920
3. *Umanità Nova*, September 6, 1921
4. *Vogliamo*, June 1930
5. *Umanità Nova*, April 7, 1922
6. *Il Programma Anarchico*, Bologna, 1920, in this volume, pp.173–88

24. Expropriation

1. *Il Programma Anarchico*, Bologna, 1920, in this volume, pp.173–88
2. *Umanità Nova*, June 19, 1920
3. *Umanità Nova*, April 1, 1920

25. Defence of the Revolution

1. *Fede!*, November 25, 1923
2. *Umanità Nova*, August 27, 1920
3. *Umanità Nova*, October 7, 1922
4. *Pensiero e Volontà*, October 1, 1924
5. *Pensiero e Volontà*, October 1, 1925
6. *Umanità Nova*, August 12, 1920

26. Anarchist Propaganda

1. *Umanità Nova*, September 2, 1921
2. *Pensiero e Volontà*, April 1, 1924
3. *l'Adunata dei Refrattari*, December 26, 1931
4. *Umanità Nova*, February 27, 1920
5. *Pensiero e Volontà*, January 1, 1925
6. *l'Agitazione*, September 22, 1901

27. An Anarchist Programme

1. *Il Programma Anarchico* was drafted by Malatesta and adopted by the Unione Anarchica Italiana at its Congress in Bologna (1920)

Notes for a Biography

1. *Pensiero e Volontà*, July 1, 1926
2. Max Nettlau, *Errico Malatesta—La Vida de un Anarquista* (Buenos Aires, 1923)
3. Armando Borghi, *Errico Malatesta* (Milan, 1947)
4. Errico Malatesta, *Scritti Scelti* Vol. 2 (Naples, 1954)
5. George Woodcock, *Anarchism—A History of Libertarian Ideas and Movements* (London, 1963)
6. Max Nettlau, op. cit.
7. Max Nettlau, op. cit.

8. Luis Fabbri, *Malatesta* (Buenos Aires, 1945)
9. Max Nettlau, op. cit.
10. Armando Borghi, *Mezzo Secolo di Anarchia* (Naples, 1954)
11. *Pensiero e Volontà*, July 1, 1926
12. *Pensiero e Volontà*, September 16, 1925
13. Max Nettlau, *Bakunin e l'Internazionale in Italia dal 1864 al 1872* (Geneva, 1928) preface by Malatesta
14. Luis Fabbri, op. cit.
15. Max Nettlau, *Errico Malatesta—El Hombre, el Revolucionario, el Anarquista* (Barcelona 1933)
16. Luis Fabbri, op. cit.
17. Angiolini quoted Nettlau, *Errico Malatesta—La Vida de un Anarquista* (Buenos Aires, 1923)
18. Max Nettlau, op. cit.
19. *Questione Sociale* (Florence, 1884) quoted Nettlau op. cit.
20. Max Nettlau, op. cit.
21. Max Nettlau, op. cit.
22. Malatesta in preface to Nettlau op. cit.
23. Malatesta in preface to Nettlau op. cit.
24. *Questione Sociale*, quoted Nettlau, *Errico Malatesta*
25. *Questione Sociale*, quoted Nettlau, *Errico Malatesta*
26. Max Nettlau, op. cit.
27. Max Nettlau, op. cit.
28. Malatesta, in preface to Nettlau op. cit.
29. *Umanità Nova*, March 11, 1922
30. *Pensiero e Volontà*, July 1, 1926
31. Malatesta in preface to Nettlau, op. cit.
32. Luis Fabbri, op. cit.
33. Errico Malatesta, *Scritti* Vol. 3 (Geneva, 1936)
34. *Umanità Nova*, August 24, 1921
35. op. cit.
36. James Joll, *The Anarchists* (London, 1964)
37. Luis Fabbri, op. cit.
38. Errico Malatesta, *Scritti Scelti* (Naples, 1954)
39. op. cit.
40. Armando Borghi, *Errico Malatesta* (Milan, 1947)
41. Luis Fabbri, op. cit.
42. *Freedom*, July 1914
43. James Joll, op. cit., see Appendix I
44. *Freedom*, April 1916, see Appendix II
45. *Freedom*, December 1914
46. *l'Adunata dei Refrattari* (Newark, NJ, September 3, 10, 17, 24, 1932)
47. See Ugo Fedeli, *Errico Malatesta—Bibliografia* (Naples, 1951)
48. Luigi Fabbri, *Malatesta l'Uomo e il Pensiero* (Naples, 1951)
49. Trento Tagliaferri, *Errico Malatesta, Armando Borghi e Compagni davanti ai Giurati di Milano* (Milan n.d. 1921?)
50. *Il Libero Accordo* (Rome, 1920–1926), *Fede!* (Rome, 1923–1926)
51. *Pensiero e Volontà* (Rome 1924–1926)
52. Max Nettlau, op. cit. (Barcelona, 1933)
53. Max Nettlau, in *Freedom Bulletin*, December 1932
54. See Appendix IV
55. Max Nettlau, op. cit. (Geneva, 1928)
56. *A proposito della Piataforma in Risveglio* (Geneva, December 14, 1929)
57. *Freedom Bulletin*, December 1932
58. See Borghi, Fabbri, Nettlau, op. cit.
59. See Nettlau, *Errico Malatesta Vita e Pensiero* (New York, 1921) Chapter 11
60. Only quite recently a Spanish syndicalist of mature years expressed to me his admiration for Malatesta's ideas but repeated as a fact that Malatesta always managed to get away when things were getting "too hot." He was most surprised when I told him that Malatesta had spent some ten years in the various prisons of the world!
61. *Umanità Nova*
62. Trento Tagliaferri, op. cit.
63. op. cit.
64. *La Protesta* was a daily paper for 25 years. See Rocker, *Anarcho-Syndicalism* (London, 1938)

65. Luis Fabbri, op. cit.
66. Errico Malatesta, *Scritti Scelti* Vol. 1 (Naples, 1947), Vol. 2 (Naples, 1954)
67. Luis Fabbri, op. cit.
68. Max Nettlau, op. cit.
69. Armando Borghi, op. cit.
70. See Appendix III
71. P. Kropotkin, *Memoirs of a Revolutionist* (London, 1899) Vol. 2, pp.59–60
72. E.H. Carr, *Michael Bakunin* (London, 1937)
73. Luis Fabbri, op. cit.
74. James Joll, op. cit.

Appendix—III

1. MacMillan (New York, 1932)
2. Armando Borghi *Errico Malatesta* (Istituto Editoriale Italiano, Milan, 1947) pp.136–37
3. *Man!*, March, 1933
4. *Avanti!* October 3, 1897. Reprinted in *Scritti Scelti* (Naples, 1954) p.54
5. Borghi op. cit. pp.135–36
6. *Anarchism: A History of Libertarian Ideas and Movements* (Cleveland, 1962)
7. Pelican Books (London, 1963)
8. See "Anarchism and the Historians" by V.R. in the monthly journal *Anarchy* 46 (Freedom Press, London, December, 1964) for a detailed analysis of the escape, fact and fiction.

Malatesta's Relevance for Anarchists Today

1. Karl Mannheim, *Freedom, Power and Democratic Planning* (London, 1951)
2. Pierre Besnard, *Les Syndicats Ouvriers et la Revolution Sociale* (Paris, 1930)
3. Wilfrid H. Crook, *Communism and the General Strike* (Connecticut, 1960)
4. Katharine Chorley, *Armies and the Art of Revolution* (London, 1943)
5. I do not agree with all the evidence with which Lady Chorley builds up her case. For instance I would consider more significant as a revolutionary portent the weakness of the government, following the repression of the Asturian Rising and the mass imprisonment of the revolutionaries, to assert itself dictatorially, and the more or less free elections (by Spanish standards) which it found itself obliged to hold, than by the results! From an anarchist point of view Lady Chorley's conclusions and observations are so valuable because if anything they stem from personal convictions which at most are orthodox Labour Party, and her Spanish sources, Jellinek, Atholl, et alia, are the kind I spent my time denouncing!
6. Max Nomad in *New Leader* (New York, December, 1964).
7. Woodcock and Avakumovic, *The Anarchist Prince* (London, 1950)

Index

"Passim" (literally "scattered") indicates intermittent discussion of a topic over a cluster of pages. Page numbers in *italic* refer to illustrations.

Vernon Richards

Vernon Richards (born Vero Recchioni) the writer, publisher, translator, photographer, and organic gardener was born July 19, 1915 and died December 10, 2001 at the age of 86.

During his life he was involved in the publishing of many anarchist periodicals. *Italia Libera* (Free Italy) a collaboration with Italian anarchist Camillo Berneri. *Spain and the World* published along with veterans of *Freedom* as an English-language news source for Spanish anarchists during the civil war. At the end of the civil war the paper was renamed *Revolt!* and by the start of the second world war was known as *War Commentary* (during which time he served a nine month prison sentence for inciting disaffection in soldiers) before finally returning to the title *Freedom* in 1945. Richards was editor of *Freedom* from 1952 until 1964 and continued to write for the paper until the 1990s.

Among his other publications are *Lessons of the Spanish Revolution, 1936–1939; George Orwell at home (and among the Anarchists): essays and photographs; Violence & Anarchism: a polemic;* as well as several volumes of photographs.

Carl Levy

Carl Levy is a professor of politics at Goldsmiths, University of London. He has published extensively on anarchism, comparative history, and politics.

About PM Press

politics • culture • art • fiction • music • film

PM Press was founded at the end of 2007 by a small collection of folks with decades of publishing, media, and organizing experience. PM Press co-conspirators have published and distributed hundreds of books, pamphlets, CDs, and DVDs. Members of PM have founded enduring book fairs, spearheaded victorious tenant organizing campaigns, and worked closely with bookstores, academic conferences, and even rock bands to deliver political and challenging ideas to all walks of life. We're old enough to know what we're doing and young enough to know what's at stake.

We seek to create radical and stimulating fiction and nonfiction books, pamphlets, T-shirts, visual and audio materials to entertain, educate, and inspire you. We aim to distribute these through every available channel with every available technology, whether that means you are seeing anarchist classics at our bookfair stalls; reading our latest vegan cookbook at the café; downloading geeky fiction e-books; or digging new music and timely videos from our website.

Contact us for direct ordering and questions about all PM Press releases, as well as manuscript submissions, review copy requests, foreign rights sales, author interviews, to book an author for an event, and to have PM Press attend your bookfair:

PM Press • PO Box 23912 • Oakland, CA 94623
510-658-3906 • info@pmpress.org

Buy books and stay on top of what we are doing at:

www.pmpress.org

MONTHLY SUBSCRIPTION PROGRAM

These are indisputably momentous times—the financial system is melting down globally and the Empire is stumbling. Now more than ever there is a vital need for radical ideas.

In the seven years since its founding—and on a mere shoestring—PM Press has risen to the formidable challenge of publishing and distributing knowledge and entertainment for the struggles ahead. With over 300 releases to date, we have published an impressive and stimulating array of literature, art, music, politics, and culture. Using every available medium, we've succeeded in connecting those hungry for ideas and information to those putting them into practice.

Friends of PM allows you to directly help impact, amplify, and revitalize the discourse and actions of radical writers, filmmakers, and artists. It provides us with a stable foundation from which we can build upon our early successes and provides a much-needed subsidy for the materials that can't necessarily pay their own way. You can help make that happen—and receive every new title automatically delivered to your door once a month—by joining as a Friend of PM Press. And, we'll throw in a free T-Shirt when you sign up.

Here are your options:

- $30 a month: Get all books and pamphlets plus 50% discount on all webstore purchases
- $40 a month: Get all PM Press releases (including CDs and DVDs) plus 50% discount on all webstore purchases
- $100 a month: Superstar—Everything plus PM merchandise, free downloads, and 50% discount on all webstore purchases

For those who can't afford $30 or more a month, we're introducing ***Sustainer Rates*** at $15, $10, and $5. Sustainers get a free PM Press T-shirt and a 50% discount on all purchases from our website.

Your Visa or Mastercard will be billed once a month, until you tell us to stop. Or until our efforts succeed in bringing the revolution around. Or the financial meltdown of Capital makes plastic redundant. Whichever comes first.